Book 9 in the

PINE BOX PAROLE

TERRY FITZSIMMONS
AND THE QUEST TO END

SOLITARY CONFINEMENT

& OTHER TRUE CASES

Book 9 in the Durvile True Cases Series

PINE BOX PAROLE

TERRY FITZSIMMONS
AND THE QUEST TO END
SOLITARY CONFINEMENT

& OTHER TRUE CASES

X

John L. Hill

Foreword by Raphael Rowe

Afterword by Keramet Reiter JD PhD

DURVILE IMPRINT OF DURVILE & UPROUTE BOOKS
CALGARY, ALBERTA, CANADA
DURVILE.COM

Durvile Publications Ltd.

DURVILE IMPRINT OF DURVILE AND UPROUTE BOOKS

Calgary, Alberta, Canada
www.durvile.com

Copyright © 2022 Durvile Publications

LIBRARY AND ARCHIVES CATALOGUING IN PUBLICATIONS DATA

Pine Box Parole
Terry Fitzsimmons and the Quest to End Solitary Confinement
& Other True Cases
Hill, John L.

1. True Crime | 2. Prison
3. Canadian Prison | 4. Solitary Confinement

Book 9 in the Durvile True Cases Series
Series Editor, Lorene Shyba

ISBN: 978-1-988824-85-7 (print pbk) | ISBN: 978-1-990735-02-8 (e-book)
ISBN: 978-1-990735-03-5 (audiobook)

Cover design: Austin Andrews | Back cover photo Gary Mulcahey
Book design: Lorene Shyba

Canada Alberta
Government

Durvile Publications would like to acknowledge the financial support of the Government of Canada through Canadian Heritage Canada Book Fund and the Government of Alberta, Alberta Media Fund.

Printed in Canada
First edition, first printing. 2022

We wish to acknowledge the ancestral and traditional lands of Indigenous Nations all across North America. They help us steward this land, as well as honor and celebrate this place.

This book is dedicated to the memory of
John Peters Humphrey
who played a foundational role in the creation of the
Universal Declaration of Human Rights (UDHR).

Humphrey was a noted Canadian lawyer, scholar,
and one of the key drafters of the *Declaration.*

The rights set out in the *UDHR* extend to prisoners;
they do not lose their rights by virtue of their incarceration.

Prisoners are entitled to a fair trial and to be free from
arbitrary arrest, detention, or exile. Moreover, prisoners
should not be subjected to torture, or cruel, inhumane,
or degrading treatment or punishment.

CONTENTS

Foreword   *Raphael Rowe*   *ix*

Preface   *1*

PART I The Story of Terry Fitzsimmons   5
Introduction, Part 1   6
1995: The End of the Beginning   9
1993: First Contact   18
The First Meeting   23
The Rasky Murder   29
The Fernand Talbot Murder   39
The Don Hebert Murder   48
The Details   57
The Ride Home   69
The Theory   77
The Grassian Meeting   83
The Next Meeting   88
Call To Action   96
Negotiations   101
June 1994, Ottawa   109
Toronto   121
Montreal   125
Reflections   131
Aftermath   136
Later Revelation   146
The Inquest   151

Afterword, Keramet Reiter   *157*

CONTENTS

Part II Other True Cases   163

Introduction, Part II   165

Clifford Olson, Legendary Evil   167

Susan Wood, Love Is All You Need   178

Joseph Stanley Faulder,

     A Tale of Two Families   195

Allan MacDonald, Trapped   223

David Bagshaw, Kids Who Kill Kids   233

Inderjit Singh Reyat, Air India   251

Acknowledgements   272

About the Author   *274*

FOREWORD

Raphael Rowe

EVERYONE RIGHTLY CONDEMNS criminal activity. But there is sometimes an accompanying evil—injustice. Injustice takes place when the rules of civil society are set aside and an outraged general public demands the spectacle of punishment, no matter the consequences. I know this firsthand. I am Raphael Rowe and my career was born as a result of spending 12 years in prison for crimes I did not commit.

The German philosopher Friedrich Nietzsche once wrote, "What doesn't kill me makes me stronger." Most penitentiary inmates, at least those who survive suicide, would agree. Terry Fitzsimmons, the subject of this book, suffered not only the horrors of imprisonment but was one of the many who died an unnatural death in prison. Others, like myself, used the experience to continue to fight the injustices that abound in a prison environment. I was one of the fortunate few who overcame the financial and social challenges I endured growing up in a deprived area scarred by racial discrimination and inequality. I went from there to prime time television and a career in investigative journalism that has taken me around the world.

Would Terry Fitzsimmons have been able to extricate himself from the torments he experienced in prison? Or was it inevitable that he would become a statistic of imprisoned men and women who, in numbers disproportionate to the general population, choose to end their lives? When a person is so broken by the prison experience, the desire to fight unjust treatment dies first.

During my career, I have been fortunate enough to encounter individuals who have left a permanent mark on how correctional systems operate. One of these individuals is a Canadian lawyer and author of this book, John L. Hill. He confronted the torture of extended solitary confinement experienced by his client head on. The story told here is not a story of instantaneous victory over the evil confronted. John Hill was one of the first to challenge a deficiency in the humane treatment of prisoners. Following these initial steps, other lawyers and reformers came forward and continued the struggle with the result that in Canada, the courts have held that solitary confinement is unconstitutional. Canadian courts have gone even further by compensating prisoners who have been in solitary confinement for inordinate time through a class action lawsuit.

The quest described in this tale is based on a desire to end the imposition of solitary confinement as a means of punishment. It is a story of one man's efforts to bring the ground-breaking research of psychiatrists like Dr. Stuart Grassian to the attention of the courts. Fitzsimmons did not have the stamina to see the venture to conclusion but the effort was commenced. It was the beginning of a legal journey that in Canada would be successful.

In fact, the story has its analogy in Canadian and British history. In 1845, Captain Sir John Franklin departed England with two ships, the HMS *Erebus* and the HMS *Terror*, in a quest to find an easy route by ship between Europe and Asia by plotting a course through the Arctic waters, hoping to find a northwest passage. Winter cold trapped the sailors and their ships in extreme conditions and the expedition failed. But the effort was made. It was the desire to fight for a better way of doing things that lived on.

The struggle to end solitary confinement also lives on. The practice continues (even in Canada, but under the new name "Structured Intervention Units"), mostly because it is something most people have never experienced nor could even contemplate experiencing. There is simply no public outcry for reform. It goes by different names in different jurisdictions: isolation units, special handling or housing units (SHU), supermax cells, management control units, security threat management units, protective custody, or permanent lockdown. Most prisoners just refer to it as "The Hole." The names may be different but conditions are remarkably similar, including:

- 22-to 24-hour confinement behind a solid steel door;
- Limited contact with other human beings;
- Extremely limited opportunities to contact people on the outside;
- Limited or no opportunity for rehabilitative programming;
- Inadequate access to medical and mental health professionals;
- Sensory deprivation including exposure to bright lights, temperature extremes, and forced insomnia.

In the United States it is estimated that upwards of 20 percent of state and federal prison inmates and 18 percent of local jail inmates are kept in solitary confinement or another form of restrictive housing at some point during their imprisonment. Solitary confinement generally comes in one of two forms: disciplinary segregation, in which inmates are temporarily placed in solitary confinement as punishment for rule breaking; and administrative segregation, in which prisoners deemed to be a risk to the safety of other inmates, prison staff, or to themselves are placed in solitary confinement for extended periods of time, often months or years.

A brief history of solitary confinement would note that its practice arose with the insistence by religious groups such as the Quakers demanding that imprisonment should result in repentance and rehabilitation. The practice expanded in the 19th century because it was seen as a humane alternative to the brutality involved in the prevailing methods of punishment such as public flogging. However, early in the 20th century, because of the practice's high cost and questionable ethics, the practice declined. It did return during the 1980s and 1990s when there was political appeal for the notion of getting tough on crime.

Indeed, the system has expanded even though reformers have brought legal challenges attempting to overturn the continued use of the practice.

In the United Kingdom, the situation is somewhat better but much the same. Prison rules allow solitary as a punishment not to exceed 21 days. *Her Majesty's Inspectorate of Prisons* described conditions in its 2012–2013 *Report* and described segregation cells. It noted,

...[a]part from a shower and a phone call, most prisoners remained locked in their cells nearly all day with nothing to do. There is no time limit for prisoners (including children) kept in isolation for good order and discipline if it appears desirable, for the maintenance of good order or discipline or in his [the prisoner's] own interest.

In the 2020-21 *Report*, the horrendous conditions of solitary confinement appear not to have improved. The report noted,

At Erlestoke, we found that prisoners had been held in degrading and inhumane conditions for weeks at a time. Many cells were damaged and lacked running water or working toilets. At Long Lartin, one prisoner had been segregated for over two years and the average length of stay was in excess of 200 days; there were no reintegration plans to help prisoners aim for a return to life among the general population.

In New Zealand, where there is no legislated authorization for dissociation and, theoretically, it is a crime to hold a prisoner in solitary confinement, the practice has been "overused." A human rights expert, Dr. Sharon Shalev, in a report funded by the United Nations, has found the use of segregation to be four times higher than in English prisons. As in most countries, the practice of isolation is often overused on distinct minorities. In New Zealand, Māori People and women were found to be over-represented.

The situation in Australia has also resulted in criticism. Kriti Sharma, a Human Rights Watch campaigner toured Queensland prisons for a 2018 report. She concluded that, "there was no excuse for Australia to be using solitary confinement against prisoners with disabilities in 2020." But, she added, "The major issue in Queensland is that it's legal."

The Covid-19 pandemic made the use of solitary confinement even more prevalent. Some prisons used the device as a quick-fix method of controlling the spread of the virus. But torture, even if applied for humanitarian purposes, is still torture.

Most people grew tired of the restrictions and lockdowns imposed to control the spread of illness. Imagine if the lockdowns imposed were for weeks, months, or even years at a time. The call to end solitary or at least make its imposition more tolerable is, in essence, a call for humanitarian treatment to end an injustice.

I spent 12 years in prison for crimes I did not commit. The only reason I am here now and able to share my story with you is because I never stopped fighting to prove my innocence. Eventually, I won and my convictions were overturned by the Court of Appeal in 2000. I was free — but changed forever. I knew, firsthand, what injustice felt like, looked like and what prison can do to a human being. I am scarred by my life experience but I have not allowed it to hold me back.

It is unlikely the concept of imprisonment will end anytime soon. The onus is on those who want to see a prison system that prizes rehabilitation and avoids injustice to never stop fighting.

—*Raphael Rowe, 2022*
Author of Notorious *and host of Netflix'*
Inside the World's Toughest Prisons

PREFACE

John L. Hill

WHAT IS THE AIM OF JUSTICE IN CRIMINAL LAW? That was a question I would commonly ask of students in my teaching days. The students' usual reply was, "Making the punishment fit the crime." I would then try to convey that such a response was inconclusive because concepts of what are considered punishment and crime are constantly evolving.

Take the word 'crime'. In the early 1800s, in many areas it would not have been considered a crime to buy and sell human beings at a slave auction. But today, we consider such a notion appalling and slavery is prohibited around the world. Sadly, that is not to say the concept is not alive and well in different forms such as debt bondage or child labour.

Early colonial settlers in North America felt it was right and proper to dispossess Indigenous Peoples of their lands and traditional methods of support because they were 'savages'. These people did not share the language, religion, and culture of the colonizers. In many parts of Canada and the United States, government turned the task of integration of an Indigenous population into the colonial standard of mainstream. Today we are horrified by such a concept and strive to rename our streets, towns and municipalities where the surname belonged to such vile people. We tear down their statues because as Shakespeare had Marc Antony say at Caesar's funeral: "The evil that men do lives after them. The good is oft interred with their bones."

It was not that long ago that homosexuality was outlawed by what were called 'sodomy laws'. Same sex marriage was considered anathema if it was considered at all. Today homosexuality is no longer listed as a mental illness in the DSM and most people have no concern with the issue, even though it is still considered newsworthy when an NFL star tweets his situation. The act or condition has not changed; attitudes have.

The same fluctuation of attitude applies to the concept of punishment. While visiting Rome I had the opportunity to stand in the prison where St. Peter was kept until his crucifixion. It looked nothing like a jail; it bore more resemblance to a hole in the ground. That is because the penitentiary as we think of it today is, in historical terms, a rather recent concept. Jails existed only as temporary holding areas until the real punishment could be administered: flogging, drawing and quartering, and various means of capital punishment. All involved the physical destruction of the body. There are countless cases where people were bled or tortured because the dominant explanation for societal indiscretions was blamed on evil spirits. There was no concept of mental illness or alternatives to the notion that "the devil made me do it."

In or around the year 1800, most places in the world realized that not all crime necessitated death or physical mutilation. Reformers such as Jeremy Bentham, John Howard and Elizabeth Fry thought the best way to treat criminals was to ensure they were cognizant of their misfeasance. Allowing God's grace to enter their souls would allow wrongdoers to become penitent.

Thus, a new word was coined where this would occur—penitentiary. Inmates could view the sky and pray for their forgiveness rather than rotting away in a dank hole *in durance vile.*

The transition is evident if one tours the Kilmainham Goal in Dublin, Ireland. Now a museum, it exemplifies how the new concepts of punishment took structural form. That is not to say it is not a site where lethal punishment was administered, such as gunning down the Irish rebels as were the leaders of the 1916 rebellion.

The concept of physical punishment continued. One need only look at the quarries on Robben Island off the coast of Cape Town, South Africa to observe how prisoners were forced into hard labour to atone for their misdeeds. All the while, the concept of rehabilitation was ignored. Hard labour became a standard practice in most institutions. The chain gang, a feature of the Paul Newman movie, *Cool Hand Luke,* is representative of the attitude that prisoners were subservient individuals lacking in rights. The chain gang was recently restored in the State of Alabama.

Regression to older and outdated concepts of physical brutality continue to be used and are justified by our inherent belief that, "it's the way we've always done it" and it must be right. Criminologists tell us that many of these outdated concepts of punishment are misconceived and can actually endanger society.

However, modern times have generated modern solutions. Advances in the field of psychiatry demonstrated that criminal behaviour could be explained or modified. Sex offender clinics were opened in many institutions to use the concept of behaviour modification to ensure that sexual deviance could be cured or at least that the risk could become manageable.

Unfortunately, the desire to associate the brain with miscreant behaviour also led to abuses. We no longer use frontal lobotomization as a correctional tool, and drug therapies have established their own challenges. Nonetheless, psychiatry offers us the best hope of humanely dealing with society's wrongdoers.

So, while the concepts of crime and punishment have been undergoing reinterpretation, the concept of justice is also fluid. That is why I have coined a new definition for the word 'justice'. I take it to mean the concept that involves the authoritative imposition of social norms.

I include the word 'authoritative' because no one could ever consider vigilantism as justice. Mob rule leads to excess and perhaps the opposite of what a society would consider appropriate. Similarly, social norms are the purview of the legislatures and the courts. As society changes, so must our laws and our interpretation of them. It is therefore appropriate that when one sees an inhumane practice in our criminal justice system that one uses the courts and even the press to influence public opinion. It is important to change practices that are outdated and that work against the wishes of society to be safe from the criminal acts of others.

Even with the advances in penology, certain abuses continue. At a very early stage in my criminal and prison law practice I focused on solitary confinement as one of the dinosaurs that continued to exist even though other medieval modes of punishment had long vanished.

The Terry Fitzsimmons story is one of Canada's first forays into bringing the torture of solitary confinement and its aftermath to the courts. It was not the end, but it was one brick in the road to a safer and more humane correctional system.

PART I

THE QUEST TO END SOLITARY CONFINEMENT

THE TRUE CASE OF TERRY FITZSIMMONS

INTRODUCTION, PART I

THE TERRY FITZSIMMONS STORY

PHOTO: GARY MULCAHEY

I AM A CANADIAN LAWYER who defends criminals and penitentiary inmates. I am also a citizen that wants to live in a safe community where the law is fairly, impartially, and humanely applied. Because of my work, I realize that there are inequities in not only our laws but more so in the way they are applied that can result in our society being less safe.

Part I of this book tells the story of my dealings with Terry Fitzsimmons and my quest to halt the imposition of the use of solitary confinement. This story is not told in linear fashion. I begin with Terry's demise and then try to explain what led to the tragic outcome.

Part II is included to tell the stories of other cases that I have worked on in order to show that even with successful challenges to solitary confinement brought by others after Terry died, our judicial and correctional systems continue to be flawed.

In a sense, the way the Terry Fitzsimmons story is set out is how I envision it would be told if this were a television miniseries. The difference is that while a dramatic presentation would likely include the words, "Based on a true story," or "Inspired by a true story," this is actually a true story.

Timeline of a Short Brutal Life

Terry Fitzsimmons was born in 1964. He dropped out of school at age 15. He had a series of run-ins with the law as a youth but at age 18 received his first penitentiary sentence of 3 years. While on that sentence he was involved in a prison stabbing that added another 9-year sentence.

As a result, of the new offence, Terry served a total of 6 years in solitary confinement before being released directly to the street on December 31, 1992. Release did not go well. He violated the conditions of release on April 23, 1993 but his suspension was cancelled on July 13. He bolted from release once again making his way to Toronto and over the span of five days committed three murders. Once returned to prison, he died on March 30, 1995 by strangulation.

Accurate Portrayal

I took careful notes during my discussions with the persons named in this account and I am confident that when I put their words in quotations, it is an accurate portrayal of what they said. Dr. Stuart Grassian was even so kind as to review the section of the book dealing with him and to confirm the accuracy of the description of our meeting.

I want to assure readers that in telling the stories in this book, I am careful that I have not breached lawyer-client privilege by disclosing information intended by the client to be kept confidential. Everything recounted in the following pages is information from public records or material the client has allowed me to repeat.

Terry Fitzsimmons challenged me to make our system of justice and corrections better. By telling his story and the stories that follow, I am hopeful that others might be inspired to work toward what we all want: a system of justice and a system of corrections that is rehabilitative, fair, and humane. In the end, the result will be a society less terrorized by crime and its perpetrators. The punishment for crime need not be brutal.

— John L. Hill, 2022

ONE

1995: THE END
OF THE BEGINNING

■ ■ ■

Hᴏᴡ ᴄᴀɴ ʏᴏᴜ defend someone you know is guilty? As a criminal defence lawyer, especially one who looks after penitentiary inmates, it is a question I hear often. In most cases, I simply reply that I never ask whether a person is guilty or innocent. After all, proving innocence is not my job. There is a constitutional right in Canada and in the United States to be presumed innocent unless proven guilty beyond a reasonable doubt before a court of competent jurisdiction—not the court of public opinion. It is the prosecution's responsibility to prove guilt beyond a reasonable doubt. At the heart of the question, however, is an ethical dilemma: Am I not supportive of criminal activity if I provide excuses as to why criminal activity took place?

What follows is the true story of Terry Fitzsimmons, which was told to me by Fitzsimmons himself. It is also my recollection of the thought processes that I endured while acting on Terry's behalf. It's my answer to the question of how I can defend someone I know is guilty.

Behind Locked Doors

Nobody knows what goes on behind locked doors. That is especially true in the historic and picturesque city of Kingston, Ontario and in the Kingston Penitentiary, located on the shores of Lake Ontario. Built in 1835, there have been daring escapes, riots, and even a visit from British author Charles Dickens. It was not the exciting times for which the prison was appreciated; it was the drudgery in the day-to-day lives of the two hundred to four hundred men and the custodial staff behind locked doors, many in solitary confinement.

It came to pass that on March 30, 1995, a male correctional officer made his hourly rounds on an upper tier, expecting to see nothing out of the ordinary. His flashlight discerned the lifeless body of a young, caged man. A call went out to other guards that the cell occupant had "strung up." Nothing had alerted staff that an inmate had decided to kill himself. Indeed, it would have been rare for such an intention to have reached staff. Every institution has a Preventive Security Officer whose job it is to collect and ascertain the validity of rumours, but the system breaks down when those rumours are not spread.

The dead man was Terry Fitzsimmons. He was wearing the typical inmate garb: green shirt, jeans, and running shoes. He was 31 years old but looked younger than his calendar years. His brown hair was cut short, close to the scalp (as he had worn it since shaving his head two years previously). His body was short and compact, well-defined from years of lifting weights. His clothing was never disheveled in life or in death. Although Terry believed he did not care about much, he was meticulous in ensuring that he was clean and dressed as neatly as possible. He was also clean-shaven. He sported a neatly trimmed beard at one point in his life, but it too had been removed at the time he shaved his head and he made no attempt to regrow facial hair. Since returning to Kingston Penitentiary, Terry had no plans whatsoever for the future. Starting a beard would be just an excuse to live longer. He had no intention of doing that.

Most people put up a struggle even while attempting suicide. Not Terry. He had a mission, and he was out to achieve it. In fact, the whole procedure had not taken long. He made a plan as he always did—just wait until an officer passes by while

Terry Fitzsimmons upon entering penitentiary.
Guards must carry the inmate's photo any time a prisoner is
transported outside the institution should there be an escape.

doing his rounds and then secure a cord that he had pilfered
from maintenance snuggly around his neck and kick the stor-
age trunk out from beneath him. He tried with all his might
not to make a sound, but a loud gasp was inevitable. He had
planned it to go smoothly, but his legs flailed about in search of
a solid surface. His hands grasped inadvertently at the ligature
around his neck but it was so tight he could not squeeze his
fingers between his neck and the cord. Suddenly, all motion
ceased. He had taken his last breath. He had taken his fifth life:
his own.

An emergency response team arrived within an hour of
the notification of the incident. Terry's body was cut down.
Some perfunctory attempts were made at resuscitation, to no
avail of course. Just as quickly, medical staff were called and
promptly made it official. Terry died from a self-strangulation.
There was nothing more to do but to remove the body and have

the Warden's staff prepare an official media release and contact next of kin. That would wait for normal business hours.

Inmates with cells on the range (the common area viewed from individual cells) are certainly aware of when there is an episode taking place. No one needs to be briefed on any occurrence. When staff move in groups larger than two and spend time at a cell where no yelling or fighting is heard, one just knows that a fellow inmate has strung up. Terry had been in a single cell. Sometimes when inmates are 'double-bunked', meaning two to a cell, voices are raised, and yelling precedes a possible inmate-on-inmate assault. Most everyone on the range has had experiences when one inmate has taken a 'shiv' to another, even if a stabbing does not occur. But there was none of that.

A Death and an Inquest

Since his return to custody, Terry had been sullen. He had not engaged frequently with others. He had kept pretty much to himself. The other inmates knew full well what had happened and the body bag that passed their cells merely confirmed their suspicions. There was no sadness and there were no tears. Terry had gone the way he wanted to go. Nobody even asked why.

The body was taken to the makeshift hospital where medical staff could complete a full inspection. That was necessary. The guards were all required to complete an Incident Report. Words of resentment were spoken about the paperwork that was incited by the dead inmate's act.

Whenever a death occurs in a state-run facility, an inquest is mandatory in Canada. All paperwork and medical staff notes would be turned over to the coroner. That would be the procedure in the case of Terry Fitzsimmons. The prosecuting Crown attorney in Kingston would be advised. Another medical doctor would be appointed to preside over a coroner's court, and five jurors who by and large were ignorant of prison practices and procedures would be summoned and asked to make recommendations as to why such an incident happened and what steps, if any, could be taken to prevent such steps from reoccurring. The findings would be published and sent off to the government ministry responsible for corrections. There are procedures for this. All procedures would be followed as laid out in the Commissioner's Directives, the rules formalizing the day-to-day operations of Canada's prisons.

My office received a telephone call from the Warden's secretary the next day. My assistant was told that Terry Fitzsimmons had taken his own life and that a memorial service at the prison would be held at some time in the future so other inmates could attend and show their respects. No future date was mentioned. No notification was left as to how the body would be transported or who would be in charge of a burial or cremation.

I knew Terry's parents lived in the London, Ontario area but I did not know if Terry had contacted them after his return to prison for the last time. From a call I had with Terry's mom and dad two years previously, I assumed they wanted nothing to do with him. I had hoped they had come to a reconciliation, but I seriously doubted it.

The suicide rate in Canadian prisons is six to seven times that of the general population. In the United States, the rate is generally four times higher. Suicide is the leading cause of unnatural deaths of federal inmates. In any given year, suicide makes up twenty percent of all deaths in custody. Nonetheless, the Correctional Service of Canada vigilantly denies that its treatment of prisoners, including its use of solitary confinement, accounts for these statistics.

It may well be that prisoners with suicidal ideation are more common than in the general population because both Canada and the United States have closed down psychiatric institutions. The result is that many of those who would formerly have institutional psychiatric treatment wind up in the correctional system. But could it be that the prisons and the ways prisoners are treated creates mental disturbance?

There was never a doubt in my mind that Terry Fitzsimmons was a deeply flawed individual. As a youth he had sought out the respect of his peers and rejoiced in the admiration of those around him, even though what they were cheering on was criminal behaviour. He was prone to substance abuse even before he first became known to police. Once he breached parole and committed drastic crimes, he was vilified in the press. But was he the monster that the Toronto media made him out to be? Or had that designation of "monster" been my own doing?

In life, Terry used me for his own purposes; I used Terry. I had been hell-bent on getting recognition that solitary confinement was wrong. There had been great work already done on building a legal basis to challenge the use of solitary confinement in court, and there would be even greater steps taken in the future. Terry died. He could not be counted on to assist in the challenge further. I had worked on his case, and he had been at the top of my mind for almost two years. Yet I had to admit I really felt nothing, or at least I was able to repress my emotions. I was a prison law lawyer. I also handled high-end criminal cases like murder and major drug conspiracies. There are, of course, boundaries that all professionals must keep by constantly reminding clients (despite an intense personal involvement in the clients' lives), "I am your lawyer and not your friend." Yes, I had gotten to know Terry and despite his crimes, I had come to like the man. But my professional obligation was to let it go. Professionalism requires that one maintain boundaries. Yet Terry had wanted his story told. He had talked openly with a reporter for the *Globe and Mail* before his death.

Terry had made a plan and I knew, without specifics, that it would end this way. I already knew I would not be attending the memorial service at the prison chapel; I also knew I would not be attending the inquest. But I recognized that Terry had given me a hell of a ride, and I had fun.

Earlier Facts About Me, John L. Hill

I didn't start out as a criminal defence lawyer. I hadn't started out to be a lawyer at all. I was the first in my immediate family to attend university. I enrolled in political science and stayed on to complete a Master's degree in Politics with a strong recommendation from my faculty advisor to complete a Ph.D. program at an American university. However, my housemate, while living off-campus, wanted to be a lawyer and was about to take the LSAT exam before applying. He promised his girlfriend would provide a roast beef supper if I were willing to take the test alongside him. Who would turn down a home-cooked meal? I agreed to take the test as well. When I got the LSAT results, I found I ranked in the top five percent of all those taking the test. My plans abruptly changed. I was off to law school.

My parents were pleased with the change of plans. I had never known my parents to hire a lawyer and they really had no business sense as to what my long-term goal would be. My only recollection of my parents talking about law was when my father would refer to a tragic murder of a young girl abducted and killed after stepping off a school bus in Grafton, Ontario, a neighbouring village. My father never named the assailant. He probably never knew the name. The individual was referred to in our household only as "the guy who killed the little girl in Grafton."

It was troubling, therefore, when I advised my parents that I had turned down a job offer in 1974 from the firm that had hired me to do my articles of clerkship (at the time a mandatory one-year apprenticeship prior to completing the Bar Admission course). The offer was to hire me with the firm to do corporate-commercial law. Rather, I wanted to be a litigator.

The day after completing the six-month bar course and being called to the bar, I rented space above a real estate agency in London, Ontario and started my own practice. I concluded rapidly that I did not like the work that is bread and butter to most small firms, real estate transfers and wills and estates. Instead, I found a niche: representing patients at the nearby St. Thomas Psychiatric Hospital.

I represented and secured the release of a woman who saw herself as a male and who had murdered a cabbie in Toronto to secure his genitals. She then Krazy-Glued these genitals to her vagina to convince her girlfriend's father that she was really a man.

Stories like this did little to assuage my father's regret that I was throwing away the opportunities he never had growing up in the Great Depression and serving in World War II. Most assuredly he resented it when I told him about my most-recent client at the psychiatric hospital whom I simply called "the guy who killed the little girl in Grafton."

"I hope you lose!" was his only comment.

Besides my involvement with this type of client, I handled other criminal cases and became comfortable arguing clients' cases before juries. In the first few years of practice, I landed defence of my first murder trial, an experience seldom encountered by someone so fresh out of law school.

My other preoccupation was my involvement with the London Humane Society. In my initial years in practice, I had married a woman from London and acquired a dog. Not content to lead a simple home life, hours at work in the law practice were matched by my work on the board of the LHS and ultimately becoming president of the operation.

It was revealing to me how similar it was seeing dogs ripped apart from their homes and transferred to cages and seeing men and in some cases, women, cast adrift from their families to endure excessive periods of being locked away.

But my time away from home was costly. In March 1985, after only a few years of marriage, my wife and I decided to separate and ultimately divorce. On the same day we had agreed to separate, my business partner announced his leaving to take a corporate job on the east coast, and my legal assistant tendered her resignation.

Everything I had worked at to develop a practice seemed lost. I was depressed and staring at my desktop early in the afternoon when the phone rang. I answered it. It was Professor Ron Price at Queen's University.

"We've been hearing of the work you've been doing at the St. Thomas Psychiatric Hospital. Is there any chance we could lure you away from private practice to join us on faculty at the law school to head up our Correctional Law Project?"

Professor Price gave a brief description of the work involved; I would be teaching up to a dozen second- and third-year law students and overseeing their clinical involvement with federally incarcerated prisoners.

"I know you'll need some time to think this over. Could you get back to us within a week?"

Not to show my desperation, I agreed to a callback before the week was out.

Within the week I was able to sell my firm and list my house in London. There were good people at the Humane Society who would carry on so that was of little concern. One board member commented that now I will be able to look after people and not just animals.

Humane treatment of all living creatures had become my passion.

I was excited about the prospect of moving and starting a new career. I was looking forward to involving myself with prisoners. Little did I imagine that while I was readying myself for a move to the city of Kingston, inmate Terry Fitzsimmons was preparing to leave its prison. In less than a year, on July 20, 1986, Terry Fitzsimmons would be involved in an incident that not only would preclude his release but also would lead him into years of brutal solitary confinement. It was an incident that ultimately would bring the two of us together. My drive to see all humans and animals treated fairly would be put to the test.

TWO

1993: FIRST CONTACT

■ ■ ■

IT WAS A WARM AND SUNNY summer afternoon in mid-August 1993. I intended to spend part of my weekend at the marina in Cobourg, my birthplace and new home, after leaving my teaching responsibilities at the University of Windsor Law School. It was back in 1985 that I had left private practice in London, Ontario to become Director of the Correctional Law Project at the Faculty of Law at Queen's University in Kingston. I taught second- and third-year law students the ins and outs of prison law, a unique blend of criminal and administrative law concepts. From there I moved on to the University of Windsor, supervising students in a legal clinic operated by the university but while earning extra income teaching my old prison law course in the Departments of Sociology and Criminology.

The teaching experience became somewhat frustrating. My academic colleagues were first rate but I sensed it was a closed community. Important revelations about the wrongs in society became objects of debate in peer-reviewed articles unread by the masses who would be responsible for making changes in a democratic society. I believed there was a failure of our criminal legal system to take seriously violence against women, children and other vulnerable groups.

I decided to leave teaching in large part because of this failure—indeed the refusal—of our criminal legal system, from police, prosecutors, defence counsel/lawyers, judges, correctional services to assist men to take responsibility and remedy criminal sexual harassment, abuse and other forms of misogynistic violence. But misogyny was only a part of the problem. I was deeply troubled by the cruelty of many prison practices. I needed to get back into the trenches.

I enjoyed teaching, but I also missed private practice where I felt I could have greater influence in addressing the wrongs I perceived to exist. I was recently divorced and had no attachments to any particular community or thing, except for my dog. When my aunt's home in Cobourg became available, I decided to buy it and return to Northumberland County. I limited my practice to high-end criminal cases and worked with penitentiary inmates when prison issues arose. Ordinarily, my prison practice was assisting inmates going up for parole or defending them before the National Parole Board (as the Parole Board of Canada was then known) for violations of conditions of parole, dealing with disciplinary infractions while a sentence was ongoing, or suing the Government of Canada for violation of an inmate's rights when institutional staff stepped out of line.

There were very few legal practitioners who knew about correctional law (or for that matter, wanted to know about it). That being the case, my name spread rapidly within the prison population. Sometimes inmates (or their families) could rustle up my fees but, more often than not an inmate would claim to be impecunious and obtain financial coverage through Legal Aid.

Legal Aid, a provincial initiative to give the poor access to justice, never paid as well as a private retainer, but since I could work from my home (I didn't need an office since my clientele could not come to me), I had little need of luxurious office space or extensive support staff. With a simple office and minimal staff acting as telephone receptionist and bookkeeper, I could operate efficiently. Thus, by focusing my practice on a limited range of issues, I could live comfortably and become expert in an area of law that few had interest in pursuing.

Saturdays were usually days to unwind. I had purchased a 36-foot yacht (secondhand, but in reasonably good condition), and Saturdays provided an opportunity to visit the boat and scrub away a week's deposit of seagull droppings. Or at least that was my intention.

Before I could assume the role of Captain Bligh on this sunny day in August 1993, the phone rang. It started in the way in which I had become accustomed: "You have a collect call from..." the mechanical voice intoned, leaving room for the caller to state a name. "Terry Fitzsimmons," the voice added quickly (but distinctly) before the pre-recording resumed. "If you wish to accept this call, say 'yes' now." I consented immediately, cutting the mechanized list of options short and starting directly into conversation.

"Hello," I began.

"Hello. Is this John Hill?"

"Yes, who am I speaking with?"

"You don't know me. My name is Terry Fitzsimmons. I got your number from another inmate at the OCDC."

The call was originating from an inmate of the Ottawa Carleton Detention Centre, a provincial jail and remand centre just outside the nation's capital.

"How can I help you?" I asked.

"I just got arrested for murder. I don't know if you can help me or not. Buddy here thinks I should talk to you anyway."

"What's the charge?"

"Murder. First degree. Times three. You must have seen it in the papers."

"I didn't," I replied. I failed to state that I rarely paid much attention to criminal cases reported in the newspapers, especially when they involve inmates whom I may be called upon to represent. I believed they usually approached their coverage in a sensationalistic manner and parroted information divulged from police. I knew there was always another side to every story, and it was unfair to prospective clients to have my perceptions of a situation molded by biased coverage. If I was going to be effective in representation, better that my biases tilted toward the client.

Terry recited the names of the people he was charged with killing. I scratched those names onto a scrap of paper that I could refer to in writing up a memorandum to a file yet to be opened.

"Hold on, Terry," I cautioned. "Don't say anything over the phone. You know that jail authorities can and do monitor calls. I will arrange to get up to Ottawa to meet with you in person."

"I want to see you right away."

"You will," I promised. "In the meantime, be sure not to say anything to anybody until I show up."

"Okay", Terry agreed, "But make it soon. I need to speak to you right away." That concluded our first contact.

An Emotional Roller-Coaster

Getting into a provincial remand centre is not as simple as showing up at the door. One must telephone the jail and set up an appointment to see a client. Even after a booking is made, the process is never assured. A single range or even the entire jail may be under lockdown, preventing an appointment from taking place. Lockdowns are never announced. They could result from a criminal action in the jail, such as an inmate being stabbed or murdered, or that a quantity of narcotics was found during a routine cell inspection.

I certainly did not want to undertake a three-hour drive from Cobourg to Ottawa only to be sent home. But that's the downside in a practice such as mine. A call to the institution prior to leaving certainly helps, but it's never a guarantee of entry. Another potential problem exists with new clients. What if the lawyer arrives and the client refuses the visit? Some inmates call several lawyers, trusting their fate to the counsel who arrives first and simply giving short shrift to anyone who arrives later.

A first meeting always includes a discussion of retainer. That can mean having a client without means calling in Legal Aid to take an application and waiting for approval before a certificate guaranteeing payment is issued or getting a list of people who might be willing to ante up the funds for a private retainer. My suspicion was that for a young man (or at least who sounded young on the telephone) in jail for murder times three, Legal Aid would be the likely option.

I knew full well that accepting a Legal Aid certificate would guarantee funds, albeit at a lower rate than my normal billable hour fee, but it would also require strict adherence to any conditions of the certificate. For example, unless the certificate authorized travel time and mileage, I could be on the hook for the hours on the road and the cost of transportation. All this was on my mind, but it was only a minor distraction to the thoughts racing through my brain as I considered the telephone call.

I had done several murder trials in the past. Even with many such trials under my belt, I foresaw that just listening to the tale would be emotionally draining.

I recalled the emotional roller-coaster I endured on my initial contact with my first client accused of murder who I defended in my first few years of practice. I recalled that after being told the horrors of the crime, the shock at meeting the accused person was disconcerting. I could not believe that the vicious allegations could be committed by an individual very similar to someone I could meet every day at a supermarket or while getting gas at the local service station. I did not seek out any reported background stories that had been published. I knew I would await the story from the man himself.

The following day, I made the call and arranged an appointment at the end of the week for my first visit with Terry.

THREE

THE FIRST MEETING

■ ■ ■

UPON ARRIVING at the Ottawa Carleton Detention Centre, I took mental note of how dissimilar the experience was from my arrival at federal penitentiaries. There were no high fences or walls, just a rather modern-looking brick building without towers and with the exception of an outdoor yard, minimal fencing and barbed wire. It was a long driveway leading up to 2244 Innes Road in the Ottawa outskirt municipality of Gloucester. Unlike most penitentiaries I had visited, it looked quite modern. (It was opened in 1972.) Nonetheless, this provincial facility was more despised than federal penitentiaries by its inhabitants.

The OCDC houses female as well as male prisoners, whereas federal facilities are segregated according to gender. Still, there is no intermingling of prisoners. Each gender is confined to a separate area. Provincial jails are largely remand centers with most inmates awaiting trial—technically innocent people. All provincial jails are maximum security, whereas federal pens are maximum, medium, and minimum secured institutions. Because convicted inmates in provincial institutions serve at most a sentence of two years less a day, there is never a feeling of having to make the place your home, as federal inmates so often choose to do. There is little by way of treatment programs and an overarching feeling that an inmate's physical safety is always at risk. This is largely due to the fact that remand prisoners who are too dangerous to make bail prior to trial quite often suffer mental conditions with limited treatment options.

Upon entry, I went through the usual process of obtaining a locker to store my keys, briefcase, and wallet. No metal is allowed. I could only take in a pen and pad of paper, and I had to walk through a metal detector and surrender my 'bar card' proving I was a legitimate lawyer. I was then escorted to an open interview area by a white-shirted guard, who had a badge sewn on each shoulder bearing the coat of arms of Ontario and the words "Correctional Service" printed in a circle surrounding the coat of arms. Guards rarely spoke and seemed like they did not like being spoken to. I kept quiet as I was taken to a glassed-in interview area to await the arrival of my client. The interview room is basically an office with a desk and two chairs with windows allowing custodial staff to watch without hearing anything discussed.

Terry arrived, looking pale in an orange jumpsuit and blue running shoes, the standard dress for prisoners locked up in a provincial jail awaiting trial. There was a small desk, and instead of sitting across from one another, I felt a more effective interview technique would be to assume a seat where I would be sitting beside the prisoner.

The individual who sat beside me was nothing exceptional for a man in his late twenties. He was about five foot seven and solidly built, the orange jumpsuit covering what I suspected to be a muscular frame. In other circumstances, he would look like a good prospect for a college football team. His face was round, and he approached with a friendly smile even given the known reason for the visit. His face was clean-shaven, and his light brown hair cut short.

Terry sat down next to me and immediately the smile vanished. He put both hands over his face. "I can't take it in here," he said. His voice was loud and clear. He spoke in crisp clear tones, but the first words felt more like exasperation than sorrow.

"What's the problem?" I asked, thinking it unusual that we weren't getting immediately into the details of his charges.

"This place is a fucking hellhole. The guys on my range are all nuts. They think they're all tough guys. I have to sleep with one eye open so I don't get a shiv rammed through my neck."

"Is it just the group of inmates close to you? Can I do anything to get you to a better range?" I asked, not knowing what, if anything, could be done. Terry's indication was that the whole jail was a freak show.

"I just forgot how these provincial prisons are such bullshit," he added. "I would just like to get back to KP." He was referring to Kingston Penitentiary. Federal offenders often refer to an institution by its initials—a common practice not only with inmates but in the Correctional Service as a whole. One unfamiliar with the use of initials and acronyms within the system can easily become confused.

"You are a federal offender?"

"Yeah, I got released on stat from KP. That's where I heard your name. You were the guy who got us hot water and cable TV, right?"

Without admitting it, I was very grateful that my work had been appreciated. When I first started work at Queen's Law School, Kingston Penitentiary was on the verge of riot. I had met with some of the inmates and promised that I would use my office to try to ameliorate some of the conditions that they objected to. The first two items on the list of demands were for making hot water available in the cells of the ancient building, and for a cable TV outlet to be installed in each cell so that inmates who saved enough money to buy their own television could watch a wider array of programming than what was available with a set of rabbit-ear antennas.

To that end, I set up a meeting with Solicitor General (now called Minister of Public Safety) Perrin Beatty in Ottawa. At the meeting with the Minister and high-ranking Correctional Service of Canada officials, I had been asked to provide a list of inmate demands. Hot water and cable TV were among those reforms being sought. Beatty asked for six weeks to study the issues at which time I would meet again to hear the government response. In the meantime, I was told to tell the inmates that nothing would be given if there was any violence while the study was going on. I relayed the message to the inmate leaders and all threats of violence came to an end. When I returned to the meeting in the Ottawa Parliament buildings, I was more surprised than anyone to learn that the government had decided to accede to all the demands.

"Well, it wasn't just me, Terry. In my view, Perrin Beatty really knew his portfolio and was willing to take action." Lawyers like to drone on about their past perceived victories, but Terry didn't want to hear my old war stories. He had something more pressing on his mind.

"What brings you here?" I asked, wanting to hear what Terry had to say.

"You got to stop the fucking lies!" he said. I could see the anger in his eyes.

"What lies are you talking about?"

"The fucking *Toronto Sun* is calling us Canada's first gay Bonnie and Clyde. And I'm not gay."

"Okay, okay," I interjected. "What's that all about, anyway?"

"Haven't you read it? Haven't you read it? The paper is calling me and Don Hebert the gay Bonnie and Clyde cuz we robbed a bank in Toronto. I'm not gay. You gotta stop this!"

I thought I was here to talk about murder, and now I see that Terry's first concern was possible libel and slander.

"Slow down," I said, "Start at the beginning. Why would the paper call you that name?"

"After I got out of prison, I took money from my family in Kingston and moved to Toronto," said Terry. "I knew that the gays were a repressed minority, so I decided to hang out in the Gay Village."

I underlined his words 'repressed minority' thinking

it unusual terminology to hear in such an interview. I knew that many (if not most) inmates upon release feel discomfort in open society. It's a feeling that everyone is staring at the released offender in a condescending manner. Obviously, Terry had experienced this discomfort but analyzed his emotion and formulated a plan on how to deal with it.

"I met up with Don Hebert. He's gay and has AIDS. He really liked me, and I liked him, so we hung around together. We both got into crack cocaine but when I ran out of money, Don came with me and we robbed a Canada Trust branch on Yonge Street. A few days later we went back and robbed it again."

A Need For Respect

I had been dealing with penitentiary inmates for so long that I found none of this shocking. Substance abuse was common in the inmate population. What I found surprising was that, despite knowing the seriousness of the charges Terry faced, his seemingly sole concern was that the press had linked him to an outlaw gang and called him gay. It was not a classic case of homophobia. Terry clearly had sought out the gay community and had sought the friendship of a man who was certainly well-known in that community. I concluded (without saying it aloud) that Terry felt he was being disrespected. Within the inmate population, it was no problem being labelled a murderer. Being laughed at in the press though, that was a different matter. Terry seemed like a man who demanded respect from those around him and was very troubled when he was powerless to enforce that need for respect.

"I guess some of the guys we met at the Sailor—it's a local gay bar that Don liked—suspected it was us and reported us to police." Terry continued. "We had to go into hiding, so we stayed put in Don's apartment at 80 Charles Street. Then the fucking press got hold of it and started calling us 'Bonnie and Clyde.' It's not right. I want you to stop it."

"But there's more to your story than this," I insisted. "You said on the phone that you've been charged with three murders. Surely that is a bigger concern than being called a name in the newspaper?"

After all, Bonnie and Clyde were folk heroes in Depression-ridden America. They robbed banks that were seen as enemies of the poor. They were like Red Ryan or the Boyd Gang in Ontario: they robbed banks and were lionized by the media for so doing. It didn't make sense that being likened to a folk legend was worse than being called a murderer. I understood Terry was being charged with murder and the most certain way to negate a folk hero image is to turn against the folk.

"Yeah, they charged me with three first-degree murders, but Don Hebert is the finest man I've ever met," said Terry. "He doesn't deserve to be made a laughingstock. I turned myself into police. I told them everything. So, in defending me, just have fun with it. I've already given myself capital punishment, but I want to look out for Don."

Never before had an alleged criminal hired me with an order that I "just have fun" with the defence.

"I promise that I will do what I can about the name calling," I said. "But let's review what you told police about each of the murders. I've got a few hours booked here, so take your time. It's all new to me, so I may have some questions along the way."

I was totally unaware during this initial interview that there was a massive elephant in the room. Terry had not yet mentioned to me that he had spent six years in solitary confinement.

Terry started recalling the murders, one by one.

FOUR

THE RASKY MURDER

■ ■ ■

A S TERRY FITZSIMMONS' LAWYER, I deemed it essential that I get a synopsis of the circumstances that led to his arrest on three first-degree murder charges. I knew very well the provisions of section 231(1) of the *Criminal Code* of Canada.

Murder can be either first-degree or second-degree. First-degree murder is planned and deliberate. Second-degree murder requires an intent to kill but is not premeditated or planned in advance. Although both first-degree and second-degree murder require a jury to find that the accused acted with intent, the degree of premeditation lies at the heart of the distinction. The distinction is crucial since it determines the penalty. Both first-degree and second-degree murder are punishable by life imprisonment. But since Canada has abolished the death penalty, the difference focuses on the extent of parole ineligibility. Contrary to what some people say, a life sentence in Canada means a life sentence. A person convicted and sentenced to life will be under state control for the remainder of the offender's natural life. Some 'lifers' casually refer to death as a "pine box parole." Even with first-degree murder, however, there can be light in the tunnel. Parole is always discretionary and requires the granting of parole by the Parole Board. Thus, it is possible that some lifers will never walk the street in free society ever again. But for first-degree murders, there is but one sentence: Life in prison without parole eligibility for 25 years. That means for a person convicted of first-degree murder, one must serve at least 25 years in federal prison before an application can be made to serve the remainder of one's life on parole.

If the charge can be reduced to second-degree murder, the jury has the responsibility of not only establishing the factual elements of the crime, but it can also recommend to the judge that the sentence imposed can include a period of parole ineligibility of between 10 and 25 years. A life sentence remains, but there is some wiggle room on parole ineligibility.

There is also the crime of manslaughter to be considered. Manslaughter is also homicide, but it does not require intention. There may be an intention to cause harm, but if no intention to kill is established, a manslaughter conviction may be sought. The penalty can also be significantly less. While a life sentence can be imposed, the manslaughter sentence usually involves a sentence specifying a term of years of imprisonment ranging from four to seven years (at the low end) to life (at the high end).

Unless a judge specifies a specific number of years, parole eligibility would occur when one-third of the sentence is served (with Parole Board authorization) to mandatory release at the two-thirds mark (independent of the Parole Board) unless a recommendation is made to detain the inmate beyond the two-thirds point in a special hearing commonly referred to as "gating." [The concept being that as the inmate approaches the front gate of the prison, the Parole Board orders his return to incarceration.]

Of course, if an accused person cannot be found to have committed a homicide beyond a reasonable doubt, said accused is entitled to an acquittal. My intention of having Terry recount the facts of his alleged crimes was to determine how the facts, if proven, would substantiate a possible plea of 'guilty' of first-degree murder, second-degree murder, manslaughter or 'not guilty'.

Norman Rasky was a dentist and a member of a
prominent and well-respected Toronto family.
He fell on hard times following a drug conviction.

"Let's start with the first murder," I said. "Just tell me in
your own words what happened. I will ask questions if anything arises."

"Well, I arrived in Toronto. I didn't have a place to stay,
and I decided that I had to hide out in the gay community."

"I'll stop you there. Why would you need to hide out?"

"Well, I was on stat release when I got out of KP on
New Year's Eve last year. I just couldn't handle all the noise
and confusion. I got along fine with my ol' lady while I was
inside. But once I got out, it was just full-time nagging and
complaining. So I just scooped some of her jewelry and cash
and got a train to Toronto without anybody knowing."

"Did you know that travelling outside your radius would
trigger the Correctional Service to seek a warrant of suspension, meaning that they could haul your ass back into
prison?"

"Yeah, I knew that, and I had no doubt my wife would lodge the complaint once she knew I was gone. But when I was inside, I'd heard stories that gay men were picked on. And so, I figured that if I could find a few who could sympathize with my situation, I could stay free a lot longer than if I just roamed around on my own."

"So how did you get involved with Toronto's gay community? How did you know where to go? You didn't know Toronto, did you?"

"It changed a lot since I was a kid. I just asked. I got to the Union Station terminal, and I just walked up to some cool-looking dude and asked where I could find gay guys in Toronto. He didn't even blink. He said I should get a subway, get off at the Wellesley Street Station and walk east to Church Street. There would be lots of bars there.

"I found a couple of places and went in for a beer. It was daytime, and nobody was particularly friendly. I asked where all the action was, and one bartender told me that nothing really picks up until around 10 o'clock at night. So, I just did some sightseeing and headed back in the evening. And yeah, things had picked up."

Terry went on to describe that his first few days upon reaching Toronto developed into a routine: He's sleeping in the park, spending his days hanging out there as well, and heading back to the bars in the evenings hoping someone would buy him a drink.

"I went to a bar—I can't remember what it was called. I stood at the bar and just hung out sucking on a beer. After about twenty minutes, this guy approached and asked me if I hung out at this bar often. I told him I was new in town. I said I'd just arrived a few days before and wasn't familiar with the city. He asked me if I had a place to stay. I told him that I didn't and without anything further he asked me if I needed a place to stay that night. So, I took him up on the offer. It was only then that he told me his name—Don Hebert—and I told him mine.

We shook hands and he commented that I had a good build."

Terry stated that he had been approached in the same bar by a few other men but not one of them were as friendly and open as Don Hebert. Terry described Don as "immediately likeable."

"In prison, guys work out—not so much for the exercise but to get compliments from other prisoners. It adds to your self-respect to know that other guys are appreciative of the hard work you do lifting weights and that shit. He told me he was 30 and he had a ground-floor apartment nearby."

"Did you suspect that Hebert might just be trying to get you in bed with him?" I asked.

"I didn't care. I needed a place to stay and if some guy wants to blow me, what's the big deal?"

His response caught me off guard in that it just seemed a bit too cavalier. So, I then posed one of the questions I sometimes ask inmates.

"Were you ever sexually or physically abused as a child?" Over the years I learned that a very high percentage of inmates confirm that they experienced some form of abuse. While I never kept statistics, I had come to realize that toxic shame was often at the heart of addictions and criminal behaviour.

"No," Terry answered. "Things were great growing up. I was raised north of London. We even had horses."

From our initial conversation, I assumed that Terry may have been close to his parents at least at one point in his life, though sorting through the familial bonds would be a topic for future conversation. Terry then gave me the highlights of his early life.

I gathered that Terry was not much of a scholar. Hanging out with anti-social younger pals and early involvement with alcohol and drugs were other points to be raised later, as these raised the specter of early childhood trauma. (There is a more significant link between early childhood trauma and addiction than there is between obesity and diabetes.)

I took his denial of abuse at face value but as the interview continued, I was determined to see if I could spot any indicia of trauma.

"How come you're so liberal about having sex with men?" I asked.

"You see a lot of things inside. It scared me early on but after a while, I just accepted it. Guys talk a lot about being queer in prison. It's no big deal. You just accept it."

"Did you go to Hebert's place that night?" I asked.

"Sure", he replied. "We were both kinda drunk when we left the bar and we walked up to Charles Street. Don had an apartment on the first floor, and when we walked in there was an old guy sitting on the couch. Don introduced me to him as Norm Rasky."

I later learned that Norman Rasky was a 62-year-old retired dentist. He had been divorced from his wife for 20 years. He had three grown daughters when his drug dependence interfered with his professional and social life.

Rasky had graduated at the top of his class at the University of Toronto School of Dentistry. He maintained a very successful dental practice in Toronto until January 1988. A tip to Crime Stoppers led to a raid in which 380 grams of cocaine was found. Police valued the street value of the drug to be $228,000. It was commonplace to overvalue the worth of seized substances since ordinary folk would have no idea this price was probably six times its actual value on resale, but it allowed the police to portray themselves as stalwart protectors against the evils of the illicit substance. Rasky, then 56 years old, found himself facing jail time for trafficking and a dental practice that was worthless.

Rasky's crime did not result in significant time in jail. Indeed, by the time he met Terry, he was on probation.

"He seemed like a nice old man." Terry continued. "He had white hair and seemed a bit out of it. Don asked if Norm had been smoking, and Norm admitted he had."

"What had he been smoking?" I asked.

"Crack. He used to be a dentist. A regular guy with wife and kids. But then he got involved with coke. Just couldn't handle it. He tried living alone but couldn't handle that either. He'd bring old homeless guys back to his place until his landlord got sick of it and kicked him out. I don't know how he met up with Don. I didn't question it. But he just hung out with us. He was pretty quiet. I knew he was listening to everything we said, but we just continued on.

I questioned Terry on his use of crack cocaine. He said, "I don't think I ever did crack before that night. I'd tried powder coke before, but this stuff gave you an instant high. Didn't have to inject anything. Just a single drag and you're racing."

"Did Don have the equipment to smoke it?" I asked, seeing if I could get a glimpse of how extensive the drug habit was by his answer.

"You don't need any equipment," Terry shot back as though I were a complete novice, which indeed I was. "You just get a toilet paper tube. Punch a hole on it and get some aluminum foil stuffed into the hole to form a bowl. Then take a needle and punch a lot of little pin pricks through the aluminum, fill it with tobacco ash, lay on a rock and ignite. That's all there is to it. You block off one end of the toilet paper tube with your hand and suck all the air out of the tube while you're lighting the bowl. Instant high!"

"How long did this go on?" I asked.

"We passed the pipe around all evening. One after the other. By the time it had been passed around the high wears off and you're ready for another hit again. So, we did that until late, until it was all gone. Then I tried to sleep. When you're on the run and you're so high you can't sleep, the paranoia gets the best of you. So, we were determined we had to get more.

"The next day, everybody was out of cash. We were craving more crack. And then the idea came to me. If you can't get cash legally, you can always get it illegally.

"So, I ran the idea by Don about pulling a score with me. He seemed pretty excited about the prospect. We didn't plan anything. It was July 27th. We just went to a Canada Trust, walked in, and told a teller we didn't want anyone to get shot and to just hand over the cash. She got this scared look on her face and shoved a wad of cash our way. We grabbed it and ran.

"Don knew a place to buy crack. There were street hustlers willing to supply us, so we spent the bulk of the score on more drugs.

"When we got back home, the old man was sitting on the couch and asked us where we'd been. Don told him we found a place that handed out cash, and so we bought more crack. And we spent the rest of the day and most of the next day puffing away.

"Then we ran out again. So, we went to the same branch on the 29th and pulled the same stunt. Just like taking candy from a baby. Like shampooing your hair, do it once, then repeat.

"We were into our second round of getting high when the old man said he heard a rumour that police were passing a picture of us around at local bars. Being high and paranoid, we felt that somebody would be at the door within minutes. We wondered how the old man heard the rumour, given that he had never left the building. Maybe he was making the story up.

"Then Norm says he has to see his parole officer and that he would be leaving shortly.

"Bullshit I thought. The old man is a snitch. He's about to go to the police. He's going to turn us in. Maybe even collect a Crime Stoppers reward. I called Don aside and he was just as paranoid as me. We can't let this happen, so we told the old man that we were going to put a supply of crack in a locker in the basement for him to use if we were gone when he got back home. We asked him to follow us downstairs to show him where it was. He agreed. Once he was downstairs, we accused him of trying to rat us out. He said he wouldn't do that but both Don and I were so paranoid, we wouldn't believe a word he said. So, we started smacking him around a bit and he started shouting. So, we got a knife and stabbed him over and over again until he was dead.

"Don wondered what the old man had seen that he could report to the cops. We were both so paranoid we didn't even appreciate he was dead. So, we agreed he should never be able to see anything anymore. So, we took the house key and gouged his eyes out.

"There was blood everywhere, so we dragged the body up through the lobby and left it in the building next door.

"Even all mixed-up as we were, we knew we had to get out. So we went to the apartment and I shaved off my beard and then cut off my hair. Don did the same. We had enough cash to get us to the train station and buy two one-way tickets to Montreal. If police were looking for a bearded guy with long hair, it wouldn't be me.

"Funny, we both slept most of the way to Montreal."

Terry advised that he later learned the police spent considerable time questioning Hebert's associates after Rasky's body was discovered. People knew that Rasky was living at the Hebert apartment, and Hebert was missing.

Terry continued, "The questioning led to the police hearing stories of Don's new acquaintance, me, Terry Fitzsimmons. Police would have my mug shot and putting two and two together—suspected that Hebert was on the lam with me rather than being a missing person himself."

An Unconnected Murder

Nothing of the Rasky police investigation was revealed to the press. There was tension between the police and Toronto's gay community ever since Operation Soap when Toronto police raided four gay bathhouses in February 1981. News of gay men being murdered provokes public distress. But that could not be avoided when the body of a 58-year-old man was found on the second floor of a Collier Street apartment, just north of

Toronto's Gay Village, and a fire started in a first-floor closet. The man who was killed had left his home at midnight on August 1st and driven to an area known as a hang-out for male prostitutes. He picked up a 24-year-old street hustler and the two returned to the apartment to party and play. After ingesting large quantities of valium and alcohol, the hustler killed his john.

Police determined quickly that there was no connection between the Rasky killing and the Collier Street murder, but these unusual occurrences in the peaceful gay section of Toronto led to significant public anxiety. This put enhanced pressure on police to solve the crimes.

I had heard stories of shootings and stabbings before. Indeed, I had represented people who committed such acts. Yet I was immediately struck by Terry's admission that he was an enucleator—someone who gouges eyes—and it took me aback. That was a practice I associated with serial killers or mentally deranged individuals. I needed time to digest Terry's story and asked no further questions about Rasky at that time. There was a pause in my note-taking while I buried my shock.

"What happened once you got to Montreal?" I asked. I knew the answer would shock me as well.

FIVE

THE FERNAND TALBOT MURDER

■■■

"Montreal turned out to be a bit disappointing." Terry said. "Don and I were not French speakers and you had to start a conversation in French before whoever you were talking to would switch to English. Plus, we didn't know our way around the city. We were both afraid that the police would be hunting for us."

"I guess you weren't there for long?" I queried.

"Basically, just overnight. Don kept talking about Rasky and telling me that it was the most gruesome scene he ever witnessed but also the most thrilling. It was only then that Don told me he was dying. He told me he had AIDS."

In the 1980s and early 1990s, a diagnosis that one was suffering from AIDS was considered a death sentence. No treatment existed. Terry recounted how Don Hebert suspected that he would be immobile within months whereupon he would slowly and painfully waste away. Terry told me didn't believe Don at first and that he would continually assure Don that he would be fine. It was only when Don showed him the large black spots developing on his arms and chest that Terry realized Don was serious. Don had been either an airline attendant or a travel agent, Terry said. Terry was unsure which. Don was always in good spirits, but he'd become sullen when talk came of his pending demise.

"There's one thing I want to do before I go," Don told Terry while he was in one his more withdrawn moods.

"What's that?" Terry asked.

"I want to kill a guy like you did in Toronto," Don exclaimed. Terry was shocked by the request. It took a while before he realized Don was serious.

"Why?"

"Because I have never done anything exciting in my life," Don answered.

I then made the connection as to why Terry and Don related as they did. For Don, Terry's appeal was physical. Terry was a buff, good-looking young man. Don gave Terry respect. I had come to know that in prison, the amount of self-esteem inmates have could be measured with a thimble. Terry found it both odd and comforting that Don saw him not as a worthless charge on society, as many people saw inmates both while in prison and upon release, but as a role model or a mentor capable of providing excitement that Don had wanted all his life.

Terry was overwhelmed that the Rasky murder had so impressed Don that he wanted to mimic Terry. As Terry digested the request, he realized that Don saw Terry as a role model and could understand that Don wanted to bind himself more emotionally than physically with his new-found friend. In the most bizarre way, the two men had bonded.

Partners in Crime

Terry described a conversation he had with Don that I recorded in my notes. Terry advised that the conversation went something like this:

"The first thing we have to do is make a plan," Terry told me that he said to Don. "You don't just go into the street and mow somebody down. You gotta think of how you can get away. If you don't have a plan, you will surely get caught. You know the consequences."

"What type of plan are we looking at?" Don asked him.

"It has to be something that fits our natural movement of

Fernand Talbot was a 58-year-old independent cab driver
working for the A-11 company. His taxi was not equipped with a radio;
He picked up fares from the street.

getting from A to B," Terry explained.

Don was worried and said, "I don't get you."

"Well, where do we want to go?" Terry asked. "Obviously, we don't want to stay in this goddamn town any longer. So where do we go?"

"We can't go back to Toronto," Don reasoned. "We'd be picked up immediately."

"Where then? The further east we go, the more French we get. Where else?"

"There's always Ottawa. It's only a few hours' drive from here. Or maybe we could take the train. I know we are low on cash, how about another robbery?"

"Too much heat," Terry told him. "We'll have to steal a car. And then there is the cost of gas. We don't have the bucks to do that. What if we wait until dark and hail a cab? Cabbies usually carry cash. Are you up for a kill?"

Terry explained to me that Don was delighted by the prospect of a kill. He was about to get his dying wish, and it wouldn't be a trip to Disneyland.

"So how do we go about it?" Don asked Terry.

"I still have the knife I took downstairs when we killed the old man. I didn't want to leave fingerprints lying around."

I stopped Terry's story dialogue right there and asked, "When you went downstairs at the Charles Street apartment, did you arm yourself with a knife?"

"Of course," Terry said without hesitation. "We couldn't let the old guy get away with ratting us out."

There goes one defence, I thought to myself.

This was a significant admission. Terry had willingly taken a knife downstairs to kill Rasky which qualifies as planning and deliberation—first-degree right off the bat. While a lawyer must use every opportunity to get the best outcome possible in the trial process, a bedrock principle is that a lawyer cannot mislead the court. Ordinarily I would not directly ask if a person had committed the crime alleged, but Terry's circumstance was different. He had talked to police. I needed to know the scope of his involvement.

"Why is that so important?" Terry asked.

"It just means that if we go to trial, I can't ask you to take the stand and lie that the killing was unintentional or a spur-of-the-moment happening." I reminded him that if we are to go to court, it would be up to the prosecuting Crown attorney to prove all elements of an offence beyond a reasonable doubt. It was not our obligation to provide the prosecution with the ammunition to do so. We could proceed to trial and simply not call Terry to the stand, thus ensuring he wouldn't give evidence against himself. Juries always like to hear the testimony of an accused, but in instances such as this, it just couldn't happen.

Terry reassured me that he had no intention of telling a false story. He didn't even seem bothered that I would have to conduct a defence according to my own standards of conduct.

He just wanted, at this moment, to unburden himself with the memories of a very bad week.

"Carry on," I suggested.

"Don wanted to do the deed," Terry continued. "So, we worked out a plan. I would hand Don the knife, which he would keep hidden under his jacket until we got into the taxi and Don would sit in the rear seat directly behind the cabbie. I'd get in the front seat. We would go a few blocks, and when I saw the proper place with minimal traffic, I would ask the driver to pull over. As soon as we came to a stop, I would nod my head. Don was to take the knife and reach around and jab the cabbie in the chest. We'd grab his cash, dump the body and drive to Ottawa."

Again, obvious planning and deliberation, I reasoned.

"Is that what happened?" I asked.

"Well not exactly."

The unsuspecting cab driver was a 58-year-old bachelor named Fernand Talbot. Talbot's car lacked a radio; he was an independent and liked working evenings and nights.

"Don hid the knife as we discussed and got into the back seat directly behind the driver," Terry continued. "I went to get into the front seat, but the driver was upset and signaled he wanted me in the back as well. I pretended I could not make out his directions due to a French accent, and just loaded myself in the car as we planned. I pointed that I wanted to go in a particular direction. And the cabbie started driving even though he seemed irritated. We came across a dark barely populated street. I shouted out that I wanted to stop here. The driver looked puzzled, but he did as he was told. I nodded.

"At that point Don pulled out the knife and reached around and started poking the driver with knife. He didn't use a lot of strength, though, and any stabbing was nothing more than a couple of pin pricks. The driver was confused as to what was going on and startled when he saw the knife. He reached to open the driver's side door to escape. I just grabbed the knife from Don and in a circular motion imbedded the knife deep within the cabbie's chest. I must have hit his heart since he keeled over almost immediately."

A passerby made a call to the Montreal police after seeing significant blood stains inside an empty cab. Talbot's body was found in an industrial park near 6396 Côte-de-Liesse in St. Laurent, a municipality just outside Montreal. That was August 1st, 1993. Police noted the deceased man's pockets were empty and formed a theory that the motive for the killing was robbery. There was no money, nor any identification found.

"I pushed him out of the driver's side door onto the pavement. Don jumped out and grabbed his wallet and cash. We then stole a car. Don sat on the passenger side, and I took the steering wheel, and we were off.

"We barely spoke all the way to Ottawa. It was nighttime and we didn't see any cops. We knew we'd have to ditch the car on the outskirts of Ottawa. There was some blood on my clothes—not a lot, but I would have to hide out until I could get something else to wear."

Terry explained that the two men spent the rest of the night in a park and "didn't see a soul." Once the stores opened, he sent Don out to buy replacements for the shirt and pants Terry wore that could be used as evidence if the two men were apprehended for Talbot's murder. Don made the purchases in short order. "I guess he was better at shopping than I was," Terry joked. "When we met up again, I trashed the blood-stained clothing and we set out exploring."

Don came up with the idea that the two men could go to a bathhouse in Ottawa, check in, get a room, and get a few hours of shut eye. A bathhouse room was far cheaper than a hotel.

"Don was still pretty calm even though he knew we'd fucked up. I had never been to a bathhouse before. Guys just walk around with a towel around their waists. Both Don and I were in pretty good physical shape, so we got the eye of a lot of guys who wanted to party back in their own rooms. We'd just shake our heads. We were sitting in the sauna and this mid-dle-aged dude nods his head and asked if we ever tried cocaine. Party boy invited us back to his room and measured out lines for both Don and I to snort.

"Then he says he owns a club downtown. I seriously doubted it. But he had some nice clothes and I think liked por-traying himself as some sort of bigshot. I think some gay guys think that if they look rich, it will be a way to capture young handsome guys. Just like old straight men think they can score a trophy wife by flashing their wallets."

I let Terry continue his narrative. I have observed that cli-ents who have spent time in prison are far more prone to accept stereotypes than those of us on the outside would deplore as politically incorrect. I did not press Terry further about the identification of the man he referred to as a "bigshot." If this matter were to go to trial, that individual would likely deny drug usage or even encountering Terry and Don. My interest was ascertaining the basic facts as Terry could recall them.

He continued, "This bigshot wanted us to drop by his club. We told him we were just visiting town. He insisted that we come by his bar later that evening. He'd show us a good time. He asked where we were staying. We admitted we had not checked in anywhere. So, he said that was great; we could sleep over at his place."

Patrons of the gay bar were taken by the sight of two attrac-tive men, Terry and Don, entering the club together. Their heads were shaved, and they both wore matching baseball caps and team jerseys. They stood together at the bar, ordering vodka and lime juice. Occasionally, a bar patron would approach and try to engage in conversation. Terry would answer any ques-tion posed politely but sent the signal he was not about to get involved in small talk. Persons who stopped to chat would be on their way in short order.

Don did not discourage patrons who wanted to chat so easily. He seemed somewhat nervous, fiddling with a book of matches that advertised the bar and lying on the counter. Even though he was not smoking, Don stashed the match book into his pants pocket. At one point he left Terry to make a call to a woman he worked with at the travel agency in Toronto. The co-worker was named Liz. She considered Don to be a good friend. Don was nervous on the phone and asked Liz if there was any scuttlebutt about him in Toronto. All coworkers were aware of where Don lived and when it was revealed that a body had been discovered near Don's residence, suspicion was raised that unbelievable as it may seem, Don might somehow be connected to the murder.

"Don't believe anything you read in the paper," Don cautioned and then added it would be unlikely that he would ever come home again.

Terry's Own Words

Here is how Terry described his memories in his own words: "The guy at the bathhouse gave us directions. We went to his club, or what he claimed to be his club. It was a gay bar in the market area. He met us at the door and kept us in booze until rather late and then told us to meet him at his car and we could get a lift to his house. He didn't want anyone seeing him with us as we left the club around midnight. We did as he asked. He drove us to his place. The house was fairly big. Only the three of us there. Buddy brings out a bag of powdered coke and puts it on the glass top of his coffee table. He separated them into lines with a playing card and then rolled up a twenty-dollar bill into a tube and we each took turns sucking back the shit.

"As we were getting loaded, buddy strips off and says he wants us to do the same. It was his dope and neither Don nor I were shy, so it seemed like a small price to pay. Except for the nudity, there was no sex—we just partied on until almost morning.

"It was during this session that bigshot slips out of the room and returns carrying a big plastic bag of powered cocaine and a bag of syringes. I had seen guys in prison shoot up, but I had never done it myself. Both Don and I were so high, we just couldn't say no.

"It's a big step, to go from snorting to shooting," I interjected. I suspected that Don was also new to taking cocaine intravenously.

"Don couldn't believe that the blood drawn into the barrel of the syringe looked black instead of red, and buddy said this proved Don was a rookie. Don was mildly embarrassed and kept his head down as the needle went into his left arm.

"Don and I each shot up maybe four or five times. The effect was instantaneous, and the high just made us want more. There was an instant burst of energy after we poked ourselves in the arm; we would get up and strut around, just experiencing the rush. I knew buddy was getting his rocks off, having a couple of well-built young men prancing around in the nude.

"When the sun was about to come out, Mr. Bigshot told us to get dressed and that he'd drop us off somewhere where we could get a coffee. He was very polite, but we knew we were being kicked out. While the dude was out in the kitchen, Don spotted half a baggie of coke and the bag of syringes sitting on an armchair in the living room. He pocketed the stash, and party guy didn't even realize it was gone.

"We were still high and without sleep when buddy dropped us off in some godforsaken part of town. We found an abandoned Red Barn restaurant nearby; it was all boarded up, but at least we could lay down. And at least we were safe from prying eyes.

"After the coke wore off, I was finally able to get some sleep. I had no idea that would be the last time I'd see Don in good spirits. Right now, though, I just wish I hadn't woken up."

SIX

THE DON HEBERT MURDER

■■■

A<small>S I WAS MAKING MY NOTES</small> on a lined legal pad I wrote the numeral 3 and put a circle around it. It was the third murder I came to talk about. But something inside me hesitated as I wrote "The Don Hebert Murder" beside the circled numeral. I was getting the impression that while the other two killings were impersonal for Terry, killing Don was somewhat different. I sensed an emotional attachment between the men. I wanted to discern if my instincts were on point, or if Terry was a psychopath incapable of feeling human emotion.

When I talk to friends about murderers, my usual comment is that murderers by and large are like most of us in the general population. A murderer could be the guy sitting in the next bar stool just as easily as if he were a pipefitter. Never have I witnessed a convicted murderer in the stereotypical pose with intense eyes like one might imagine in a horror movie.

Whenever I did parole hearings, the Parole Board often started by reviewing an inmate's criminal history and asking the prisoner to comment on each entry. This procedure could take up a fair chunk of time before a personal interview by the Board would begin. For murderers, my experience was just the opposite. The Board would look at the offender's criminal record and, in most cases, see only one entry: murder. Murder is usually a crime of passion. A husband may catch his wife in bed with the next-door neighbour and completely lose it. Of course, there were those cases of professional hit men in organized crime circles. They acted more as trained military assassins. But the murderers I encountered most frequently were those guys (and with few exceptions it was guys) whom I labelled 'temper losers'.

On the other hand, I feel the most dangerous criminals, at least the ones I would be less likely to relate to, are fraud artists. These individuals have no soul. They look you in the eye and smile while stealing every last cent you have. Greed is their primary motivation. They are liars of the first order making you believe they have your best interest at heart, all the while robbing you of every dime in your pocket. So successful are they that I recall conducting a parole hearing for one Ponzi scheme 'financial advisor' where his victims showed up to support him at his parole hearing.

Parole Hearing Assessments

At a parole hearing, I would be furnished with psychiatric and psychological assessments conducted during an offender's stay. The one that would often be influential in determining the outcome of a hearing would be the score obtained after an inmate had been interviewed by professionals in accordance with the Hare's Psychopathy Checklist. The diagnostic tool was developed by a Canadian, Dr. Robert Hare, and continues to be used to determine if an individual has a personality disorder, with impaired empathy and remorse. In short, I needed to know if, despite his actions—Was Terry truly a cold-blooded killer?

The ballpoint on my pen underlined the numeral 3 on the page as I thought about how I would ask Terry about Don Hebert's murder. Rather than attempt an untrained psychological analysis, the kind I knew Terry was adept at answering during his past prison stay, I decided it best to shelve my concern and make my own assessment after the initial interview was complete.

"So, what happened next?" That was the best I could think to ask at the moment.

Terry described that he and Don had had a rough night. While they were sitting in the abandoned Red Barn Restaurant, the effects of the drugs dissipated and each became irritable and tired. At one point or another both men fell asleep. Terry was roused from his sleep on a few instances. Don was making a lot of noise as though he were in real pain. Terry sloughed it off as reminiscences of the gory few days they had just endured.

However, as summer morning sun streamed through the boards of the abandoned establishment, a new reality took hold. Don was very ill. He was pale in the face, suffering dreadful internal pain. When he did speak, it was in short bursts.

"What's wrong?" Terry asked.

"I can't breathe. My chest is aching," Don replied.

"Fuck it. I'll get an ambulance." Terry said.

"No!" Don cried out, "I'm not going to spend any remaining days locked in a cage until I die." The talks the two men had earlier about Don having AIDS returned to Terry's mind immediately. If Terry went for medical help, he would not only be condemning Don to a short, painful life in prison, but he'd also be sending himself back to the hellhole too.

"What should I do?" Terry asked in a panic.

"Let's go together," Don replied.

"You are saying that I should kill you and then kill myself?" Terry had until that point never contemplated that option. Don had never spoken of it either. Obviously, since Don was in great pain, an immediate response was necessary.

"Maybe you'll get better," Terry bargained.

"I have never felt pain like this before," Don whispered, "You wouldn't let your dog die this way."

Terry never had a dog. But he recalled his days as a boy when an animal at "the ranch" as he used to call his boyhood home, came down with an incurable condition, a veterinarian was summoned to perform euthanasia.

"You are wanting me to put you to sleep forever?" Terry clarified with Don.

Mug shots distributed by police showing
Terry and Don's appearance at the time of the murders.

"I love you, Terry. And if you love me, you will do it. The killing has to stop."

"And then kill myself?" Terry added. Wasn't Don asking for an end to killing? But now was not the time to discuss the incongruity.

"I can't wait to be married to you in heaven." Don smiled speaking those words.

"Or hell!" Terry muttered silently to himself.

Terry really didn't have any belief in the afterlife. He was a self-professed atheist. He hated it when fellow cons would grab a bible and profess their own salvation in prison. It was total "bullshit" as Terry referred to it. An all-knowing and loving God who was looking out for his creations on Earth? Terry felt this super-loving deity had forgotten about him and bestowed him with a life more miserable than anyone could have predicted. Terry felt that it was his own vengeance that should be meted out. Rather than say he despised God, it would be more hurtful to a Supreme Being, whoever or whatever that may be, to just deny its existence.

But this was no time for theological discussion. Don was experiencing excruciating pain, lying on a dirty floor in squalid conditions. He just wanted to be put out of his misery.

"Okay?" Don asked.

Terry nodded his head signifying his intention to proceed. How could he do it as painlessly as possible? This is my friend, he thought, indeed, this is a man who wants to be my husband. Terry realized he had not to his knowledge ever been fully loved by anyone ever before, not even, he suspected, by his parents. And then, for the first time Terry consciously heard a wee small voice inside his own head say that he too loved Don. Just as on the farm, he could not see this man die without dignity.

Terry took off his shirt and wrapped it around Don's neck and pulled the ends together ever tighter against Don's throat. As expected, Don let out a few moans as his oxygen levels dropped. Terry looked away not wanting to see Don's face as he was fading away.

Instead, as he looked away, he saw an elderly woman walking her dog staring through an opening in a boarded area on a window that had previously allowed sunlight to brighten the area. The woman not only cut off the sunlight but posed a threat to the continuation of the gambit. Terry immediately loosened his grip. Don's breathing returned, a bit shallower than before. How could he explain that he failed to grant his friend, his lover, his only request?

The woman scurried away. Where to? The police? Now was not the time to ponder potential outcomes. The decision to off Don was not planned as he had liked. And now he was in the middle of a situation and had to scramble to escape it.

Almost without thought, he reached and found the knife that had been used on Rasky and in the same swooping motion was now buried deep with Don's chest, piercing his heart. Death was instantaneous.

According to Terry, the feeling of loneliness was worse than solitary confinement. He wept.

Next to Don were some remaining syringes. Terry grabbed one from the pack. He shoved the needle into Don's arm and withdrew an entire cylinder of Don's AIDS-tainted blood and plunged it into his own arm. Once emptied he repeated the process. This is what Terry meant when he had told me that he had sentenced himself to capital punishment.

"This is how we die together."

Terry mixed up two more syringes with the water/cocaine mix, capped the needle, and shoved both inside his jacket pocket.

Terry bent over and placed his dead friend's head on his knee. He then bent down, kissed Don's forehead, and left the building and the body within it.

It was not until the next morning that police were alerted to the presence of a body in the empty building. Police took note of the smartly dressed body and good shoes and immediately suspected that they were not dealing with a homeless transient. A matchbook with the name of a gay bar gave police another clue to investigate.

Patrons of the bar readily recalled the two newcomers and identified the dead man's picture as being one of the two strangers who had passed the evening hours at the bar.

Ottawa police were able to make a connection with Toronto police and were then able to piece together the connection between Terry Fitzsimmons, Don Hebert and Norm Rasky.

Reeling from the Events

It was August 5, 1993. Terry was still reeling from the events of the day before. He had thought about dozens of options of what to do now and finally settled on the one that seemed the most logical. Terry walked toward the Ottawa police station. Just before entering he fished the syringes from his pocket and injected the contents into the vein at the elbow of his left arm. He then entered the building. The station was a large concrete building on Elgin Street. Terry showed no hesitation as he pushed the glass door to enter.

No one seemed particularly interested that a young man, high on cocaine, was standing at the visitor's portal. A uniformed officer with 'Special Constable' emblazoned on his uniform was writing, no doubt completing one of several forms so necessary for police to record every movement of their existence.

The officer was young as well, maybe 25, dark hair and a thin long face with prominent chin, cleanly shaven. His dark brown eyes stared up at Terry. Terry looked quite the opposite. His head was shaved—his hair had not regrown since he'd shaved it in Toronto. Terry's more rounded face and less prominent chin face sported a couple of day's stubble. His green eyes were, no doubt wild, from the drugs.

"How can I help you?" the officer queried.

"I'm Terry Fitzsimmons. The killing has to stop."

The young officer looked perplexed. Was this an admission of murder or was this a private citizen reporting a grisly incident? Either way, it certainly wasn't run-of-the-mill daily activity at the front desk.

"Could you kindly take a seat on the chair just behind you. I'll call a detective who I'm sure would like to speak with you."

Terry complied immediately. A detective wearing a suit was summoned. The detective appeared to be in his fifties. His comportment reminded Terry of the no-nonsense aura his father projected whenever they sat down for discussions. It also reminded him of the way parole officers look, taking their jobs very seriously without displaying any hint of humanity in their work. Terry could tell by the way the detective approached that he had been interrupted from something the detective considered to be far more important.

"Yes?" the detective introduced himself "How can I help you?"

Terry repeated the words he had told the young constable at the front desk. "My name is Terry Fitzsimmons. The killing has to stop."

Terry went on to fully describe to the detective the actions he had related to me — the events that had taken place in the six frantic days between the time he met Don in Toronto and showing up at the Ottawa detachment. Terry was placed in a holding cell for further questioning. The detective took extensive notes.

A squad car was dispatched to the abandoned Red Barn. Don Hebert's body was recovered and identified by his Toronto family. Despite being told of Hebert's involvement in murders, the Hebert family did not hold it against their deceased relative. The body of the prodigal son was welcomed home.

A large well-attended funeral took place. Of course, Terry did not attend. He had been transferred from the station to be held awaiting trial at the Ottawa-Carleton detention centre. He was taken to court two days later where the charge of murder in the first-degree of Donald Hebert was read aloud. No plea was entered, and a duty counsel attended with Terry at a rather perfunctory hearing where he was detained in custody. Duty counsel told him bail in such circumstances was extremely unlikely and there were no prospects of his having a surety. Terry gave instruction to waive any prospect of bail and the Crown attorney was so informed.

It was at the OCDC that Terry started to open up to some of his fellow inmates. He was still grieving Don's loss and he had not talked much of anything to anybody. But once he disclosed the seriousness of the charges, he had decided to obey the suggestion of a fellow inmate who said, "Man, you'd better call a lawyer."

Hebert's Loving Family

I later had further confirmation that Don Hebert had a loving family. A nephew posted a comment on a summary published about the Fitzsimmons crime spree.

He recalled his Uncle Don fondly and explained Don was troubled about being HIV positive and had fought bipolar disorder for many years. The nephew was aware that Don was infatuated with Fitzsimmons and may have been manic at the time—the robberies supported a cocaine addiction which likely fueled further mania.

"He was not a monster as I remember him," the nephew stated.

The funeral parlour in which Don's body rested was crowded with well-wishers. It was standing-room-only with much support from his coworkers and the community—certainly not the kind of service one would expect for an alleged spree killer.

Obviously, the family was magnanimous in their regard for the man. It would have been much easier to attempt to disown a wayward family member. They did not do so and should be commended for their bravery in standing tall while exemplifying their forgiveness.

SEVEN

THE DETAILS

■ ■ ■

TERRY WAS RELATIVELY EXPANSIVE in his recollection of events. Most clients, whether they are newly arrested or having years of incarceration behind them, tend to be brief in their synopsis of events. After all, they are talking to a stranger for the first time and it takes a while to trust an unknown person with deep and dark secrets, even if those memories can be of substantial assistance with one's defence.

This was my first meeting with Terry. He had expressed himself openly beyond my wildest expectations. But a 'Just the facts ma'am' approach is never sufficient for a criminal lawyer. Defence counsel must know the human being behind the story. Although a history of the criminal acts was necessary, I needed to delve deeper to reveal the personal history of the person I was dealing with.

I knew there may be many explanations as to why a human being may act out antisocially: trauma caused by beatings, molestation, rape, childhood abuse or neglect being among them. I hoped clues to Terry's criminal conduct could be uncovered in casual conversation.

"Have you or anyone in your family ever undergone psychiatric treatment?" I asked.

"Nah," Terry replied giving his head a slight nod indicating no.

"Do you have any scars," I continued. I was curious because

there had been some discussion in the psychiatric literature that scars may indicate physical abuse by a person in authority in the past. Again, the reply was negative.

"How was your homelife where you grew up?" was another standard lead question.

"Nothing much to speak of," Terry continued. "I was okay through public school and never got into much trouble. I did okay in school, but I was no brainiac if you know what I mean. I really didn't like school. I was always moving around and being told to sit still in class. I'd rather be out in the yard running and jumping. Just too much energy I guess."

"Were you ever diagnosed as having attention deficit or being hyperactive?" I asked.

"Nah," Terry replied.

"Were you ever given any pills or medicine to help you settle down?"

"None that I can remember. I got into using drugs when I was nine. Not the prescribed kinds though."

I think Terry sensed my shock. I did not say anything, but he noted that I stopped writing and looked directly at him.

Terry continued, "The robbery of the convenience store was my first-time offence as an adult. It was just a mom-and-pop store, a convenience store, in East London. I was just eighteen. It was close to a school, and I knew a lot of the kids who met up around there. I hung out with a group of guys who like to drink, smoke cigs and weed. We usually got a carton of beer but this night—the night of the heist—one of the gang members brought a 26er of Canadian whisky. We drank it straight, the four of us and got pretty loaded. So, we decided to do a hit on a local store. There was no surveillance. Just a simple mom-and-pop shop. It was easy pickings."

"When you say, 'as an adult', do you mean you had been arrested before as a young offender?" I asked.

"Yeah. Three years before, I got nabbed for obstructing police. The next year, I was up on four robbery charges. But I was under 18 so nothing much happened."

"When you speak of robbery, to me that means theft with violence. Did you use a weapon?"

"No," he replied. "We just roughed up a guy a little bit."

"Okay. Sorry to interrupt. Carry on about the convenience store incident."

"We walked into the store without any face masks and pretended we were armed and told the woman behind the counter to stuff the contents of the till into a plastic bag. She did everything we demanded.

"What I didn't know was there was a goof I went to school with [at the store]. He recognized me and told the store lady, who then phoned the cops."

I was taken aback by Terry's use of the word 'goof'. Although seemingly mild to those of us who have never been jailed, it is the worst insult one inmate can use against another. Calling another inmate a goof was a call to battle. The fight would be over only when one or the other inmate was dead or severely beaten. By using the word goof, it signaled to me that Terry was very immersed in prison culture.

I questioned him about the arrest.

Terry replied that he was the only name the cops knew, and he was pressured to name his associates. He refused. The police decided to have Terry's father intervene. His father met with him and urged him to be cooperative, telling Terry he was sure that he would get a lenient sentence, maybe just probation or community service.

"How did your father convince you to talk about the robbery," I asked.

"I hadn't planned on saying anything—the right to remain silent, you know," Terry continued. "Then my dad tells me that no matter how bad the whole thing sounded, it would only get worse if I didn't 'fess up.

"My dad had tears in his eyes and said that a good father never gives up when a son makes a mistake and even if I went to jail, he would continue to love me and always be there for me. My father was misty-eyed. That's the only time I ever saw him like that. He said he would rather die himself than make me, his son, feel unloved. So, I told my father I would cooperate, and he could tell the cops that I was ready to make a statement."

Terry was inexperienced dealing with police. He accepted his father's logic and named all his fellow gang members. But things did not go so well in court. Terry had entered a guilty plea but the cashier at the store told an impressive story that she was frightened as never before in her life and that loss of a substantial amount of cash had put her whole business in jeopardy of failure. The Crown prosecutor asked for a provincial custodial term, meaning less than two years. The defence lawyer recommended probation. The pre-sentence report was not helpful indicating trouble with school attendance, dropping out of school at 15, and hanging out on the streets of Toronto. There were behavioural problems at home. The sentence was sharp and swift: three years in prison. He would be eligible for parole in one year or, if he were not paroled, he could expect to be released after two years.

Whenever a judge imposes a punishment exceeding what is recommended by experienced counsel, it could be the basis for appeal.

I asked, "Did you appeal the conviction and sentence?"

"Nah. I figured I'd be out before the appeal got processed."

Immediately, Terry was handcuffed and led to the holding cells of London's Dundas Street courthouse. From there he was taken to the Elgin-Middlesex Detention Centre. He signed a paper at the jail waiving his right to appeal and within a week transported by bus to the maximum-security Kingston Penitentiary for classification and penitentiary placement.

"The other guys were under eighteen. They went to juvenile detention," Terry told me. "I guess I was held most responsible because I was the oldest and should have known better.

But I soon found out that being a rat was one way of getting killed inside. I guess my dad never realized he was setting his son up to be killed."

Terry was the third of four sons in the Fitzsimmons household. Terry believed that none of his other brothers was ever in any trouble.

"Once I was in prison, my parents really dropped out of my life, I guess we lived in different worlds. They didn't want to have any part of my world and I didn't want to have any part of theirs. I think they thought I was an embarrassment to the family."

Classification

The classification process was long and seemed longer with Terry's limited and begrudging participation. Days at a time would go by where no one on staff would speak with him. The waiting seemed endless. Finally, a determination was made that Joyceville Institution, just outside the city, would be the best fit for the young man. It was medium-security and had educational programming that would assist in his rehabilitation. It was explained if he behaved well, he could be granted parole in as little as twelve months and if he did not make parole, he would be released on mandatory supervision, now called statutory release, after two years. The classification officer felt she was delivering Terry good news, but twelve months or twenty-four months was an eternity to this youth.

Once Terry arrived at Joyceville, he felt the cards were stacked against him. One inmate called him a fish and Terry took objection. He had not realized that was a nickname for all new arrivals, because so many walk around with open mouths in their new and frightening situation. Terry was also told other helpful hints, for example, if another inmate throws a chocolate bar on your cell cot, don't accept it. Otherwise, you owe the provider services, maybe even sexual services. As it turned out nobody ever threw anything Terry's way, but he was so scared by the rumours of prison rape he decided it would be best to link up with one of the more experienced cons to look out for him.

"Did anything ever happen to you?" I asked.

"When I got into prison, I was just 18, five and a half feet tall, 98 pounds, blond hair, green eyes—just a little cutie. A week later, I got fucked.

"Looking back on it, I guess it was just part of the initiation process. By this time, I had learned to keep my trap shut. The other cons knew I could be solid after that. So, it was horrible to experience at the time but ultimately it was all for the best."

Terry paused and stared at me trying to discern my reaction to his disclosure. I made sure my expression remained stoic.

"That taught me to keep my defences up."

He met up with an older inmate whom Terry made sure had absolutely no interest in Terry sexually. The two agreed to lift weights together at the gym. Terry felt safe and learned the prison code from the older man.

But even prisoners who keep to themselves can incur enemies, especially if one loses a bet even though betting is forbidden in prison. It so happened that Terry's workout partner had run out of cigarettes. It was a time before cigarette smoking was banned in penitentiaries, when tobacco was the currency of the prison realm. Inmates could not use cash. Terry's workout partner had bet more than he could buy in several weeks spending on his minimal inmate pay at the canteen. Welching on a debt is a mortal sin in a prison context. It came to pass that while returning from the gym, an agent of the debt holder ran toward Terry's workout partner and rammed a knife through his heart with a swooping motion (the same swooping motion that Terry would later use) of the assassin's arm. The prisoner fell to the floor instantly. There was surprisingly little blood. Of course, an alarm was sounded, and everyone was questioned. It came as no surprise to the Institutional Preventive Security

Officer, or IPSO as the office was called, that everybody in the hall at the time of the stabbing was temporarily blind, or so they maintained. No one saw anything and had nothing to report.

Terry had learned his lesson in London that it does not serve an inmate well to be called a rat. He continued to maintain he saw nothing while his partner was lying on the floor beside Terry's feet. The IPSO took retributive measures. A Security Information Report (SIR) was prepared accusing Terry of conspiring with the killer. As such, he was no longer a medium-security risk, he would be involuntarily transferred to maximum-security Kingston Penitentiary. Any possibly of release on parole was now non-existent.

The transfer was accomplished almost immediately. No institutional charge was laid, and Terry never had the opportunity of defending himself at a hearing before the Disciplinary Court. Deprivation of the internal court process was of little concern to Terry. Although the Internal Disciplinary Court was presided over by someone appointed and outside the Correctional Service known as an Independent Chairperson, most inmates referred to the office as 'the dependent chairperson' believing that the office was held at the pleasure of the institutional warden to mete out the punishment the prison desired.

Terry worked diligently to remain productive and aloof while at KP. He managed to get a job working in the prison's kitchen. It was a good job allowing workers to keep exceptionally clean, with white uniforms and white hats. It often required early morning waking to get breakfast on the go. It also seemed that his fellow workers were easy to get along with. Save and except one.

That inmate was a notorious child molester and sex offender by the name of Mark Shannon. Shannon had been convicted of the murder of a 21-year-old woman who had been returning to her apartment on an October night in 1980. He dragged the woman behind a billboard, raped and then bludgeoned her with rocks. He continued his predatory behaviour in prison. He had spotted Terry early on when Terry first started working in the kitchen. Terry kept as far away as possible, and knew the other kitchen workers detested this inmate as much as he did. Four months before Terry's expected release date, he submitted a request for a transfer to another prison because he feared Shannon. Kingston Penitentiary took no action on the request.

It was July 20, 1986, two days before Terry's statutory release date. He had already met with his classification officer to set up a release plan. Everyone was in a good mood. Other inmates usually took pleasure when one of their numbers was destined to exit the prison. However, the inmate Terry abhorred came up behind him as a Sunday brunch was being prepared. With a smile on his face, he whispered in Terry's ear that before the two days were up, he would rape him.

Shannon's words, "Before you leave, your ass is going to be mine" were overheard by fellow inmate and kitchen worker, Chuck Armstrong. Armstrong had been observing that Shannon's harassment had been persistent for about two hours before Terry had had enough of it.

Terry simply lost it. Terry was holding a kitchen knife he used to cut vegetables. Shannon jumped onto the table used for cutting vegetables holding a plastic cutting board as a shield to ward off Fitzsimmons' blows. One of the kitchen crew would later testify that when he heard a commotion he turned around and saw "eggs and things flying" at the grill area behind him. Terry picked up a pan of boiling oil from the gas stove where food was being prepared and threw it toward the head of the intended seducer. Shannon ran toward the vegetable room with Terry in pursuit. All the while Shannon fended off stabs directed toward him with the cutting board. Terry aimed higher. A witness later told authorities that he saw a red spot appear on Shannon's shirt in the area of his diaphragm. The floor in the vegetable room was wet and slippery. Shannon called out, "Terry, that's enough." Terry watched and listened as Shannon fell to the floor, screaming in agony. A total of three stab wounds pierced Shannon's chest, the final one through his heart. The screaming did not last long. Before help could arrive, the screaming was over. The man was dead. A food service officer recalled hearing someone say, "My God! He's done it," as the body was taken away.

The SHU, Special Handling Unit

Terry was kept locked up in solitary until his trial was concluded in criminal court. The cells in the solitary wing were on either side of a long corridor. Each cell was about 6 x 12 feet in size. The occupant sleeps on a concrete slab a few inches off the floor. There is a thin foam mattress and foam pillow. Each cell is equipped with a combination toilet and sink. There is a solid steel door. Food trays are inserted through a slot in the door. There is an exit to an outdoor screened-in exercise yard that resembles a chicken coop. Inmates confined in solitary have use of the yard once a day, alone and for an hour maximum. Anyone walking down the corridor hears loud screams as though this was Bedlam itself. Some inmates, on the other hand, remain deathly silent. A tag on each door contains the name of the inmate locked inside.

Of course, Terry was arrested and charged with murder. He elected to be tried by judge and jury. A preliminary hearing was scheduled for November 21.

Even though it is contrary to the convict code to assist the court by giving evidence, the kitchen worker who overheard Shannon's statement, Chuck Armstrong, came forward. Chuck was a Kenny Rogers look-alike. His voice was even similar. Armstrong validated Terry's story that he was about to be sexually assaulted. Chuck Armstrong was an older inmate, and his word was gold, even to prison staff. His testimony was accepted by the criminal court and instead of murder, Terry was convicted of manslaughter. In April 1987, instead of going to trial, Terry pleaded guilty to manslaughter and received a sentence of nine years consecutive to his existing sentence. He would be out in six on stat release.

But it was not all good news. One of the rules few seem to know is that if a prisoner injures staff or another inmate, it could mean an involuntary transfer to the Special Handling Unit or SHU, as both inmates and staff call it, at Prince Albert Pen in Saskatchewan or PA as it is known. It is a super-maximum-security unit, one of two in Canada, housing inmates in solitary confinement for up to four years after which time the inmates are returned to their sending institution.

"Tell me about your four years at the SHU. How did that go? You would be in your early twenties when you first went in, right?" I asked.

"At first there is the realization this is going to mean pain," he started.

"How so?"

"When you are inside a regular prison, about the only thing to keep you occupied is keeping yourself in shape. Other guys help you out, like spotting you when you do bench presses. They encourage you to dig deeper. It's all very painful at first. Every muscle in your body aches at the start. But you press on. Day by day the pain gets less until you no longer feel it. But when you are sent to solitary, you don't have access to weights or your workout partners. You try to do sit-ups and push-ups on the floor of your cell, but it is just not the same."

Solitary Emotions

Terry was expressing a complaint about solitary cells I had actually heard before. Most inmates prize the time they spend lifting weights to maintain a muscular build. Solitary confinement deprives them of this opportunity when exercise is limited to push-ups and sit-ups inside a small cell.

"Your muscles aren't used the same way and you know that when you get back to a good workout routine you will have to go through all that pain again," explained Terry.

Not completely satisfied with the response I had received, I asked, "I can see that to be true if you are talking about a week or so in the hole at KP, but surely, it's not the same going to the SHU?" I could tell Terry was feeling some embarrassment giving me a truthful answer. The response about pain was a cover-up for a more emotional reason. But big boys don't cry, and I sensed it would be embarrassing to go deeper.

"Okay," he said, relenting and deciding to share a memory probably more painful than physical suffering. "You are alone day in, day out with your thoughts. Sometimes the walls seem like they are closing in and you feel you are going to be buried alive. Sometimes you hear things that are not there. Sometimes you see things that are not there. You get confused and just want to scream. But noise is an enemy, so you hold it in. It's total isolation for the first two years. Then I was allowed to have a radio. I got one and turned it on. But I couldn't take the noise. So, I pitched it against the wall and smashed it to pieces. I couldn't take the sound. Even footsteps outside my cell would drive me bonkers. I just started to feel that I wanted to be alone. I couldn't stand anyone being around me."

I understood that Terry didn't like talking about any weakness. I complimented him on his bravery in verbalizing those feelings.

At the end of the four years of isolation he returned to Kingston Penitentiary to serve out the duration of his sentence. However, the noise of a regular prison cell and the presence of others was so shocking, he felt he had to take steps to get away. The rage Terry was experiencing at time got the better of him.

"I punched a wall and broke my hand. They wanted to take me to the hole for that. I didn't mind that. In fact, I preferred it. My criticism was the length of time it was taking to get me there. I protested by taking a big bite of flesh out of my arm.

It took twenty-four stitches inside and 12 stitches outside to repair the wound."

He told staff he would only stop self-mutilation if he were placed in a segregation cell at KP. Staff agreed and he remained in solitary confinement until the day of his release.

In all the years I had been working with federal inmates, I had never heard such a story. In ordinary circumstances, I would outline a course of defence. I was unable to suggest a road map in these circumstances. I left it that Terry would obtain legal aid coverage as soon as possible. I had Terry get approval to place my office telephone number on his list of approved calls. I promised a return visit at my first possible opportunity.

"Be sure to get the *Toronto Sun* off my ass and calling us names." Terry emphasized. "I've already given myself the death penalty. So just have fun with it."

We shook hands and I departed the institution.

EIGHT

THE RIDE HOME

■■■

E VEN WITHOUT LEGAL AID IN PLACE, court processes
moved on. Immediately after Terry Fitzsimmons' arrest
for the death of Don Hebert in July 1993, he was brought
before a court in Ottawa. A duty counsel was provided to assist
him in initial procedures. Terry had already been denied bail.
I had yet to appear with Terry to go on record in his defence. I
expected that as a pro forma tactic, both duty counsel and the
prosecutor consented to a request from the provincial court
judge to impose psychiatric remand for up to sixty days. To
some extent, I expected the ensuing report would show that
Terry was competent to stand trial. Nonetheless, there was
the off chance of an NCR (not criminally responsible) finding, but the best I was expecting is that the remand would buy
time until a more plausible defence could be contrived. I was
exhausted not only physically but emotionally after these couple of days in Ottawa.

I would ordinarily enjoy the trip to and from Ottawa. But
this time my mind wondered continuously reflecting on what
I had heard. The trek involved travelling through an area that
included the Rideau lakes, beautiful scenery, and small towns
such as Smith Falls. Smith Falls was rural Ontario at its best
with locks on the Rideau Canal system that were designed
to prevent an American attack on Canada's capital. Queen
Victoria, in designating Ottawa as the nation's capital, had

chosen a city half-way between the former capitals of Toronto and Quebec and on the border between the two provinces but easily defensible from American attacks like those in the War of 1812. I tried to think of such visual observations as a diversion to what kept playing on my mind.

My attention driving down Highway 15 this time was not on the scenery nor the history of the locale; my mind was fixed on Terry Fitzsimmons and the horrible story I had learned from him. What would cause a human being, even one who had spent time in prison to act out in this manner?

The usual precursors of criminal activity or acting out criminally seemed to be absent. Terry did not come from an impoverished background. There was no indication that he had been physically, sexually or emotionally abused as a child. There was no suggestion he suffered from a mental illness. What could be Terry's motivation to act has he had described?

This question was one I knew needed careful consideration. Most people understand that if twelve jurors find as a matter of fact that the elements of a crime are made out, a conviction will follow. Terry was charged with committing three first-degree murders. He has identified himself as the assailant. He acknowledged to police that he knew what he was doing and knew that it was wrong. How can I participate in a trial where he has already admitted what would be the crucial facts that the prosecution must establish?

Establishing a Motivation

Modern juries, I have sensed, are less forgiving of violent conduct than juries would have been even ten to fifteen years previously. Ordinarily a criminal's motivation is irrelevant to a finding of guilt. But by giving the jury a rational explanation of why a crime was committed, it could lead to a conviction on a lesser and included charge. In Terry's case, that could result in a conviction for second-degree murder or manslaughter. Establishing a motivation that a jury could understand and sympathize with may be the best approach in formulating a defence.

Terry's killing of a fellow inmate at Kingston Penitentiary could be explained by the culture that exists in male prisons and studied in depth by criminologists. It was widely known that both prisoners and their guards suffer from what has been called 'toxic masculinity'. There is a culture that the Correctional Service has done little to reform where an exaggerated form of what it means to 'be a man' has been inculcated.

Prison guards use this to justify brutality on prisoners that would be abhorrent if the same brutality and indifference were exhibited outside the prison gates. Officers who show human concern for prisoner wellbeing are labelled 'con lovers'. This is a derisive term, and no correctional officer would accept such labelling.

Prison itself is emasculating to the men confined. They are not free in their movement or associations. They are deprived of normal heterosexual contact and are subservient to a hierarchy based on force.

Any sort of weakness is something to be shunned. A hierarchy comes to exist where exaggerated notions of masculinity prevail. The top of the pecking order is reserved for the most powerful in terms of being able to use physical force to achieve one's ends. It is like the bully in the schoolyard—the bully is not necessarily the most powerful himself, but he is the one who can best muster the force to ensure the job gets done.

These explanations may explain why Terry felt it was necessary to get into a lethal battle with Shannon, but the concept of toxic masculinity did nothing to explain why Terry was motivated to end the lives of those people he stabbed once out of prison. I knew I would have to delve deeper into the social science literature to come up with a plausible explanation. Without a plausible explanation for all three killings, the jury would conclude it was time to take out the trash and convict Terry on each of the first-degree charges. Even if his explanation were believed on two out of three, conviction on one charge alone would necessitate a judge imposing the life in prison with no chance of parole for at least 25 years.

I knew full well that the families of the victim would likely attend court positioned on the benches immediately behind the prosecutor demanding that the full force of the law be brought down upon the accused person. But there was another thought I recall that had a lasting effect upon me.

Tears of the Family

In my first year of law school, I and some of my fellow students remarked that we were learning the principles of criminal law but none of us had actually watched a trial in a courtroom. That ended when I, as a spectator, witnessed a man being sentenced to imprisonment for a crime I have long-since forgotten. What remained deeply impressed in my memory was the shock and horror expressed by the tears of the convicted man's family as he was led away in handcuffs from the courtroom.

I experienced a flashback to one day as an 8-year-old, I witnessed my cocker spaniel Blackie being struck and killed by an automobile. Not only had I experienced a sense of loss; what was more disturbing was the sense of powerlessness I felt in the situation.

Not only does the convicted person's family feel loss because of the incarceration, the more difficult emotion is the sense of powerlessness that could disrupt an entire family. Would Terry's family experience this as well? I knew that in some Indigenous cultures, a crime is not considered just an aggression against the state but is looked upon as an actual tear in the fabric of society. Restorative justice principles hope to mend that tear by making everyone impacted by the criminal act part of the process. But ours was not a society based on concepts of restorative justice. Our system of justice is adversarial. My job was to find a means of finding a way to lessen the punishment while working within a system that pits the accused person against the resources of the state.

I'll admit the contents of the interview were disturbing to me as I replayed chunks of the conversation in my mind on the ride home from Ottawa to Cobourg. I had heard gory stories before, some even more brutal than those Terry recounted. What I found more surprising was that in light of facing three first-degree murder charges, not to mention counts of armed robbery, what upset Terry most was the *Toronto Sun* coverage and the reference to Terry Fitzsimmons and Don Hebert as Canada's gay Bonnie and Clyde. What was the problem? I was puzzled. How can a comment in the press be more upsetting than the charges he faced?

Criminal defence lawyers are trained to defend their clients in a court of law. There is no law school training in how to defend a client in the court of public opinion. Yet, for Terry, he had considered this the most crucial defence.

A Populist Perspective

The *Toronto Sun* is a tabloid newspaper in Toronto. It was designed to be in a size easy to handle on the Toronto subway system. The political perspective might best be described as populist. Criminals were certainly not regarded highly by the editorial staff. The readership wanted 'tough on crime' approaches to people arrested. This was not a publication where criminals could expect favourable coverage. Many of my colleagues in the criminal defence bar refused to speak to *Sun* reporters.

If I were going to fulfill my instructions to Terry, I would have to break with the pack and try to convince the newspaper to refrain in future from writing unkind words about a man charged with three murders in a six-day period. How easy will that be?

My research showed that much of Toronto's criminal reporting had been done by a senior courtroom investigative reporter named Alan Cairns. His name always showed in the bylines. It was with some trepidation that I made the call to the *Toronto Sun* newsroom.

I was surprised how easily I reached the reporter. My call was transferred immediately to Cairns' extension.

"Cairns here." Were the first words I heard. With some hesitation I knew I had to request what I fully considered to be the most unlikely request.

"Hello, sir. My name is John Hill. I have been retained by Terry Fitzsimmons. You have done some reporting recently on his case."

"For sure." He interjected. I sensed there was a bit of a Scottish accent in his voice. I later learned that Cairns was born on July 22, 1955, in Gateshead, England. He was raised in a rather tough district of Newcastle-Upon-Tyne and had limited schooling. He immigrated to Canada at age 21 and worked several menial jobs before upgrading his skills and finding his true calling in journalism. As time moved on, I worked with Cairns on several cases. He was probably one of the most ethical and insightful journalists I had ever encountered. If I asked him to delay publication or advised that something was off the record, I learned that Alan Cairns' word was gold.

"What can you tell me?" Cairns asked.

I was a bit apprehensive conveying the message that Terry was not pleased with the reporting of his bank robberies. After all, newspapers in the 1930s covered bank robbers and in so doing elevated their status in society as modern-day Robin Hoods. Of course, there was the reference to Bonnie and Clyde, but major 'stars' of the era included Red Ryan and Edwin Alonzo Boyd. These became Canadian folk heroes. It seemed they had a symbiotic relationship with the press: They achieved fame for ripping off banks in depression-era

Canada that were seen as the oppressors of the poor and the newspapers increased circulation by glorifying the crooks and even embellishing their misdeeds.

"The only thing I can tell you at the moment is that Fitzsimmons doesn't appreciate that he and his partner are called the gay Bonnie and Clyde."

"Oh, that was about their bank robberies. I see Fitzsimmons has moved on to more serious stuff."

"The purpose of my calling you," in a voice trying to be as firm as possible, "is to politely request that you no longer use the Bonnie and Clyde reference."

"I don't know if I used that term. It could have been a phrase I used. It sounds like something I could have written. I just don't remember," he said. "How do you think is the best way we can work together to get the news out on Fitzsimmons in future?"

I'll admit Cairns took me by surprise. Instead of taking my call as a reprimand, he was enlisting me as a source. As thoughts raced through my head, I became intrigued that this could be a unique way to highlight the positives in the case and turn what Terry considered to be an enemy into a useful resource.

I reminded myself of the old days back in London when I was president of the London Ontario Humane Society and intent on ending our relationship with the city as the provider of animal control services. I had worked with several reporters with the *London Free Press* gaining favourable stories of how the Humane Society no longer wished to be responsible for slaughtering dogs and cats and wanting to establish a killfree shelter. The manipulation I was able to achieve by feeding positive stories drowned out the concern that establishing a new and separate animal control service would end up costing the taxpayers more. Indeed, it also increased donations to the shelter.

The call with Cairns ended with our exchanging personal

telephone numbers and a promise we would keep in touch as the news story developed. As time passed, I grew to respect Cairns as a most talented investigative reporter.

On the imaginary check list of Terry's articulated demands, I was able to tick that item as accomplished. All newspaper accounts from then on, and especially the *Sun*, I found were truthful and balanced in their reporting of the Fitzsimmons case.

Now the more challenging problem of coming up with a defence!

NINE

THE THEORY

■■■

T HE MOST SIGNIFICANT STEP in preparing for a criminal
defence is to establish "The Theory of the Defence." It is
really a roadmap of what will be pursued in testing the prosecution's case. Ordinarily it would start after digesting the
Crown prosecution's case. By law, the prosecution must surrender all evidence upon which it may present to counsel for
the defence at the earliest possible time. The object of the exercise is that there should be no surprises when the case for the
Crown is presented. The disclosure includes all witness statements, documents including photographs, and material perti-
nent to the prosecution's case. Although this obligation often
draws the criticism that "there is no requirement for defence
to disclose anything," the basis for one-sided disclosure is that
the Crown must prove its case beyond a reasonable doubt and
the defence should be free to raise doubt wherever possible so
that only the truly guilty will be punished.

For Terry, I did notify the Crown Attorney's office in
Toronto, Montreal, and Ottawa that I would be representing
Mr. Fitzsimmons (one always adds the honorific when speaking of the accused to ensure that the dignity afforded to an
innocent man is retained). It involved a great deal of photo-
copying and in 1993, the distribution of documentation on a
thumb drive was not in place. Even though, after talking with

Terry, I could anticipate what the disclosure material would be, I knew that it would require a significant outlay of time to read through what I expected would be multiple banker's boxes of photocopied material. Every document would have to be read and indexed for immediate retrieval, if necessary.

Because of my extensive interview with Terry, I felt comfortable that even without being in receipt of the disclosure, I could get a head start by determining, in a *prima facie* way, the theory of the defence.

Any defence available would have to be applicable across the board since even if it could be determined that Terry was innocent of two of the killings, conviction on the third would amount to the same life sentence with the same period of parole ineligibility. Losing one would be as bad in terms of the sentence as losing all three. Before the days of consecutive sentencing in murder cases, any sentence less than the 'life-25' would run concurrently. The object thus became to avoid any conviction on first-degree murder. I was reminded of a saying I often heard in prisons: "You get life-25 for the first murder; all the rest are free."

Drunk? Insane? Psychopath?

The usual defences were of little use to me:

1. Drunk on alcohol? There was no evidence that overuse of alcohol to the extent that Terry was unable to appreciate the nature and quality of his act was out the window. He was not under the influence of alcohol at least for the Hebert murder. The same thing for the belief that drug intoxication caused him to commit the acts he did.

2. Was he insane? I doubted that any psychiatrist could be induced to say that Terry did not understand the nature and quality of his act or know that it was wrong. That would be the test that would have to be met. A person can be crazy or do crazy things but unless an

expert can testify that the client meets the legal test for insanity, there would be no point bringing such a defence.

3. Was he a psychopath? Even though he expressed remorse and emotion when speaking about Don Hebert, I was not yet willing to rule out that possibility. I wanted to draw upon my experience with psychopaths to better equip me in my perception of Terry. I had known perhaps the prototypical example of a psychopath in my first few weeks at Queen's, Clifford Olson. Olson had been convicted of first-degree murder in the killing of several young men and women. Terry Fitzsimmons bore no likeness to Olson in any respect I could see, other than he was responsible for multiple deaths. There was no braggadocio about Terry like there was for Olson. He did not appear to be lying for no purpose. Olson loved self-aggrandizement.

At this point I was still willing to work with Terry. But I needed a theory.

Maybe, a more usual psychiatric defence would be possible even though the court-ordered assessment showed Terry was found mentally competent to stand trial.

In the past I had sometimes consulted with Dr. Jerry Cooper, a well-known Toronto psychiatrist who could be counted on to give expert evidence if the case required such opinion.

Dr. Cooper was well-known but what he was known for was his testimony on behalf of accused clients. The Crown attorney had its own list of psychiatrists who could be called upon to bolster the case for the prosecution. This would lead to the notion that both the prosecutor and the defence were engaged in the process of buying their desired testimony.

Indeed, a former Assistant Texas Attorney General in a *Washington Post* article explained it this way: "Expert witnesses are bought and sold. …The prosecution buys them, and the defence buys them. It is up to the jury to decide which is believable."

If Dr. Cooper would say that Terry suffered from a psychiatric condition excusing his criminal acts, would it be believed? Would it be argued that Dr. Cooper was another of these experts who could be bought and sold?

There was a further consideration. What if I could find another theory that could also explain Terry's aberrant actions once I had a fuller appreciation of the case, after disclosure was obtained and reviewed? It is a difficult if not impossible risk in a criminal case to argue defences in the alternative. Although a defence need only raise a reasonable doubt in the mind of the trier of fact, offering alternative explanations could be risky if not foolhardy. But I was getting ahead of myself. I had no credible facts that could give Dr. Cooper an avenue to suggest a psychiatric defence.

Further, my previous dealings with Dr. Cooper had never given me concern that he would parrot whatever defence counsel would say. He was always direct and honest with me. I had known others who would tailor their evidence to coincide with the theory of the defence, but I never found that to be the case with Dr. Cooper. He certainly did act for the defence and would get paid for his opinion letter and testimony. However, I always found him to be above board and he would not testify as to something he did not believe.

His reputation as a paid consultant for the defence was once put to him by a reporter. Dr. Cooper has been quoted in a *Globe and Mail* article as saying, "When I look at a case, I always ask the lawyer what he wants. When a lawyer is happy and his client is happy, then I'm happy. The thing is, I don't need it. Who can buy me? I won't go by a script. I don't mind a guy rehearsing me, but no one tells me what I am going to say. When people tell me I'm a hired gun, I laugh."

I arranged to meet Dr. Cooper at his Toronto home in the

evening. He met me at the door to his house casually attired and directed me to a meeting area in the basement. There, I gave him an overview of Terry's situation as it had been told to me. I asked Dr. Cooper if the facts as outlined would in his opinion support an insanity defence.

I was not surprised that his response was that a psychiatric defence would be a non-starter. Terry appreciated the nature and quality of his act and that what he was doing was wrong. He had already been found competent to stand trial.

Looking Elsewhere

I would have to look elsewhere to logically explain why Terry acted as he did. The inspiration came to me as I was brushing my dog. Skippy was a Samoyed-White Shepherd crossbreed whose thick white coat was constantly getting matted.

I had adopted Skippy from a breeder in St. Thomas, Ontario early in my career. I immediately wanted to learn everything I could know about the proper care and training of pups. It was then that I saw the ad that the London Humane Society was looking for volunteers to serve on its board of directors. I applied and devoted excessive amounts of time to the organization until ultimately, I became president.

I was repulsed that the Society acted as a humane operation, taking in and adopting out dogs and cats, but also acted as the local dog catcher for the city's Animal Control, euthanizing healthy animals that had been picked up as strays. As president, I vowed to institute a 'no-kill' shelter. As a board, we terminated the city contract and adopted a policy that no animal would be put down except for medical necessity with veterinarian approval.

We had noticed that many dogs would go stir crazy if confined to a cage longer than six weeks. For the dog's benefit and to avoid overcrowding at the shelter, the board approved a policy that at the six-week mark of a pet's stay, a sign would be posted outside the cage reading 'Free to Good Home'. In effect, we would waive the usual adoption fees and find a home where the animal would be well cared for.

If keeping a dog in solitary caused the dog to act out violently, was it possible that humans confined for extended periods could act out viciously as well? If so, perhaps this was the theory of the defence I was looking for.

The problem, I believed, was this methodology of forming a theory was ass-backwards. One certainly should start with the facts and formulate an all-encompassing rule. I realized I was starting out with a theory and now in search of data to support it.

Everything I could get my hands on showed that research done by the Correctional Service of Canada concluded that punishment in the form of solitary confinement even over long periods had no effect on the physical or emotional well-being of inmates. Correctional officers demanded that this form of treatment be continued since it was a powerful tool in their arsenal of ways to control an out-of-control offender.

I had just about given up my theory that extensive solitary confinement had resulted in Terry acting out as he did. Then, fortuitously, I watched an episode of the CBS program, *60 Minutes*. It was September 12, 1993. There was a segment on the work being done by Harvard Professor Dr. Stuart Grassian on the effects of solitary confinement in the Pelican Bay SHU, a supermax facility in California.

The next day, on Monday morning, my office placed a call to Dr. Grassian's office at Harvard and an appointment was arranged.

Shortly thereafter, I booked my airfare to Boston. The following week, I would be meeting with Dr. Grassian.

TEN

THE GRASSIAN MEETING

■■■

THROUGHOUT THE TIME I spent on board the plane taking me to Boston, I had the nagging doubt that this might be a complete waste of time.

Although the Fitzsimmons case was at the top of my mind, I could not forget that Terry was not my only client. I had long trips several days a week driving to various penitentiaries for parole hearings and inmate interviews; there was always research to be done, factums to write and a seemingly endless number of letters to be written and telephone calls to be answered. All my research into the effects of solitary confinement in Canada were written by psychologists employed by the Correctional Service of Canada or who were paid for their studies through government grants funded by the CSC.

In establishing an appointment with Dr. Stuart Grassian, I made it clear that I was not asking for an opinion as to the psychiatric or psychological make up on Terry Fitzsimmons. Specifically, I wanted his academic perspective on the effects of solitary confinement.

The *60 Minutes* television episode where I first heard of Dr. Grassian dealt with the research he had undertaken at Pelican Bay State Prison in California about the effects of solitary confinement on inmates. The institution had a "supermax" facility similar to Canada's SHUs in Saskatchewan and Quebec.

He had interviewed and studied forty-nine SHU inmates and prepared a lengthy report to the Federal Court in the United States filed in a class-action lawsuit concerning conditions at Pelican Bay.

His findings, according to the televised report, were shocking. According to Dr. Grassian, his research confirmed and corroborated existing studies, not cited by the Canadian correctional system, that the severe and prolonged restriction of environmental stimulation in solitary confinement was toxic to brain functioning. People with pre-existing central nervous system dysfunction or serious mental illness were especially likely to develop overt confusional, agitated, hallucinatory psychoses as a result of SHU confinement.

Grassian asked me to drive to his home. I found his residence located in a rather trendy well-to-do area of Newton, Massachusetts, just outside of Boston. Dr. Grassian met me at the front door and invited me to follow him to his upstairs home office. He was dressed casually. He appeared to me as a tall man, slim and comfortable meeting new people.

Beyond asking a few questions about my good flight and ability to find his house, there was limited small talk. Both the doctor and I wanted to get to the subject matter of the meeting directly.

"Your client did time in solitary?" he began.

"Yes," I replied and then gave a summary of Terry's time in segregation and the legal difficulties he now found himself in.

"Confinement of a prisoner alone in a cell for all or nearly all of the day with minimal environmental stimulation and minimal opportunity for social interaction. You know that it is my opinion that solitary confinement can cause severe psychiatric harm."

"I am worried that this may be in opposition to what several CSC psychological studies have shown," I added.

"It's not just me." Dr. Grassian added. "The harm includes a specific syndrome which has been reported by many clinicians in a variety of settings which are characterized by inadequate, noxious and/or restricted environmental and social stimulation."

"To what effect?" I interrupted.

"In more severe cases," he said, "this syndrome is associated with agitation, self-destructive behaviour, and overt psychotic disorganization.

"Solitary confinement can exacerbate a previous mental condition. Inmates so confined can suffer significant psychological pain during their period of isolation impairing their ability to adapt successfully to the broader prison environment and back to the broader community when released from prison."

My mind went immediately to thoughts of torture. The adage that a person is sent to prison as punishment and not for punishment, seemed to be ignored by the cruelty of solitary confinement.

"Moreover," Grassian continued, "although many of the acute symptoms suffered by these inmates are likely to subside upon termination of solitary confinement, many individuals, including some who did not become overtly psychiatrically ill during their confinement in solitary, will likely suffer permanent harm and impairment as a result of such confinement. This harm is most commonly manifested by a continued intolerance of social interaction. This is a handicap that often prevents the inmate from successfully readjusting to the broader social environment of general population in prison, and perhaps more significantly, often severely impairs the inmate's capacity to reintegrate into the broader community upon release from imprisonment."

I wanted to flesh this analysis out further. "I have clients who feel the burden of interacting with other inmates is becoming too great, especially those who may have run up gambling debts and just want to 'check in' to solitary, as they call it, to get away from potential harm. Are you suggesting that should be disallowed?"

"Not at all," Grassian continued. "However, theoretically there should be a difference between administrative segregation and punitive dissociation even though they may result in the inmate occupying the same bed.

"Punitive solitary confinement imposes deprivations in excess to those which are minimally required to maintain an inmate in segregated confinement, such as limited programming, occupational and education opportunities, visitation, use of telephone, radio, and TV. Inmates moving into admin seg should retain those opportunities and privileges enjoyed by inmates in congregate housing. Sadly, however, in practice this is, unfortunately, rarely the case."

What my expert was telling me was in effect that punitive dissociation overlooked the harsh realities of its effect on the prisoner in exchange for the notion that punishment of bad behaviour would have a deterrent effect on other inmates who might want to act in a similar fashion.

Specific Deterrence

Ever since my first course in criminal law in first-year law school, I learned that the functions of sentencing included specific and general deterrence of criminal behaviour.

Specific deterrence was the notion that severe consequences would be imposed on a person violating the law; general deterrence would be imposed to deter would-be criminals by seeing the punishment imposed on one of their community members.

The concepts never really merged with my day-to-day experience of living. As a child I recognized that there would be consequences for misbehaving. I never took it that since one of my peers did wrong and was punished, the rest of my peers would, forever after, restrain themselves from like action to avoid similar consequences. General deterrence was nonsense as best I could figure although the term was used regularly by those appointed to mete out sentences.

The use of solitary confinement as a means of general deterrence of disruptive behavior in prison was as, Dr. Grassian was signaling, "the imposition of pain of staggering proportions without the safeguards that anchor our system of criminal justice."

In both Canada and in the United States, the early prisons built in the 19th century featured isolation as a tool for rehabilitation. The massive prison walls were not so much to keep inmates in as they were to keep evil influences out. If wrongdoers could be sheltered away from all other influences, it was thought, they could reflect on their evil ways and be penitent for their sins. Thus, the origins of the word 'penitentiary.' In Kingston Penitentiary, as was the case in the Philadelphia and Auburn prisons of the United States, inmates were forbidden to speak; in many cases, they were blindfolded while being moved about. They were psychologically harmed.

According to Dr. Grassian's research the serious harm caused by solitary confinement was recognized within years of its institution in the 19th century. Clinicians in Germany were especially scrupulous in documenting the harm being done. Eventually, prisons allowed inmates to converse and socialize together.

Solitary confinement is an anachronism; it is a remnant of an outdated and tragically misguided concept of penal justice. It is a system that can and does create monsters. Perhaps putting the blame on the system was the best way to defend Terry's wrongdoings. Would Terry accept such a defence?

ELEVEN

THE NEXT MEETING

■ ■ ■

Upon arrival home from my meeting with Dr. Grassian in Boston and reflecting back also to my encounter with Toronto psychiatrist Dr. Jerry Cooper, I sensed that a defence was coming together. I put in a call to the Ottawa Carleton Detention Centre requesting that inmate Fitzsimmons call his lawyer and that I considered the call urgent.

The following day, in the afternoon, I received Terry's call. I went through the usual recorded announcement that identified the caller and confirming that I would be responsible for the charge for the call. I *did* want to speak with Terry, and I *did* consider the call urgent.

Terry was anxious about his pending charges, and I knew he wanted the legal machinery to move with haste. The only way I could keep him satisfied and convinced that the 'world is unfolding as it should' would be to use the 'project effort' concept I had learned as a law student. The concept is that a client suspects a lawyer is doing nothing unless the client receives notices from time to time showing that the lawyer is projecting effort into the case. The procedure includes sending a client a copy of all correspondence and court filings, regular telephone communication if possible, and visits to incarcerated inmate clients. When a client sees the lawyer is working hard on their behalf, there is a reduction of anxiety, greater trust in the lawyer and less likelihood of a complaint being lodged with the lawyer's professional organization. Moreover, a satisfied client is more likely to refer associates who may need legal counsel in future.

Terry was happy to be talking with me again. "How's it lookin'?" Terry began.

"I've been very busy." I replied, cutting Terry off from continuing his question. "I went to Boston to see an expert psychiatrist who can give expert evidence at your trials, and I have been doing quite a bit of research." I added. I told him there was a body of law being developed and name-dropped cases like the *McCann* case in British Columbia, the *Vantour Report*, the *McGuigan Report*, and other legal cases I had reviewed. I was certainly projecting effort but nonetheless Terry seemed displeased.

"When are you coming up to the OCDC again," he asked. "I need to talk to you."

"What's pressing," I asked.

"My wife came up to see me and I need to talk to you about it—but not on the phone."

"Wife?" I queried. "You never mentioned you were married. When did you get the time to do that?"

"It was no big deal. Six months before I got out, I married this woman who was a sister to one of the guys inside. I really didn't know her. It seemed like a good idea at the time, and it would give me a place to live when I got out. They always want to know where you'll be living. So, I needed an address."

"How come you didn't mention it before?" I wondered.

"You didn't ask. As I said, it was no big deal."

In actuality, Terry had made reference to his wife at our first meeting. I did not discover this until later when I reviewed my notes. His description of the murders was so graphic that I lost all memory that he told me he had been married.

"We only lived together ten days. Then I moved in with this chick who owned a beauty salon. I was with her until July.

She was working days, so I was able to be alone in the house most of the time. She had a whack of jewelry and so I took it, pawned it off and came to Toronto in July. That's all there was to it. But now I hear my wife is knocked up and having a kid with a guy I know from KP. I hate his guts. I want to talk to you about that. It's important. I need to talk to you in person. Can you book in later this week? I'd really appreciate it."

I promised I would attempt to drive to Ottawa once again. His pleading alerted me to the fact that Terry was down in the dumps at the time I was on an emotional high from the Grassian meeting. I remembered to warn Terry that sometimes things cropped up making a visit impossible, most notably, an institutional lockdown where all visits, even professional visits (as lawyer/client interviews were called) are cancelled.

"Oh, one more thing," Terry added. "Could you call my parents and ask if they could spare some bucks to put into my canteen account. I'm running low on cash. Every little bit helps."

He provided me with what he believed was a working telephone number for his parents' home in London, Ontario. He said he couldn't call himself because no one would accept his collect call. I gave in once again and promised I'd call on his behalf.

Non-delivered Funds

I secured a date later in the week to see Terry in Ottawa for another face-to-face meeting. I also called the London number for Terry's parents and left a message that I was Terry's lawyer, and that Terry is requesting that some money be deposited in his canteen account in the Ottawa Carleton Detention Centre. I explained that inmates need to buy their own toiletries and the cost of such items are deducted from the trust funds the institution administers on each inmate's behalf. I explained a deposit could be made by simply telling the front desk that funds are being delivered for a particular inmate. The receptionist would accept the cash and provide a receipt. I mentioned that Terry would really appreciate it.

Within the hour, a man returned the call claiming to be Terry's father.

"I'm not going to be depositing any money for Terry," the voice at the other end of the line said in a stern and deliberate tone. "Terry has got himself in too much trouble. His mother has a nice business here and we don't want that wrecked."

The voice never said, "He's dead to us" but that is the distinct impression I received. I was not looking forward to conveying the gist of the conversation to Terry.

When Terry was led to the interview room, I asked if he would care for a soft drink. There were vending machines close to the interview room. Terry said he would have a ginger ale. I left the area returning with a ginger ale for Terry and a diet cola for me. We popped the pull tabs on the aluminum cans simultaneously; we each took a swig and set the cans side by side in the interview desk table.

Terry had not cracked a smile. I knew he was pondering some serious questions and I was waiting for the dam to break before he got into them.

"Let me start off," I said nervously. "I spoke to your dad and your parents won't be delivering any cash for your account." I was dreading giving the news but better to be up front about it. I took another sip of my drink.

"You just didn't put your lips on that can did you?" Terry asked.

"Why?" I asked.

"I just drank from that can while you were talking to me."

"I had Coke; you had ginger ale. I didn't see you." I replied.

"Well, I did. Remember I have AIDS. You better make an appointment to get yourself checked out."

I looked surprised if not outright shocked. I knew that Terry suspected I had limited knowledge how an infection that was considered fatal could be spread. I realized it was not by shaking hands with or breathing the same air an infected person but I had far too little knowledge of how the infection was spread than to eliminate drinking from a contaminated soft drink can.

Terry started to laugh. He was joking. Terry wanted to see a shocked expression on my face. I realized I was set up for his practical joke. Even in the circumstances, it became clear to me that Terry had a spirited sense of humour.

A Request for Divorce

Rather than being angry or embarrassed, I realized that my news about the non-delivered funds was what Terry suspected. His request was simply to reaffirm that he was alone in the world.

"The old lady came by two days ago." Terry started, referring to his wife. She wanted me to sign papers for her divorce. I told her I would sign whatever she wanted. I said the only thing I care about is that you don't shack up with…" and Terry named a name that was familiar to me, another inmate at KP who was about to be released, or maybe even had been released at the time Terry and I spoke. I will call him Gerry Moss for purposes of this story.

I sensed that Terry was not concerned with the request for a divorce. Something more seemed to trouble him. Why the concern?

Terry told with me that when he spoke with his wife, the two separated by a glass partition and communicating through telephone handsets, Terry sensed his wife was pregnant. It really didn't matter to Terry if the woman he was speaking with was to bear Terry's child or if Gerry Moss would be the father. He was frantic that no child should be living in the same home as a sex offender.

"Is Moss a child molester?" Terry asked.

"I can't tell you that, Terry."

"I know you acted for him. You would know if he is a child molester."

"I am not allowed to give out information about other people I learn of through my work. You wouldn't want me talking about sensitive matters in your life, would you?"

"Tell anybody anything they want to know. I want people to know. I have no secrets. If telling other people about me would help just one other person, shout it all out from the treetops."

"There are plenty of avenues to protect a child that work far more efficiently than my publicizing what I know about an offender's criminal history." I said in a reassuring manner.

"Suppose your ex and this guy do have a kid," I continued.

"Don't you think your ex will be watching out or, if all else fails, the doctors, teachers, and Children's Aid Society would be on top of it? There's nothing you can do to control the situation from inside. Sometimes you just have to hope that the system works."

"Like it worked for me?" Terry asked defiantly.

"I know you're confused and angry, Terry. But let it go. You have bigger things, real things, to think about rather than a lot of 'what ifs."

"Like who is going to pay for my funeral when I'm gone? Obviously not my folks. I doubt they'll even claim the body. It will cost $135 for a cremation. The taxpayers will have to pick up the tab. It doesn't matter to me."

Putting in His Time

I could tell by his reaction that Terry need not be in a solitary cell to feel the loneliness he was now enduring. There was nothing I could say to raise his spirits. Terry was just putting in time until his time was up. Every day, every meal was just one step closer to death and he was accepting of that fate.

I briefed Terry on my interaction with the *Sun* reporter. I predicted he would not see any repetition of the nasty slur against which he had raised such an emotional reaction.

"But he'll find something worse to say once the facts come out in court." Terry suggested.

"We'll cross that bridge when it's time," I pleaded. "I'll make sure that the paper gets our version. Sure, the details are horrible. But the worst thing anyone can say to the press is 'No comment'. It reinforces in the readers any negative slant that the reporter is taking. Remember Terry, any newspaper reporter worth his salt will try to answer five questions: who, what, when, where, and why. The most important of these is 'Why'. Once we hand that out, with our spin on it, the public has its answer, and the curiosity dies a natural death. Don't let it all bother you now. Take it one day at a time.

"There is an explanation, and a good one," I added. I then reviewed with him the discussion I had with Dr. Grassian. It didn't cheer him up. It was obvious he was leaving things with me, but I sensed he was waiting for the whole ordeal to be over.

A Real Sense of Loneliness

The telephone call I had from Mr. Fitzsimmons, the father, bothered me all the way during my drive back home. I had very supportive parents—hell, they were even boarding my dog while I was away in Boston and in Ottawa. It would be supper time by the time I was at their place to pick up the dog. I knew too that I could count on a particularly good meal.

Even though I always enjoyed visiting my parents, there was always a certain amount of tension in the air when I discussed my criminal law practice with my family. On this occasion, however, there was no mention of what I was doing in Ottawa or concern that I had spent time with a criminal whose deeds would be incomprehensible to my parents who had never had legal troubles in their lives. I was sitting at the table with a fresh helping of food in front of me when my mother said, "Did you notice anything missing?"

I had been so caught up in my dealings with Terry that I had neglected to notice that my dog had not met me at the door with his tail wagging.

"What?" I said with surprise. Then it hit me. Skippy, my 16-year-old Samoyed/Shepherd sidekick was not near the table expecting treats snuck to him under the table.

"He got very sick," my mother continued. "We took him up to the vet. We know you couldn't do it."

Memories flooded through my mind of the puppy I adopted from a farm in St. Thomas, Ontario. Raising the pup in the early days of my marriage, keeping him through the divorce, the moves to Kingston, to Windsor and finally the move back to Cobourg. Suddenly, my dog was gone. In a very real sense, I could sympathize with Terry. I felt very alone.

TWELVE

CALL TO ACTION

■■■

I HAD EXTRAORDINARILY LITTLE TIME to wallow in self-pity. The long drives to Ottawa and the rescheduling of daily activities that the meetings with Terry required meant a lot of catch-up work to be done. There were numerous clients to be seen going up for parole in the month. All had to be seen and counselled on how best to answer the questions put to them in hearings by the Parole Board panel members. There was correspondence that was required. Most of the letters I received day to day were handwritten in pencil on note paper.

I enjoyed reading inmate correspondence. Inmates would pour their hearts out describing the current injustices they perceived were being inflicted on them. These were always hand written and sometimes it was difficult translating some words so poorly spelled they seemed indecipherable. Of course, inmates always used their own vernacular when writing. The favourite adjective it seemed was the misspelled word 'fucken'.

Another inmate wrote to me requesting that I sue on behalf to seek damages for a punch he received to his face when the correctional service was late in intervening into an inmate brawl: "I know you are comfortable enough in your own sexuality, John, that you can admit that before my nose was broken, I was a damn good-looking guy." Most inmate mail imploring me to take on cases contained that brutal honesty of belief in their own claim.

Many of my letters were from parents. I had noticed a trend in my practice that parents were becoming more and more involved in the care and treatment of their incarcerated offspring. It was as though their young prodigies were incapable of doing anything wrong. Perhaps this had much to do with the criminal defence strategy of seeking an acquittal and never having to admit that harm was done.

It was always a shock to these parents that a lawyer would take what seemed to be an opposite stance in the interest of the inmate client. Many parents wanted their sons or daughters to continue the position taken at trial that they were innocent of illegal or immoral behaviour. This usually cropped up when an inmate client went for parole.

Three Keys to the Prison

I instruct my clients that to be successful in obtaining parole one must be able to accept the 'three keys to the prison', as I call them. The first is to 'look inside yourself'. Since a parole board always reviews an inmate's past criminal history, success in a parole hearing means the prisoner must be aware of what he or she did wrong in the past and understood their motivation for doing so. The underlying belief is that if an inmate doesn't know why they did wrong, the likelihood is that the parolee would repeat the wrongdoing in the future.

The second key is to 'look outside yourself' and realize there are many victims to a criminal offence other than the complainant. Victims can include one's own family, especially spouses who could well do harder time on the outside than the prisoner is doing on the inside. Remorse for one's crime is an essential ingredient.

The third key is "Release Plan". It was essential that if parole is to be granted, the inmate must have a structured plan of reintegration that should include a satisfactory residence and, in the best of all possible worlds, a workplace.

Over-involvement by parents negated many of these factors. With this in mind, I was much more forgiving of Terry's parents' lack of involvement in his case. In any event, Terry was not going for parole anytime soon. His admission of the killings could be used in mitigation of a harsher sentence since remorse also is taken into account at criminal sentencing. The nagging doubt that, in a very real sense, kept me awake at night was that his admissions could also be the basis of a first-degree murder conviction.

I was having lunch at a Cobourg restaurant when my assistant arrived to give me news of a telephone call that had just come in. The Ottawa Carleton Detention Centre called to advise me that my client had attempted suicide. He had survived but was taken to hospital. He had cut his wrists, but staff had arrived in time before he suffered too much blood loss. He would be released from hospital back to the OCDC. The institution would arrange for an emergency visit once he was discharged from hospital and brought back to the institution.

About a week later I trekked back to Ottawa. I was happy to see Terry but angry that he had taken extreme measures. From the cold expression on Terry's face, I knew that he was embarrassed for trying to kill himself (or perhaps that he was unsuccessful in the attempt) and annoyed that the criminal process was dragging on so slowly while he was caged in a remand centre.

"Do we really have to go to trial in three different cities?" he asked. "Couldn't we just get it over once and for all right here? I just can't take it anymore in a place like this. Send me back to prison. At least I could live like a human being."

"It is possible to go to court here in Ottawa and enter guilty pleas. But that is only one way the matters can be resolved. You would have to plead guilty to all three first-degree murder counts. Then there are the bank robberies. Are you willing to walk in and plead guilty to everything?"

It was a pattern I had seen elsewhere, especially in my parole representation work. An accused party gets so worn down by the pressure of sitting in a remand centre that a guilty plea is an acceptable option, regardless of guilt or innocence.

When I advised parole applicants of the 'three keys', most would readily agree except for the point of admitting wrongdoing to a recorded guilty plea. Too often I would hear the comment that the plea was entered just "to get it over with." Such a comment was fatal at a parole board hearing. "If you were prepared to lie to the court, are you prepared to lie to the Board?" How many people who could in fact be found not guilty were serving time in this country's penal institutions?

I reminded myself that in Terry's situation, there would be no 'factual innocence'. He was charged with killing three people and he had killed three people. Moreover, he told the police he had killed three people. I had satisfied myself that manslaughter was not an option. The decision a court would have to make would be whether Terry should be found guilty of first-degree or second-degree murder. A 25-year parole ineligibility would be the mandatory sentence if first-degree murder was found to have taken place. The ineligibility period would be from 10 to 25 years if the outcome was second-degree.

Terry's demand seemed reasonable. He wanted things wrapped up soon. What was unreasonable was that he was willing to plead to first-degree murder when I firmly believed I could assist in having all three murder counts reduced to second-degree.

Left unsaid was my excitement that Terry's case could be the start of ridding our prison law system of the evil of solitary confinement. I saw no ethical conflict in what I perceived as advancing the client's interest while pursuing a political objective of changing the law or at least how the law was administered.

"So how would it work if we decided to plead to second-degree?" Terry asked.

"I haven't explored the situation," I said. "I will have to talk to the Crown attorneys in Ottawa, Toronto, and Montreal and see if I can work out the deal. If they agree, you can be sent over to the courthouse here and get Ottawa out of the way. Probably Toronto will be next and then Montreal."

"Does that mean I will have to be red bagged to those other places?" When Terry used the term 'red bagged' he was referring to a procedure where all the prisoner's possession in an Ontario remand centre would be placed in a red bag to be moved from the sending institution to the receiving institution.

"Yes," I said, "That's the standard procedure."

"I don't want to end up waiting in the Don Jail. That place is worse than here." Terry was referring to the old Toronto Jail built in 1864. It had a reputation for overcrowding and violence. I had interviewed several clients kept in that facility and I readily appreciated his concern."

"That is probably a good guess," I responded. "But we would work out a time when you could appear in court in Toronto and then let them know immediately that you were needed in Montreal."

Terry seemed unhappy with the prospect. "Do you think you can get the Crown to buy into a deal?", he asked.

"I don't know. I can try. I'll let you know what I am able to work out." I had no expectations what I could accomplish. With an overwhelmingly solid case for the prosecution, there was little for me to bargain with.

"Do what you have to do even if it's first-degree," Terry instructed. With that, I was on my way to the Crown attorney's office.

THIRTEEN

NEGOTIATIONS

■ ■ ■

GETTING A CASE from initial court appearance to trial often takes an inordinate amount of time. Much of this can be attributed to court backlog. But a substantial delay occurs when it is necessary to schedule preliminary inquiries. In murder cases, like all criminal cases, charges are laid by filing an indictment by the Crown attorney in the county where the transgression occurred. A preliminary hearing before a provincially appointed judge is scheduled.

The rationale for the preliminary hearing is that before the case moves forward to a superior court, the evidence before the preliminary inquiry must show that there is some evidence that a 'properly instructed' judge or a jury could use to convict. The origins of this test were set out in a Supreme Court of Canada decision known as the *USA v. Sheppard*. The purpose is to weed out those cases where there would be no likelihood of conviction and save valuable court time and expense. The bar is very low and it is almost always the case that a case completed through the preliminary inquiry stage will result in the matter going forward.

I understood that a preliminary inquiry would have to be arranged in Ottawa, Toronto, and Montreal. The resulting procedure in each jurisdiction turned out to be different in each case.

In Ottawa, to save time, I agreed to a truncated procedure I had never used before, but I was assured the transcript could be used in Superior Court just as if it had been taken in the more formal judicial proceeding.

Defence counsel use the preliminary inquiry phase of the prosecution as an additional means of 'discovering' the Crown's case. Crown witnesses are examined under oath and their testimony can be used to point out contradictions if the testimony varies at trial from the responses made at the prelim.

The Ottawa questioning took place as a transcribed interrogation before a court stenographer rather than as a proceeding before a judge in open court.

In Toronto, the Crown attorney proceeded by way of direct indictment which precluded any preliminary hearing whatsoever.

In Montreal, a preliminary hearing was called. Unlike Ontario hearings, counsel attends court fully robed. The courtroom in Montreal was arranged on one level in the form of a horseshoe. Despite wearing my barrister's robe, the procedure seemed much more relaxed and informal.

Once the preliminary transcripts were prepared, the time had come to meet with the Crown attorneys to see if resolution was possible or if a trial was necessary. First stop—the Ottawa Crown's office.

Clutter and Bankers Boxes

"May I see the Crown attorney assigned to the Terry Fitzsimmons case?" I asked the receptionist upon my entering the Ottawa Crown's office.

"Just have a seat," I was told. "I don't know if he has returned from court. I'll page him for you."

"Thank you," I said with a smile, but no doubt accompanied by an expression that showed impatience.

After what seemed an interminable wait, I was ushered

into a small, cluttered office. There were bankers boxes on the floor with the name, presumably of an accused, scrawled with magic marker on the sides of the cartons. The desk was littered with a variety of papers. A dark blue suit coat hung across the back of a desk chair. There were two chairs as well, but both were piled high with an assortment of documents.

While I was standing alone in the room, I heard a rustle at the office entrance door behind me. The assigned Crown introduced himself. He was holding a sheaf of papers.

"Nice to meet you." I said, deliberately not mentioning his name for I had instantaneously forgotten it.

"I was just reviewing the transcript of the cross examination in your fellow's matter," he declared. It was apparent that the papers he was clutching were the transcribed answers taken in private at a court stenographer's office.

Ordinarily it could take months to arrange a preliminary hearing. It had been agreed between the defence and the prosecution that to speed up proceedings, the Crown would subpoena each of its witnesses to a court reporter's office where the witness would be placed under oath and asked questions by defence counsel. Ordinarily, such an examination would be done in open court before a judge at a preliminary inquiry. This informal procedure would allow me to get the answers I would get if the matter were heard in court, but without the delay in scheduling that an actual court appearance would involve. I was able to have the examinations under oath concluded by early 1994.

"You were pretty rough on the investigating officer, weren't you?" This is not how I wanted negotiations to begin.

The officer had sworn that when he walked into the abandoned Red Barn restaurant, he observed that he saw the body of a "dead gay man' "I wanted him to tell me what would distinguish the body of a straight man from that of a gay man. I asked if there was some mark or insignia that would notify an observer that a particular individual was gay or straight. He refused to answer.

My thought was that the police officer would have answered that he had been told the victim of the crime was a man identified as gay by his cohorts in Toronto. The officer never took this easy way out. Sometimes a non-answer can be as instructive as complete answer. I did not dwell on this point, but I had seen through the cross examination that the officer was troubled by the question. Now I discover that the Crown attorney had been advised of the troubling question as well. Was the Ottawa bar Terry had visited under surveillance? Was the bar owner under surveillance? Could the police have intervened earlier? Those were issues I would want to explore if the matter were to go to trial; but that was not the purpose of my visit.

Negotiating a Sentence

I could sense that the issue of gay man/straight man had been raised in expectation that I would be pursuing the matter in a hard-fought trial.

"It really doesn't matter," I said changing the avenue the discussion was taking. "Would you consider trying to resolve the matter?"

He asked, "What do you have in mind?"

I shot back, "A plea of guilty to second-degree and a joint submission of life-10," knowing full well the proposal for the minimum length of parole ineligibility was a nonstarter.

He said, "Well, we could save a lot of time by getting this thing over quickly. I'm always agreeable to saving resources. But there is no way I can agree to 10 years ineligibility."

I asked him, "What are you looking for?"

He replied, "The lowest I can go would be life-19. We could make a joint submission on that."

When counsel agree to make a joint submission, they are agreeing to a negotiated sentence. If the sentence is in a reasonable range as to the sentence that would be imposed if the matter went to trial, it is likely that a sentencing judge would agree. Indeed, it would be grounds for appeal if the judge jumped the joint submission and imposed another figure that had not been agreed to. Of course, it is up to a judge to ensure that any joint submission is within a range that would satisfy the ends of justice.

Judges like joint submissions. One judge told me that coming up with an appropriate sentence was the hardest thing a judge must do. A joint submission eases that burden. As well, if counsel can be reasonable, it saves the cost and inconvenience of a trial. Judicial economy is highly regarded.

I asked him, "What if I were to agree to a plea but came in with a lower number? You could still ask for 19, but I could say something less and see if the judge will buy it."

Rolling his eyes, he said, "Do you really think that your guy could expect anything less than 19? You're dreaming in technicolour if you think that. What would you be asking?"

I replied, "Say life-12?"

He said, "There is absolutely no way. I think I am being generous dropping it as low as 19. If you want to ask for a lower number, it won't be by joint submission."

I snapped back, "I'll agree to that. You make your pitch and I'll make mine. But I have to get my client's consent. Without that, I cannot say we have a binding deal."

He said, "Get back to me soon. If we are going to resolve this, I want to get it before court as soon as possible. You know that without a joint submission, a judge can go higher than 19?"

I said, "I am well aware of that."

The meeting was brief but, in my opinion, productive.

A Year After the Six-Day Killing Spree

Plea deals often draw criticism from the public. Whenever counsel walk into court after such a bargain has been reached, a trial does not follow. In fact there is no trial at all. Instead, there is a plea taken to the charge; the prosecutor reads the allegations to the court in support of the charge; defence counsel agrees that the 'facts' read out are substantially correct. If the judge feels that the admitted facts support a finding of guilt, a conviction is registered, and the parties then speak to sentence. Evidence by way of calling witnesses to the stand or introducing photographic or documentary evidence is permitted on sentencing but that is the exception to usual process. There is no drama that onlookers would expect. The whole affair is done in minutes, not weeks. It is efficient and, provided the lawyers on each side have done their jobs, the result is acceptable and likely unappealable. Finality of the process is also highly valued.

It was too late to return to the OCDC. I would have to explain the negotiation to Terry the following day by telephone. It was almost a year since the six-day killing spree had begun. Terry was sullen when I reported the conversation with the Crown attorney in Ottawa.

"Do whatever you have to do man," he said. "I just want this all to be over and the sooner the better."

"This will set the standard," I commented. "If all goes well, we can ask a judge in Toronto and Montreal to set the same sentence. They will all run concurrently. All the sentences will run together," I explained should he not understand the meaning of concurrent.

"I know that," Terry said, subtlety putting me in my place.

"After we're through in Ottawa, you'll come to Toronto. I'll set things up to get it over as quickly as possible. And then, you're off the Montreal to get the thing done. It should all happen fairly quickly. Is that all okay with you?"

"Just do it. I can't take this place anymore." The call ended.

My office staff was curious how things worked out. I explained the Crown would be asking for life-19. I would be asking for something less and the whole ordeal would be over in probably a month or two.

"You're afraid to go to trial," my assistant snapped. I did not know how to interpret the comment. Was this an accusation that I was acting improperly or a statement of frustration that what promised to be a show trial was falling through?

"Look," I said. "I'm not afraid to go to trial. But this is Terry's decision. As far as I can see, it's a rational decision and I must take my client's instructions."

At home, I received a letter. Inside were two neatly folded sheets of paper, printed on one side with some sort of advertising and originally blank on the other side. But on the white backside of the paper was a neatly handwritten message from my old friend Claire Culhane.

Claire was a retired grandmother and noted prison rights advocate who spent every last one of her pennies travelling across Canada visiting penitentiary inmates. It wasn't that Claire couldn't afford decent stationery; it was that she would rather spend her money on the great cause of prisoners' rights. She was, as Nick Lowe labelled Claire in the title of his Culhane biography, a "One Woman Army."

After admonishing staff about their interference with a decision to get the criminal charges dealt with early, I read Claire's message: "I heard what you are doing for Terry. I think it's time we ended solitary confinement once and for all. We're counting on you. Keep up the battle. As I've told you many times before, we're fighting the best fight in town!"

Should I have convinced Terry to forget his inconvenience? After all, we could take the issue of solitary confinement to court. In all honesty, I believe Terry would have rejected the cause. Should he appear for trial, I had no doubt that he would have an amazing and true-fact situation to present to a court about all of his long years in solitary confinement, but he was not strong enough mentally to endure such an ordeal. Sometimes even a favourite is scratched from the starting line-up of the Kentucky Derby.

Should I have accepted a 19-year deal? Did I open the door to an even harsher sentence? Time was fast approaching when I would find out.

FOURTEEN

JUNE 1994, OTTAWA

■■■

CONTACTING three different prosecutors, trying to arrange court time and making dates mesh with limited disruption to my schedule seemed too big a task to undertake. All proceedings must be wrapped up quickly according to Terry's instructions. But all dates must be amenable to the prosecutors and the courts. Once possible early dates were canvassed, the hard part was to convince a trial administrator in three different cities to schedule early dates in summer. Judges like to get away to the cottage during warm weather like everyone else. That leaves a shortage, especially when emergencies crop up in summer months.

To my surprise, the prosecutors and administrators were all cooperative. I was to appear in the Ontario Court (General Division), now known as the Superior Court of Justice, in mid-June to early July. It was certainly a time frame that Terry could live with.

The first hearing, it was agreed, would take place in Ottawa. By mid-month, I found myself in the male barristers robing room at the Elgin Street Courthouse after having taken a brisk walk from the Château Laurier Hotel.

The enormity of the law and my place in it washed over my thoughts—it may have been the sight of Canada's Parliament Buildings off to my right as I crossed the road to head down Elgin. The Parliament Buildings are where all the laws are made and here I was, off to participate in the enforcement of the most serious offence in the *Criminal Code*.

The law says that for premeditated murder the sentence is life with no parole eligibility for 25 years. Terry had killed Don Hebert. It was premeditated. There were no factors that nullified the wrongful mental intent of his action. Justice says he should do life-25. But I am off to argue that he should be convicted of second-degree murder and the proper sentence would be life imprisonment but with a parole ineligibility below 25 years, hopefully substantially below. How can I justify that, having taken an oath to uphold the law, I will soon be arguing that less than 25 years is just?

Pine Box Parole
My memory was of an evening I had spent at maximum security Millhaven Penitentiary years before. I was called in by the 'Lifers' Group' to present a talk on the laws on homicide that saw most of my audience doomed to an unimaginable future in a cage. Some would get what inmates called a 'pine box parole' as the only way to exit the prison. And yet it was a pleasant and attentive group listening to my lecture. I recounted that when capital punishment was abolished in Canada in 1976, the political trade off was that an excessive number of years of parole ineligibility was added.

The year 1976 may be when *The Criminal Code of Canada* was amended. In fact, Canada had not seen an execution since 29-year-old Ronald Turpin and 54-year-old Arthur Lucas were hanged at the Toronto Don Jail on December 11, 1962. When the Lester Pearson Liberal Government took over in 1963 from the John Diefenbaker Progressive Conservatives, all persons sentenced to death had their date with the hangman commuted. Of those, the average length of time before being considered for parole was 10 years.

Several inmate hands shot in the air. "Does that mean if

capital punishment was never abolished, we could be looking to go before the Board in 10 years?" one inmate asked. I actually found it humorous that as my talk wound to a close, we had a group of Millhaven lifers ready to petition for the return of the death penalty.

The 'deal' made to secure passage of death penalty abolition was inherently bad. It suggested that after serving a term of years, an inmate could be so rehabilitated that he or she would be 'street ready', that is, an acceptable risk to the public. My experience taught me otherwise. Some people were so affected by being caught and tried that they would never again pose a public risk. Yet there were others I met, and even acted for, that were so dangerous, the public would never be safe.

Parliament, I envisioned, was using the cookie dough method of imposing punishment. In a recipe it may say "Bake in a 350-degree oven for 20 to 25 minutes," the assumption being that if the recipe is followed, perfect cookies will emerge.

Were people like cookie dough? Would perfection result after a sufficient exposure to intense conditions? I never believed that.

If parliamentarians could enact laws that were the end result of deal-making, then maybe it was not illegitimate for me to argue there were other factors to be assessed other than the *mens rea* (wrongful mental mind) and the *actus reus* (wrongful act).

Maybe it is part of our nature and now part of our culture that laws are not absolute but subject to a degree of manipulation to achieve a greater end. Of course, there is always the notion of deterrence. But I sincerely believed this principle was an utter sham anyways. Most crime is opportunistic. Before committing the act, few perpetrators, if any, consider the penal sanctions to be imposed on them.

Maybe when executions were public spectacle or individuals were placed in stocks in a public square, the idea of general deterrence had meaning. Now public involvement in a criminal's sentence was little more than a press release and forgotten the next day. Extending the parole ineligibility period was what it took to end capital punishment. We could rationalize the extended period of parole ineligibility as deterring likeminded offenders, but it was really just political compromise.

My Key Points in Court

Once inside the barristers' robing room, I readied my robes. The tradition in Canada as in the United Kingdom, is for lawyers to gown in black robes. In Canada though, we don't wear wigs. In the United States, lawyers proceed to court in suits.

As I affixed the tabs to my wing-collared shirt and buttoned up the black waistcoat and donned my barrister's robes, I did a mental review of the key points that I would be making. I would be arguing that despite the deplorable actions that my client had perpetrated, the real villain here was the Correctional Service of Canada for its part in the making of a monster.

Point one: Terry wasn't bad but had been made bad. He had grown up as a middle-class youth who unfortunately got into trouble with the law at an early age. Rehabilitation at that time in his life could have salvaged a redeemable individual. Instead of rehabilitation he got the unimaginable horrors of brutal sexual assault and isolation in solitary confinement for years on end.

Point two: The concept of solitary confinement was flawed in the extreme. Instead of allowing an inmate to become penitent, it warped a person's mind and caused ongoing psychological problems.

Point three: There was legislation on the books allowing the Correctional Service to refer the dangerous inmate to the Parole Board for detention until warrant expiry date, the day the sentence imposed by the court officially ends. Terry's case had not been reviewed for detention or if it was, staff at the prison were either incompetent or highly stressed such that an erroneous decision to release had been made. Terry had been released directly to the street without much by way of programming designed to get to the root of the prisoner's aberrant behaviour.

It occurred to me that the first point could be similar to any number of recidivists and was not particularly weighty to draw a judge to decide to make a substantial reduction in parole ineligibility.

Point two was really my motivation. It was what I wanted any member of the public sufficiently interested in the case to take away. Solitary confinement is an evil unto itself. I had two printouts of Dr. Grassian's papers to file as exhibits on sentencing.

Point three was really my favourite. It would be the argument I had presented to the parliamentary committee before which I had testified in support of Canada's Bill C-67, the legislation allowing the Parole Board to hold a prisoner in penitentiary to the very last day of the court-ordered sentence. Perhaps Terry should have been detained to explore programming that would make his transition to the street easier. It was a belated, "I told you so." to the academics at Queen's who berated me for my position.

The fact remained that it was indeed an act of misfeasance on the part of Terry's case managers. Why would someone with a brutal prison record, and having done so much time in solitary confinement, ever be considered "street ready"?

The CSC knew that he had done time in solitary and had made no gains. They chalked up the manslaughter conviction as an 'isolated act'. There was no questioning why a prisoner serving nine years for manslaughter never once applied for parole, not for work release, not for day parole, not for full parole. Unusual at the least and disturbing at best, it was all but overlooked in the CSC evaluation of risk.

Had this gone to trial, I would have called witnesses. A

Toronto Sun reporter had written on August 6, shortly after the 1993 homicides, that in reviewing the Fitzsimmons file and speaking to persons named only as 'prison sources', the author confirmed that case managers were lax in reviewing the Fitzsimmons case. What the reporter learned from a person or persons within the prison system was damning for an agency charged with public protection.

Dropping Like Flies

The *Toronto Sun* newspaper article quoted prison sources as saying that many dangerous inmates were not being recognized because their case workers were either incapable of doing the job or made mistakes because of stress. The report went on to note that two Kingston Penitentiary correctional officers and one from Prison for Women had taken stress leave in the two weeks prior to the date of publication. The report quoted the prison source as saying: "They're dropping like flies: it's burnout."

The submissions I would be presenting would be putting the prison system on trial, first by making a monster and secondly by releasing him to the public. I could never recall an incident in my career where I would be demeaning my client and calling him an unmanageable public risk rather than praising the individual as an ordinary law-abiding citizen unfortunately breaching the line between good and bad.

Once I was robed, I proceeded to the assigned courtroom. Upon entering I noted that the layout is like other newer courthouses in Ontario. It was a new building, and the lighting was bright but not overpowering. The floor was carpeted, and two wooden tables were positioned beside each other, one for defence counsel and the other for the prosecution. Between the tables was a lectern that counsel would use when making submissions to the judge. As I unloaded my files from my briefcase onto the defence table, I was trying to be careful not to spill any of the water kindly provided by court staff. At the prosecution desk to my right, the Crown attorney assigned to this case stood, also robed and engrossed in conversation with his junior assistant. The Crown attorney glanced my way and with a smile and the nod of his head, he acknowledged my existence but neither of us had words.

Behind me were rows of wooden seats as one would expect to see in a church. The seats were empty. On television, one is accustomed to seeing packed courtrooms. But this, despite the publicity of the crime was not a trial; it was a guilty plea, a case few would sacrifice a morning to attend. Two people I expected were reporters strolled in but neither chose to introduce themselves to either counsel. They simply took a seat and readied their notebooks. Ahead of me on an elevated platform was the judge's desk. A large leather-covered chair was angled behind it so the judge could readily take his seat once he entered the room and ascended the steps to his place overlooking the whole courtroom. Behind that was a large plaque looking like a battle shield inscribed with the French words, *Dieu et mon droit*. It was the motto of the British monarchy and symbolic of Canada's colonial past.

Shackled Hand and Foot

The court reporter was readying herself to make a transcription of the words spoken once court opened. The court clerk was seated below the judge's desk but still above the level of counsel table beside the court reporter.

Everyone stood as the judge entered from a door to my left. His white hair seemed especially white, almost shining, as he looked straight ahead and mounted the stairs to his elevated throne. In Canada, counsel bow to the judge while everyone remains standing. The judge returns the bow and takes his seat.

The clerk issued the order he recited by rote that we all take our seats. The judge nodded to the court officer that the accused be brought in from the cells and seated in the prisoner box. Terry Fitzsimmons was led in, shackled hand and foot and wearing an orange jumpsuit. His face expressed concern, but he said nothing. He gave me a quick glance that signaled I was to do whatever I thought needed to be done. The sole exception was that I was never to say anything that could even be interpreted as discrediting the honour of Don Hebert.

The charge of first-degree murder of Don Hebert was read aloud by the court clerk. Terry was asked, "To this charge, how do you plead? Guilty or Not Guilty?"

Before Terry could open his mouth, I jumped to my feet, inadvertently snagging the sleeve of my robe on the corner of the counsel table where I was seated.

"The accused pleads Not Guilty of the charge as read but guilty to the lesser included charge of second-degree murder." I stated firmly.

"Is that correct, Mr. Fitzsimmons?" the judge asked.

Terry nodded affirmatively and uttered in a barely audible voice, "Yes."

"We accept that plea," the Crown added swiftly. "I'll ask the court to amend the indictment."

With the paperwork out of the way, the Crown continued by reading the alleged 'facts'. The judge's head was lowered, and he made copious notes in his benchbook.

When the Crown concluded the presentation, the judge looked at Terry, now seated in the prisoner's box to my side and asked, "Are those facts substantially correct?"

Ordinarily I would be on my feet declaring the facts as just read out to be substantially correct. But the facts made no mention of planning and deliberation. Don Hebert's killing was indeed planned and deliberate. I felt it would be misleading to the court and ethically wrong for me to say the facts were entirely correct. What had been read out in open court was true in fact but, in law, the 'facts' could have been more fulsome. Due to the seriousness of the charge, I deemed it best to allow the accused person to answer himself. I had seen too many occasions where inmates claimed their counsel was a 'dump truck' and forced them into a situation with which they did not agree. Instead of answering the question on Terry's behalf, I nodded to Terry, asking him to answer the question.

"Yes, Your Honour." Terry said this time clearly and distinctly.

"A conviction will be entered. Is there a joint submission from counsel?" the judge asked.

"No, Your Honour. The matter of a joint submission was broached but neither my friend nor I were able to come to a resolution." In court, opposing counsel always refer to one another as 'my friend.'

"Very well," the judge intoned. "I'll hear your request on disposition."

The assistant Crown attorney then summarized the case law relating to a range of sentences applicable in cases where there had been a finding of guilt on second-degree murder. "I have therefore concluded it would be appropriate to ask Your Honour to impose a sentence of life imprisonment without eligibility for parole," the Crown attorney stated leaving the actual number hanging while he poured a glass of water and took a healthy slug.

My mind raced, thinking he was going to say 25 years. The maximum sentence had been part of the assistant Crown's earlier submission and my own research had indicated it was a definite possibility. The Crown was not bound by the offer of 19 years as we had not come to a mutual agreement even though Terry had told me he was comfortable if a 19-year ineligibility request were made.

I was tense. If the Crown were to ask for 25 years and I had not accepted the deal, would Terry hold me to account as an incompetent?

The Crown attorney set his drinking glass down and cleared his throat. "I apologize Your Honour, the courtroom is very dry." The Crown is asking that you impose a sentence of life imprisonment without eligibility for parole for 19 years."

I glanced over at Terry. He had what could easily become a smile on his face. Even though there was no joint submission, I would think that with two experienced lawyers recommending less than maximum sentence, the likelihood of an experienced judge jumping the sentence upward was minimal.

The judge nodded in my direction. I rose more smoothly this time, not catching my garment on the furniture. I had decided not to ask for a fixed number of years of ineligibility. I would submit merely "a much lesser number."

I began my unrehearsed speech making the points as I had planned. I recall myself getting quite passionate about the torture that solitary confinement represents and the science that was coming to the fore through Dr. Grassian and through German research. Even while I was speaking, the thought came to me that I wished Claire Culhane was sitting in the courtroom. This is an argument she would have endorsed fully.

I then pivoted to the blame-game of the misdeeds of the CSC, putting the responsibility of the deaths of three innocent people on the negligence of state employees who ignored the responsibility of keeping Canadians safe; namely, Canadians Norm Rasky, Fernand Talbot, and Don Hebert. Since we can't punish our government, we can acknowledge our displeasure by denying a lengthy sentence now proposed by the prosecution.

One last request: There are other matters to be litigated as a result of Terry's killings. Prison transfer must be made in short order. Would the judge be willing to sentence Terry immediately and not reserve decision to a later date?

The judge said, "I'm inclined to grant defence counsel's request for a quick conclusion of this ordeal. But we will break for half an hour while I review my notes and come to a decision. Thank you, both counsel."

"The court stands in recess for thirty minutes," the clerk cried out before the judge exited the room.

Sentencing

Terry was led out back to the holding cells. I decided not to visit him there while awaiting court resumption.

There were few observers in the courtroom. I had not turned around while court was in session to see who was there. Very often family members make up the bulk of the audience. It is always tough to acknowledge their tears as the facts of the case are read aloud and the goriness of the deeds done are re-lived by family members who were in recovery from the shock of the tragedy their lives experienced. If asked, they would say they were after "closure" and a desire to see the accused "brought to justice." I considered closure for the family members of murder victims to be a myth. What is justice when one loses a loved family member?

Instead, if family members are present, they are there to observe not so much the law meting out punishment in proper proportion, but what was more realistically a game show of 'Let's Make a Deal' where a judge has to determine which of three prison doors the accused will be sent through.

I was particularly hopeful I would not see Don Hebert's brother or other family members. The *Toronto Star* had interviewed family members at Don's funeral. The quoted remarks I read were skeptical that the focus of justice is on protecting the public. Indeed, it was suggested that everything is focused on the criminal's rehabilitation, without concern for victims. A family member recounted how Donny, as the family knew him, was a decent man who had spent a Christmas two years prior tending to an ailing grandmother in a nursing home.

There is no doubt that the Hebert family were genuine in their love for Donny, regarding him as a "really a terrific person." It was not unusual that family members blamed the justice system and adopted the position that convicts should serve their full term in prison. I took this to mean the maximum term allowed by law.

Had I met a representative of the Hebert family, I am sure

I would have said I was essentially making the same argument. Had Terry served out his term and acquired the skills, especially the psychiatric and psychological skills to deal with the damage done by solitary confinement, Don Hebert would likely be alive going about his business.

Family members were not in the courtroom, and I was not forced to apologize for my client's action, an apology I expected would be rejected as insincere.

Thirty minutes is never thirty minutes in court time. It was the best part of an hour before court resumed. The clerk called the session back to order, the court reporter placed the transcription mask over her mouth and the judge entered.

Counsel once again bowed in the direction of the judge and he too returned the traditional greeting. We all sat and awaited the decision.

There was a synopsis of the facts read into the record by the judge and his finding that the guilty plea had been properly accepted. Justice Robert Desmarais asked Terry if he wished to say anything before sentencing. Terry opened his eyes wide, somewhat in shock. He had not prepared to speak in open court. Nonetheless he stood and addressed the judge.

"Donald Hebert was my friend, and I regret that he's dead. I hope he's in a lot better place than I am. I didn't meet Don to say, 'one day I will kill you'.

"My intention was to live, whether it was the proper way of living, it doesn't really matter. He experienced something, I experienced something. And I'll remember—always."

The judge commented on the ugliness of the crime but that the professionalism of respective counsel had saved not only the state but the victims a great deal of stress. Accordingly, he was agreeing that considering the guilty plea as a mitigating factor and the fact that Terry had been traumatized by years of isolation, it was fitting that an appropriate sentence in this case was life imprisonment with no eligibility for parole for 15 years.

Terry looked at me and winked.

FIFTEEN

TORONTO

■ ■ ■

THE OTTAWA SENTENCING WAS, to use an analogy, an 'off-Broadway' performance. The main stage would be at 361 University Avenue in Toronto. The press coverage for a year had been centred in Toronto. If there was a judicial circus to be held, one would expect it would be here.

Of course, Terry had objected to being transferred to a Toronto jail to await sentence. As much as he had wanted to get out of Ottawa, he was no more satisfied with conditions at the ancient Don Jail. The institution was noisy and crowded. It took everything I could muster to convince Terry to calm down as it would be only for a few days before the sentencing, and then off to Montreal.

The Toronto sentencing was scheduled for June 28, 1994. Once again, I gowned in my black barrister's uniform. This time I was told that the judge wanted to meet with the Crown and me in his chambers.

The Crown attorney, Paul Culver, was Toronto's head Crown attorney. The sentencing judge, David Watt often presided over sensational trials. Judge Watt was known to be a pre-eminent criminal judge. Tall, dark haired, and lanky, he impressed always as a brilliant jurist and was revered throughout the bar as even-handed.

With a great judge and an impressive Crown as prosecutor,

I convinced myself this was surely to become a feeding frenzy for the local media. There were reporters in the courtroom and television remote trucks parked along University Avenue.

The Crown attorney and the judge knew that proceedings could go astray. It was decided that the lawyers and the judge would have a pre-trial meeting in the judge's office before going into court.

The judge's chambers consisted of a small room off the main courtroom with a window overlooking University Avenue, a main street outside the high-rise courthouse. The judge was robed, as were counsel who were ready to enter the courtroom once preliminary conversations were complete.

In chambers, counsel agreed on the facts, and I advised the group of the sentence handed down in Ottawa just a little over a week before. In methodical but less passionate tones, I listed the same points I had tried to make in Ottawa. Instead of concentrating on the Toronto murder of Norm Rasky alone, the Crown attorney was prepared with an overview of the entire spree of killings.

The judge commented that he would accept a joint submission of life-15, the same sentence that had been meted out in Ottawa, and since one could not be subjected to consecutive life terms (at least in those days), 15 years ineligibility seemed appropriate. It would show appreciation for the guilty plea but still be five years above the statutory minimum, indicating to the public the court's abhorrence of the brutality involved in the murders.

Knowing the outcome, I proceeded to the courtroom. I entered not through the main doors as would ordinarily be the case, but from the doors that the judge would enter since I was coming directly from the judge's chambers. I was able to observe a large number of people sitting in the body of the court. They were sitting together. They were neatly groomed and dressed well for the occasion. This was the Rasky family.

I had a flashback to the apprehension I always felt when

defending a violent criminal. In court the families are never confrontational, but the hate stares normally evinced was enough to have the defence counsel miserably aware that the lawyer was held in no higher regard than the prisoner who had been responsible for the agony experienced by the family.

I was therefore somewhat taken aback when a well-dressed woman stood up from the group and started walking toward me. I had no idea what she expected me to say. Until the outcome was announced in court, I could not reveal what had been discussed in chambers.

I imagine I just stood there looking apprehensive. The woman did not introduce herself other to say that she was speaking on behalf of the entire Rasky family.

"I just want you to know that I am speaking on behalf of the whole family." The woman spoke in a crisp, clear voice. "We all appreciate how difficult it must be to act on behalf of some of the people you represent. We admire you for doing such a job. The whole family has no animosity towards you whatsoever."

The woman smiled, clasped my hand momentarily and returned to her seat. I had never experienced such a confrontation before. I had known of the Rasky family and how Norman's brothers had distinguished themselves in literature and the arts. I had no idea that any family could be so thoughtful as to recognize the stress that counsel feels in trying to justify acts that are way outside the moral compass of the lawyer. I will forever hold the Rasky family in high esteem for their generous comment.

The Victim Impact Statement

The order of proceedings was similar to what had transpired in Ottawa.

During the admission of facts, prosecutor Culver called a Detective Sergeant to the stand. The police officer had led the investigation of the Rasky homicide on behalf of the Metropolitan Toronto Police. He spoke of the brutality of the attack on the dentist. The officer testified that Dr. Rasky had

been strangled, stabbed and bludgeoned first with a cast-alumi-
num ashtray and then with a brick. There were thirty wounds
attributable to the stabbing. Once Dr. Rasky was dead, both
Hebert and Fitzsimmons took off their pants to mop up the
blood. They fled the scene but first shaved their facial hair
and heads, cleaned up somewhat, and finally took a taxi to
Scarborough where they boarded a train to Montreal.

A Victim Impact Statement written on behalf of the
deceased's family was read aloud by the Crown attorney. In it,
the family asked, "Wouldn't capital punishment be effective in
such cases as this?" Obviously the Rasky family was capable at
drawing a distinction between lawyer and client. I sensed the
words were as much frustration as anger. How could anyone so
cruelly deal with what everyone regarded as a kind and gentle
man? But judges cannot order the execution of convicts. Capital
punishment had been abolished, however raising its spectre
was sufficient to exemplify the loss felt by those left behind.

The sentencing judge carried through by imposing a 15-year
parole ineligibility, but his words likely comforted the family
members listening to his comments. "There is nothing positive
to say of this offender" except for the fact he had pleaded guilty
and spared the family the ordeal of a long trial.

Following court, it was necessary to wend my way through
a crush of reporters asking for my reaction to the day's events.
I kept to my script and advised the media that I would carry
on imploring the Solicitor-General to end solitary confinement
and closing special handling units in Canada's penitentiary system. With respect to the allegation that correctional staff were
malfeasant in the execution of their duties, I commented "We've
had no cooperation from the Commissioner of Corrections in
terms of investigating this situation and we received a letter
from the Commissioner saying he doesn't feel it is necessary."

Terry would now be transferred to the Parthenais detention
centre in Montreal in advance of a July 4 hearing date.

SIXTEEN

MONTREAL

■ ■ ■

It was all set. The final sentencing hearing would take place at the Palais de Justice on July 4, 1994. I had used the same sentencing submissions twice now and I felt I was adept at running through my arguments in conversational tone having delivered essentially the same speech twice. I could use the days between my Toronto and Montreal appearances to get caught up on pending files at the office and visit clients in penitentiaries in Ontario to ready them for parole hearings or advance their arguments in civil court for violations of inmate rights. Then, the phone rang.

Terry had been transferred to the Montreal detention centre and was now in hospital with a suspected heroin overdose. Worst of all, authorities in Quebec had removed Terry from general population and placed him in segregation.

Terry's telephone message was brief and to the point: "I'm in the hole. I need to see you." Terry knew enough not to talk about the drug overdose issue while on the line. All inmate calls are monitored, and it was far too easy for authorities to investigate issues of contraband by listening in to calls—even calls to a lawyer.

I made an emergency trip to Montreal. I had never entered the Parthenais institution before. Despite its size, it was still a remand and detention centre, a high-rise building in downtown Montreal. Since the visit had to be booked, staff at the jail were well-aware of my visit. I signed in as I would at any other institution, but instead of having my briefcase inspected and walking through a metal detector, I was asked to follow a white-haired gentleman into a closed room. Inside was a middle-aged woman standing beside an X-ray machine. I was asked to place my briefcase on the conveyor belt to be scanned. This is a familiar process for me at every prison I enter and to most people who take commercial flights from an airport. The briefcase was declared clean. Then I was told to put my suit jacket on the conveyor belt and then my shoes. The white-haired man continued with petty conversation about my drive, the weather and life in Ontario.

I realized that with Terry having overdosed, the institution was on a mission to find a drug supplier. I was not at this moment just Terry's lawyer; I was a suspect.

I believed that if the X-ray had shown anything suspicious, I would be apprehended by the white-haired man. Had I been set up? Had Terry given my name as a supplier to get out of a stint in the hole? I've seen prisoners questioned and dire threats made unless they gave up the source of the contraband.

I also knew that security at prisons always suspected lawyers as a gateway for drugs entering jails. Lawyers had open, face-to-face contact with their clients in soundproof rooms that were also supposed to be free of audio or visual monitoring. Indeed, I was familiar with cases where lawyers had been caught. In Ontario, I believed my reputation was solid. I have never participated in delivering contraband to any client even after being told that I would be fired as solicitor if I failed to bring in cigarettes, cannabis, cocaine or any other illicit substance. In some instances, I terminated the solicitor/client relationship when such a demand was made and at other times, I stated I would continue to act unless a similar demand was repeated in future. In such cases, I never had a client ask me again to import contraband.

With the scanning complete, I was told I was free to proceed by elevator to an upper level where a correctional officer would direct me to an interview room.

Once seated, it was a short wait until Terry arrived. He was in a mood that I could only describe as distressed. He was fidgety and remained seated only minutes at a time before getting up and walking around.

I related my story of the examination upon entrance and revealed that I was of the belief that I was suspected as being the trafficker.

"This place is a supermarket," Terry said. "I wouldn't ask you to bring anything in. Why would I do that?"

The question made me wonder again if indeed my name had been mentioned as a possible source. I was so shaken by the experience on entering that I was willing to tell Terry our relationship as solicitor and client was over.

"No. It was easy to get. There is a guy in here that has it brought in by a guard. They wanted me to rat him out but I stayed firm. I'm no cheese eater."

As my anger subsided, I questioned Terry about his reason for using heroin when he was so close to the finish line.

"If you thought Ottawa was bad, this place is ten times worse. I just want it done with. Let me get back to KP. I'll be by myself, and I don't have to live with assholes only in jail long enough to change their socks. They can put me in seg. I can do my time there. I'm in no hurry to get back into gen pop."

Prison Practices

General population had been a problem for Terry ever since having met him a year previously. His acting out was his way of relieving the tensions that built up when confronting social situations in which he felt ill at ease.

Perhaps Terry's acceptance of solitary confinement was why the practice has continued in penitentiaries since the eighteenth century.

As far back as 1787, the well-educated in Philadelphia, including Benjamin Franklin, saw solitary confinement as an alternative to degrading prison practices such as corporal punishment or prison labour. Unfortunately, solitary became an 'add on' rather than an alternative to other forms of punishment.

It was the Quakers who felt it was proper to protect a man from harmful associations. If an inmate could live like a monk in a cell and meditate on his wrongdoing, he would come to discover the error of his ways. It became known as the Philadelphia system.

By 1818, New York State opened its second prison at Auburn. Its first warden, Elam Lynds (later to become warden of Sing Sing), modified the Philadelphia system by having prisoners work as a group during the day to pay for their upkeep.

The prisoners working in what became known as the 'Auburn system' or the 'Congregate system' had their heads shaved or closely cropped, worked in silence, and walked in lockstep an arm's length away from his fellow prisoner. Prisoners ate in a communal dining room. Once off work, strict solitary confinement was enforced. The goal was that instead of finding God, inmates would come to appreciate the value of hard work, respect for property and the rights of others.

These systems even though they became widespread throughout Europe came under criticism. Charles Dickens toured prisons in Canada and the United States in 1842 and found that the adherence to solitary confinement damaged the mind. He observed in his travelogue *American Notes for General Circulation,* "I hold this slow and daily tampering with the mysteries of the brain to be immeasurably worse than any torture of the body…"

Terry's mind was definitely damaged, I observed. His mood was more frantic than I had seen him in the past. Although he asked me to make a special trip to Montreal, he had extraordinarily little to say. Instead of being angry that the trip was pointless, I consoled myself that the brief visit might be enough to prevent Terry from doing something more drastic before July 4.

Terry left the interview room, and I was taken to another room where I was asked to wait. I subsequently found out that after my visit with Terry, he was strip searched for contraband. Only after concluding nothing had been passed to Terry during my visit was I permitted to board the elevator to the ground floor and leave the institution.

Upon returning to Montreal on July 4, I had not spoken to Terry. I had hoped to visit him in the cells prior to his being brought into the courtroom. I was told that the judge would be entering to begin proceedings imminently and there was no time to speak to my client. Any talking would have to occur in the courtroom.

Terry was escorted into the prisoner box by two burly guards. He appeared upset. However, before I had the opportunity to speak with him the court was called to order.

The proceedings were in English, although the accents of the judge and the Crown attorney betrayed the fact that they would have been much more comfortable were we to proceed in French, Canada's other official language.

I went through my prepared argument as I had done twice before. This time the judge was more argumentative and challenged me on certain assertions. Most of all, when I reminded him that two judges in Ontario had imposed life-15 sentences, he countered by stating that what those judges concluded had no precedential value on him.

Terry was not helpful. Instead of sitting quietly in the prisoner's box, he called out during both my and the Crown's submissions. He was clearly tired of the whole procedure and just wanted it to be over.

Different Emotions for Each Murder
In the end, the sentence was life-16. The case of the Terry Fitzsimmons murder spree was now concluded. I asked Terry

if he wanted me to come down to the holding cells. He shook his head no. He just wanted out of provincial lockups and a return to federal penitentiary custody. I told him that immediately upon my return to my office I would forward the jailer a notice that no appeal would be commenced and so the 30-day holding in provincial custody pending appeal could be waived. Terry smiled.

One of the last conversations with Terry was in the months before he died. He was interviewed by Cynthia Amsden of the *Globe and Mail*. She asked him if he had time to reflect on the killings he had perpetrated.

He responded, "I wish none of the murders had happened but wishing isn't going to change it." Terry thought for a moment. "They're very deep experiences, very violent experiences, and I don't think one is easier to live with than the other," he continued. "I have different emotions for each of them."

He was asked to list how he regarded and what he felt for each of his victims.

Terry replied, "Hatred for Mark Shannon. Rasky? Pity. The cab driver? I wish it had never happened. Don ... the best friend I ever had? I miss him but I'm happy for him because he's where he wanted to be. I believed in our friendship. I believe that if he was willing to die by my hands then I should be willing to die by his blood. That's why I injected his blood into my arm."

SEVENTEEN

REFLECTIONS

■■■

TERRY FITZSIMMONS was charged with three first-degree murders when we first made contact. He told me he had already imposed capital punishment on himself by injecting AIDS-tainted blood from his last victim, Don Hebert, into his own bloodstream. He told me he had made a complete confession to police. His instructions were to "have fun" with the case.

Having fun would not describe the work and thought that went into formulating a defence. At best, the outcome would be convictions of second-degree murder in all three cases. As the judge in the Toronto sentencing hearing had said in open court, the likelihood of Terry Fitzsimmons ever being released from prison was remote.

The defence I chose to advance was to put the penitentiary system on trial. I would convince a court to find that it was the Correctional Service of Canada that had taken a young man and, through the use of solitary confinement, had created a monster that led to the loss of life for several individuals.

The CSC was an easy scapegoat. They had relied on solitary confinement as a rehabilitative tool. It was not. They had failed to provide the necessary programs to have a young man treated and reformed. They had not carefully evaluated a release plan when mandatory supervision (release after serving two thirds of a sentence) was imminent. They failed to make a referral to the National Parole Board (now called the Parole Board of Canada) to have Terry detained until warrant expiry date (the conclusion of the court-imposed sentence) so that necessary treatment could be given. The prison system drove Terry crazy.

CSC is a governmental agency designed first and foremost to protect society at large. Indeed, the Office of Solicitor General is now renamed the Ministry of Public Safety. The Ministry oversees the CSC, the RCMP, CSIS, and the CBSA, acronyms for Canada's agencies to gather information and defend us from foreign and domestic threats.

Casting the Net of Blame

Upon reflection, perhaps I had cast the net of blame too narrowly. After all, Terry had been a young man abusing alcohol and drugs in his teenage years.

When Terry was convicted as an adult he was sent to prison. Perhaps there is a mistaken belief in our society that we are all better off if we remove troublesome members from our midst. Jail seems to be the default option when an offender poses a problem for law enforcement.

Some jurisdictions are coming to a different realization. I learned this years later when I attended the City of Austin, Texas with two eminent Canadian psychiatrists for a meeting with then-Texas Governor George W. Bush. We were there to try to convince the Governor to impose a 30-day postponement of the execution of Stanley Faulder, a Canadian on death row in the Huntsville Penitentiary. Faulder had been sentenced to death for the murder of an elderly Inez Phillips, matriarch of the Jack Phillips Oil Company who had made a fortune in bringing in several oil fields in the United States. Bush refused to grant an extension and Faulder was ultimately killed by lethal injection. I resented the State of Texas for its action believing it to be a brutal example of justice, until I found out that the State of Texas does not incarcerate first-time non-violent offenders.

Texas requires them to undertake rehabilitative treatment on the street. At the same time, the Steven Harper Conservative Government in Canada abolished accelerated parole release, a policy that had the Parole Board release non-violent first-time offenders after serving one-sixth of the federal penitentiary time imposed by the court. Canada was more vindictive to non-violent first-time offenders than was the State of Texas.

All our parliamentarians seemed to neglect any notion that jail may not be the best solution to resolve problems manifesting themselves in criminal activity.

Anecdotally I had come to realize how proper intervention could benefit not only the prisoner but society as a whole. I once had a client who was constantly being returned to prison for breach of an abstinence from alcohol condition of his release. The first time, the Parole Board reviewed the situation and returned him to the street. On the second breach, he was reincarcerated. I was perplexed why a man would continue his drinking when he knew a return to custody would be inevitable. I reviewed his psychology files and could find not even the hint of an explanation. By chance, I asked the inmate a simple question, "Did anything ever happen to you before you started to get into trouble that you can recall?" I was fishing for previous sexual or emotional abuse, as these had cropped up so many times when interviewing inmates. His answer astounded me. "I saw my mother being murdered," he replied.

There was absolutely nothing in this inmate's files to suggest this incident happened. I requested and received his permission to forward his answer to the psychiatrist at the prison. Counselling was undertaken and to my knowledge that inmate was released and has been crime-free since.

Underlying Factors

Statistics from the United States suggest there is an underlying factor manifesting itself in crime for some individuals but certainly not all.

Nine percent of men, over six million, experience depression daily. About half that number deal with daily anxiety problems. Schizophrenia will be diagnosed in 3.5 million men before they reach the age of 30. One out of five men will develop an alcohol dependency during their lifetime.

Psychological and psychiatric disturbances result in the statistic that suicide is the second-most common cause of death for every age group for men aged 10 to 39.

As a youth, Terry was flawed. He suffered from addictions and had alienated himself from family. Did he have underlying mental health issues as a youth? We will never know but the probability is high that he did.

A major societal problem was that then, as now, it is not okay for a man to admit depression, anxiety, or feelings of alienation. One is simply told to "Man up." Instead, many young men and to a lesser degree, women turn to alcohol or drugs as much for self-medication for the temporary alleviation of psychological problems as for the desire just to feel good.

Maybe the net of blame for what happened to Terry should cover society as a whole rather than just the Correctional Service. This goes against the commonplace view that the perpetrator of a crime must accept responsibility for the consequences of his act. Of course, someone who commits an offence, if sane and unimpaired in judgment, is primarily responsible for any criminal actions. But it is self-delusion that there are no factors contributing to criminal acts over and above the bad choices of an individual and that person alone is responsible for his or her wrongdoing. Are we not as complicit when our health care system ignores people with serious mental health issues?

We continue to see people suffering with addictions and mental health problems as pariahs in our social system, rejecting to offer a helping hand that could alleviate much of the turmoil in a person's head that ultimately leads to criminally acting out.

At election time, one group of politicians accuses another group of not being "tough on crime." The response is the imposition of harsher punishment. A slogan amongst inmates seems to bear some truth: "Get tough on crime and crime gets tough on you."

In my experience, when the Correctional Service does a good job, the results are excellent. I have witnessed many inmates released having undergone extensive rehabilitative programming and the recidivism is minimal. There are certainly far more good stories than bad ones in release from imprisonment. Most of the good comes from progressive attitudes within the CSC such as assessing and developing programs to deal with mental and physical health. In prison industries, inmates can, perhaps for the first time, be exposed to a work ethic and managing finances.

It is when the CSC imposes ancient and regressive forms of punishment such as solitary confinement that problems develop. I argued that solitary drove Terry crazy. Maybe he was crazy to start out with. We will never know. But if society would stop stigmatizing mental health issues, it might be a trivial question to take into the future.

EIGHTEEN

AFTERMATH

■■■

IT IS COMMON FOR LAWYERS to want to brag about their victories but say precious little about their defeats. Although Terry asked me to "have fun" with his case, my goal was to go on the attack against indefinite solitary confinement as a correctional tool. Terry was too fragile mentally to allow me to make the aggressive battle I had imagined. What resulted was not a victory in terms of changing the law and probably not considered as even a skirmish in the war.

But in all campaigns, one must live to fight another day. The battle against solitary confinement did indeed live on. The McCann case in British Columbia in 1975 had been the first successful foray into the cause and it was followed by the publication of Professor Michael Jackson's book, *Prisoners of Isolation* in 1983. Both these indictments of the use of solitary confinement were overlooked by the Correctional Service of Canada and legislators who could have enacted rules against unlimited solitary confinement.

Women Inmates
About the same time the Terry Fitzsimmons story was unfolding, there were tensions building at Kingston's Prison for Women, at the time Canada's only female penitentiary. The events at the P4W, as it was known, by standards known to

people familiar with prison operations were not abnormal. On Friday, April 22, 1994, a violent confrontation broke out between six of the prison's 142 inmates, about half of the women at the time serving federal custodial sentences in Canada (most serving sentences less than two years were in provincial facilities). There were about 14,500 men serving time in federal penal institutions. The six women involved in the altercation were removed to segregation cells. Tensions were high in the segregation unit. Three other inmates who were also in segregation on April 24 variously slashed their arms or wrists, took a hostage and attempted suicide.

Correctional staff demonstrated outside the prison the following Tuesday demanding, amongst other things, that the segregated inmates be transferred to a supermax facility known in Canada as a Special Handling Unit (even though Canada's two SHUs are male facilities.) That evening, the Institutional Emergency Response Team from the Kingston Penitentiary across the street arrived and aggressively performed a cell extraction of the eight women in segregation including the six who had been placed there on the 22nd. The cell extraction and the strip searches of the women by the male members of the IERT team was videotaped. The women were provided with paper gowns and left alone in separate cells shackled with leg irons. The six inmates originally involved in the ruckus were placed in solitary confinement for several months.

The CSC convened a Board of Investigation that seemingly white-washed the April events. That board's findings were criticized by the Office of the Correctional Investigator, Canada's prison ombudsman. The whole matter may well have been swept under the carpet but for the fact that excerpts from the IERT videotape were obtained by the CBC and shown on the network's investigative journalism program, *The Fifth Estate*.

It's no secret that what happens in prisons is the least understood part of the criminal justice system. The airing of the video resulted in an outcry too loud for the politicians to ignore. Thus, Madam Justice Louise Arbour of the Ontario Court of Appeal (later appointed to the Supreme Court of Canada) was named to head up a Commission of Inquiry looking into the events that transpired at P4W in the latter part of April and subsequently.

The Arbour Commision Report and Ashley Smith

The Arbour Report was released, and it detailed a long, wide, and deep list of violations of the law and directives governing the treatment of the women. Arbour noted that prison psychologists observed that the prolonged deprivation and isolation associated with the segregation of these inmates was seriously harmful to them. They suffered perceptual distortions, auditory, and visual hallucinations, flashbacks, increased sensitivity and startle response, emotional distress, and anxiety. Arbour commented: "If prolonged segregation in these deplorable conditions is so common throughout the Correctional Service that it failed to attract anyone's attention, then I would think that the Service is delinquent in the way it discharges its legal mandate."

The Arbour Report not only commented on the effects of solitary confinement, it went further and said the whole process was flawed as it applied to both male and female inmates. Nonetheless the CSC tried to exonerate itself by pointing to experiments that found no serious impairments were created by segregation. These psychological studies carried out in controlled situations led to a vastly different conclusion than studies undertaken by experts such as Dr. Stuart Grassian. Where there was conflict in findings, Commissioner Arbour stated bluntly she accepted the Grassian conclusions. The Commissioner, as part of several recommendations, stated that "the practice of long-term segregation be brought to an end."

The Arbour Commission Report did ultimately lead to some behaviour modification by the Correctional Service. However, with respect to solitary confinement and the treatment of inmates with severe psychological and psychiatric conditions, very little change was implemented.

One wonders that if the recommendation of Madam Justice Arbour had been given serious consideration, would 19-year-old Ashley Smith be alive today. Ms. Smith died by self-inflicted strangulation in October 2007 as correctional officers looked on, ordered not to render assistance.

A 2013 coroner's inquiry into the death of Ashley Smith made 104 recommendations including the abolition of indefinite solitary confinement and limiting stays in solitary to 15 days and an annual cumulative total of 60 days.

There was no doubt that Ms. Smith had been disruptive and maladaptive in prison. The CSC response was to transfer her seventeen times in one year between three penitentiaries, two treatment facilities, two hospitals and even a provincial jail. Reasons for transfers included lack of cell availability, incompatibility with other inmates and staff fatigue. It became obvious to any onlooker that Ms. Smith was a troubled young woman. However, with each transfer, the 'segregation clock' was reset to zero. Corrections had no accurate tally on the amount of time she had spent in isolation. In fact, she had spent more than one thousand days in solitary.

Edward Christopher Snowshoe

Three years later, on August 13, 2010, guards at Edmonton maximum security penitentiary found the lifeless body of 24-year-old Edward Christopher Snowshoe. He had hanged himself in the 2.5-by-3.6 metre cell on the 162nd day of the inmate's confinement in solitary. His story has been recounted by *Globe and Mail* reporter Patrick White in a series of articles for the newspaper.

There is no doubt that Eddie Snowshoe had mental problems. He had tried unsuccessfully to end his own life before by slashing and hanging. This time he covered the cell floor with dandruff shampoo to make it so slippery he would not involuntarily rescue himself if his bare feet touched the floor.

The suicide rate in federal penitentiaries is substantially greater than in the country as a whole. Nearly half of all prison suicides take place in segregation cells. The explanation is obvious. Dogs are pack animals. So are human beings. Living in isolation deprives us of the stimuli we need to survive. Without stimulation and the ability to respond, our minds play tricks, the same tricks that Stuart Grassian reported in his studies.

Even though policy prohibits the use of segregation to manage suicide risk, it is commonplace to place mentally disordered inmates in segregation even though they are at elevated risk for suicide or self-harm.

In my days with the London Ontario Humane Society, I recognized that animals confined in cages for extended periods responded aggressively. Why do we think that humans, being pack animals too, will respond differently?

With lack of public response and the lack of parliamentary oversight of the correctional system, the answer ignored the problem. CSC no longer publishes an *Annual Inmate Suicide Report*. The last one issued was for 2010-2011.

Howard Sapers, who served as Canada's Correctional Investigator, the corrections ombudsman, has stated that federal prisons "are fast becoming the nation's largest psychiatric facilities and repositories for the mentally ill." As many as 80 percent of all federal inmates, Sapers found, have some manner of mental-health problem and about 20 percent require psychiatric involvement.

In 2015, the British Columbia Civil Liberties Association and the John Howard Society of Canada joined forces to bring suit against the Attorney General of Canada to finally implore the Court to end or severely modify the dreadful practice of solitary confinement. The lawsuit brought in the Supreme Court of British Columbia was joined by the West Coast Women's Legal Education and Action Fund and by the Criminal Defence Advocacy Society as intervenors.

On January 17, 2018, Mr. Justice Leask delivered a lengthy judgment. In the landmark decision, the court held that segregation "places all federal inmates subject to it at significant risk of serious psychological harm, including mental pain and suffering, and increased incidence of self-harm and suicide." The court found that the continued practice constituted cruel and unusual punishment and a violation of a citizen's right to life, liberty and security of the person as guaranteed by Canada's *Charter of Rights and Freedoms*. These are constitutional rights. So as not to usurp the authority of Parliament to make laws consistent with the constitution, Justice Leask granted the federal government one year to enact legislation to make its despicable treatment of prisoners comply with the constitution.

The Minister of Justice and Attorney General was Jodie Wilson-Raybould. She was widely perceived because of her own background to be a force for advancement of rights of Indigenous Peoples. Indigenous people are greatly over-represented in Canada's prisons. Prison rights activists eagerly awaited a government response.

That response was timid to say the least. A bill was introduced to limit solitary confinement to 15 days and to implement an external review of all cases of confinement. The plaintiffs in the 2015 case continued to maintain the government response still did not pass constitutional muster.

The Canadian government's response was to replace administrative segregation with "structured intervention units" to emphasize "meaningful human contact". The Bill did not include hard caps on how many days or months inmates can be isolated from the general prison population. Jodie Wilson-Raybould, who had exclusive authority to act, appealed the British Columbia case and thereby put the decision regarding the practice of extended solitary confinement's constitutionality on hold.

As delays continued, legal pressure mounted. In March 2019, Ontario Superior Court Justice Paul Perell considered a class action suit for damages to segregated inmates. The law firms Koskie Minsky LLP and McCarthy Tétrault LLP had commenced a class action against the Attorney General of Canada alleging systemic infliction of prolonged administrative solitary confinement upon prisoners incarcerated in federal correctional institutions. The Statement of Claim defined prolonged administrative solitary confinement, existed where prisoners are placed in small cells and are denied any meaningful human contact for at least 22 hours per day, for a period of at least 15 consecutive days. This treatment is often imposed in instances where the prisoner had done nothing wrong and was not being punished.

The claim alleged that by virtue of this practice in federal correctional institutions, Canada had been negligent, had breached its fiduciary duties, had breached various rights under *The Canadian Charter of Rights and Freedoms*, had subjected class members to false imprisonment, intentional infliction of mental suffering, assault, and battery, and had been unjustly enriched. The class action was successful and damages were awarded.

Compensation
To receive compensation the person who experienced greater than 15 days of continuous segregation must specify that he or she (a) spent at least 16 consecutive days in segregation after March 3, 2011, or (b) spent more than 15 days in continuous segregation after July 20, 2009 and was diagnosed with a mental illness prior to or during the stay in segregation.

The civil award required the federal government to pay $20,000,000 earmarked to enhance mental health supports in correctional facilities. The judgment was upheld by the Ontario Court of Appeal in 2021.

When the Terry Fitzsimmons case was analyzed and the questions raised as to why Terry was not considered for detention when he was about to walk out of prison without rehabilitative programming, the answer was that the resources were not available so that staff in prisons could do their job thoroughly and accurately. One would think that with the passage of time, these deficiencies in the system would also be remedied?

Yet in May 2019, a Report by the Union of Safety and Justice Employees (USJE) was released. That report, calling itself the first of its kind to investigate the deep challenges faced by Parole Officers (the title given to CSC employees who manage inmate caseloads and prepare reports on their progress), painted an alarming picture of a federal correctional system that was extremely stressed and nearing a breaking point due to massive budgetary cuts to the Correctional Service under the Deficit Reduction Plan of the Harper Conservative government in 2012.

The Report also notes the changing face of corrections as it must deal with increasingly complex offender populations where staff must deal on a day-by-day basis with issues involving intensive substance abuse including deaths due to fentanyl, gang violence and mental health issues.

The Report raises a warning flag that public safety continues to be at risk if the employees working within the correctional centres must meet modern demands for more individualized offender treatment but without the financial resources to meet that end.

Unaddressed Concerns

One of the most unaddressed concerns is for people, like Terry, who have been released without a structured support system that will address issues such as institutionalization when an inmate is released.

Institutionalized inmates have spent so much time in penitentiary they actually fear a return to free society. The world has changed for the released prisoner. The manner of how to navigate the new terrain will be perplexing. Even though there are charitable organizations whose purpose is to help re-integrate prisoners with the community, the prison system feels it has no responsibility once an inmate reaches warrant expiry date (the court-ordered end of a sentence). Even for those inmates who are released prior to warrant expiry date, a constant criticism of parole officers supervising parolees in the community is that they seem more like state police—more than willing to see an offender's return to incarceration than in being a helping hand and a resource for assistance.

Prisons are not much different than when I first became involved with the system in the 1980s. Prison walls and fences are as much to keep public interest out as they are to keep prisoners in. Most criminal defence lawyers lack other than cursory knowledge of what goes on after a client is convicted and led away from the courtroom to begin the sentence.

Get tough on crime and cries for law and order continue to resound as election ploys. It goes well with the crowd who have no knowledge of what takes place inside a prison.

Some politicians advance well-meaning concepts of how the system can be improved. We vote for visionaries, but we elect managers. Once elected, the concept of reform fades due to the day-to-day necessity of running an industry efficiently without undue public notice. The vision of a system that treats prisoners legally and fairly gives way to the operations of making do with the resources available—to do not what should be done but just to do the best we can.

The United States and Solitary

I was not the first to raise the horrors of solitary confinement in court. In 1890, the United States Supreme Court in the Medley case came close to declaring the process unconstitutional. In his majority opinion in the case of a Colorado murderer who had spent a month in isolation, Justice Samuel Miller held the experience had revealed "serious objections" to the method of treatment noting that "a considerable number of the prisoners fell, after even a short confinement, into a semi-fatuous condition." After this, prisons and jails slowly moved away from using solitary confinement.

The United States saw an increased use of solitary confinement in the 1960s, when prison administrators, once again, increased usage of solitary confinement to deal with violence and overcrowding. Then came the explosive construction boom of prisons designed specifically for isolation. It is estimated that in the United States almost 20 percent of prisoners and 18 percent of jail inmates have experienced solitary confinement. In both the United States and Canada there is disproportionate use of segregation for racialized inmates, people suffering mental illness, and other minority populations.

In typical years, there are more than 80,000 men, women and children in solitary confinement in prisons across the United States according to the US Bureau of Justice statistics. Confinement ranges from months to years. There are cases of prisoners spending more than 25 years in isolation.

The Covid-19 pandemic has worsened the situation with more than 300,000 people held in solitary between June 2020 and April 28, 2021 the *Washington Post* reported.

The Mandela Rules proclaimed by the United Nations, stipulate that any stay in solitary should not extend past 15 days before its toll on a prisoner's mental health kicks in. Nonetheless, the use of solitary confinement in US prisons is rising: Before 1990, the use of 'supermax' prisons (what in Canada are called Special Handling Units or SHUs) was rare. The American Civil Liberties Union has found that now 44 states and the US federal government have such facilities.

NINETEEN

LATER REVELATION

■ ■ ■

TERRY HAD ACCEPTED HIS SENTENCES and seemed relieved to be returned to Kingston Penitentiary. But the nagging question in my mind was why he would take the extreme measure of strangulation to end his life. I learned of one explanation offered by another person who had come to know Terry subsequent to his returning to prison. I have no proof the explanation is historically accurate, but it sounded plausible.

The tale recounted to me was that while Terry was serving his time at the prison, another prisoner named Gerry Moss was picked up by the Ontario Provincial Police Penitentiary Squad for a parole violation.

One need not commit a criminal offence to be recommitted. A simple suspected breach of a condition of release is enough to trigger a warrant of suspension. I also heard but cannot confirm that Gerry Moss was placed on the same range as Terry Fitzsimmons. I immediately recalled how angry Terry had become that he suspected Moss to be a sex offender and, worse yet, a sex offender who prayed upon children. Terry's wife had given birth and it continued to nag at Terry's brain that Moss would be so close to an innocent infant.

Terry had now received a medical diagnosis that he was suffering from AIDS and in Terry's mind he had nothing to lose should he take the life of Gerry Moss. There are no reports that Terry and Moss ever had physical contact. More likely it was a smirk that Gerry flashed as he caught sight of Terry in a food line.

Macho Code

In Canadian prisons men are expected to live by a code of conduct. Part of the expectation is an attitude that can be described as misogynist. This applies to both prisoners and guards. In the 1980s female correctional officers were introduced. After a two-year trial period, female guards were hired to work in all-male institutions. Their introduction did not go smoothly. There were several reports of the more senior male officers ordering a female junior counterpart to strip search a male inmate. It was not for reasons of discovering hidden contraband; it was to humiliate both the female officer and the inmate at the same time. But the male inmates too exhibit a similar unhealthy bias. The situation continues.

Almost 40 percent of female employees of Correctional Service of Canada do not feel mentally or emotionally safe at work. The perpetrators of the harassment or violence is most likely to be a co-worker in a position of authority (55 percent), according to the results of CSC's *2021 National Employment Equity Survey of Women Employees.*

CSC has a policy for precisely this scenario: "We do not tolerate harassment or inappropriate behaviour by staff and we remain steadfast in our commitment to build a respectful and harassment-free workplace where women feel mentally and emotionally safe.

Yet only 36 percent of respondents agreed CSC has 'appropriate' support measures to combat gender discrimination, and less than 50 percent agreed CSC "works hard" to prevent it. The survey found: "In fact, nearly every one of CSC's measures currently in place to fight gender-based harassment or violence received a failing grade from survey respondents."

In prison, men like to have it known that they have a wife or girlfriend waiting for them on the outside. Some inmates leave letters from women where other inmates can read them, especially if the text of the letter contains sexy or suggestive passages. Many inmates post pictures of their wives or girl-friends on their cell walls. It is all part of an attempt to portray a macho image. Some inmates have their female allies smuggle drugs or other contraband in for them. Once again, it is an example of supercharged masculinity to be able to show fellow prisoners that one's "ol' lady" will do as she is instructed.

In Terry's case, he entered prison without a female part-ner. It took some convincing, but Terry eventually persuaded a fellow prisoner to set him up with that prisoner's sister. The 'romance' was swift and shortly before Terry's release he was married. The marriage that occurred between Terry and his newfound friend was more for convenience to demonstrate his masculinity and gain respect than it was from a deep and abid-ing love between the parties.

Terry found it was difficult adjusting to a home life once released from prison. In the penitentiary, Terry followed the prison routine, and his off hours could be enjoyed as he pleased even if it was just lying on his cell cot. In the 'real world', it was strangely different. There was no routine. Terry found he was taking orders from his wife, and he didn't feel he had the con-trol he had imagined he would have in domestic life. After all, in prison, the accepted standard is one must have control of the woman.

For Terry's wife, there was also a noticeable change from visiting a boyfriend or a spouse and having that person at home full time. Women have their own ways of doing things that are completely disrupted when this stranger/spouse enters the picture.

Living at home with his wife caused both Terry and his wife to experience frustration. It came as no surprise to either of them when after ten days, Terry walked out of the marriage and found a new girlfriend, a local hairdresser named Cheryl, who was willing to take him in. Yet this arrangement suffered the same pressures as the old one. After a while, Terry knew he would desert Cheryl as well. Fortunately for Terry, Cheryl had a stash of jewelry that could be pawned to affect his getaway.

Then why was it so upsetting when Gerry Moss would smirk at Terry? Terry read the look as a silent acknowledgment that Moss was saying that Terry was not man enough to hold on to his wife. Moss would be silently indicating that he held a masculine winning hand, and it was time for Terry to fold.

That silent smirk was no less a challenge to Terry's self worth as if Moss had called Terry a goof. In Terry's assessment, the bastard had to die.

A Secret Plan

Terry kept his silence and made a plan. Secretly, Terry procured a long piece of metal that could be transformed into a shiv. He pictured himself ramming the homemade knife through Moss' heart like he had done to his other victims.

Killing Moss would end his mental turmoil and rid the world of the perpetrator of what Terry considered the worst crime possible.

Terry planned and rehearsed his movements where the fatal blow would be administered. Then a passing thought reverberated throughout his head. He secretly believed the child his ex-wife bore was his own son. Then Terry's memory of his father, teary-eyed expressing fatherly love to his errant son and his father's words that no matter how much trouble a child gets into, that child is still loved. Terry then recalled Don's final words: The killing has to stop. He relived the moments they had discussed a suicide pact.

How could the child that he knew was alive and well living somewhere in Kingston go through life knowing that Terry, perhaps the child's real father, could murder the man the child believed to be the father in cold blood? Is this the way to honour

Don? Terry settled on the notion that if he really loved the child the way a child should be loved by a parent and to uphold his commitment to Don, the best way to suppress Terry's inner turmoil would be to become his own victim. Terry changed plans. Instead of assembling the material to construct a knife, he scrounged the materials necessary to fashion a noose.

TWENTY

THE INQUEST

■■■

IN 1996, about a year after Terry's death, an inquest was held at the Frontenac County Court House in Kingston. The courthouse is an impressive limestone structure of neoclassical design imposing on a park-like setting just to the east of the Queen's University Campus. And a bit further to the west lies Kingston Penitentiary.

An inquest is called to comply with Ontario's *Coroner's Act* that requires an investigation into the deaths of persons dying in state-supervised facilities. An inquest has all the trappings of a court but there are substantial differences. A jury is sworn but there are only five jurors rather than twelve as in a criminal case. The proceedings are overseen by a coroner, a medical doctor appointed by the Chief Coroner of Ontario. The purpose is not to assign blame or determine guilt or innocence. The jury is there to determine the cause of death and to hear evidence on the situation that resulted in death. Using this information, the jury is entitled to make recommendations so that needless loss of life can be averted in future.

After deliberation, the jury returns a verdict setting out the cause of death and recommendations.

The verdict into the death of Terry Fitzsimmons was received on April 10, 1996. The determination made was never really in dispute:

The Kingston Court House (here seen in 1860) was designed
to house the Parliament of Canada when Kingston, Ontario was
considered as Canada's permanent capital.

1. Name of deceased: Terrance Allan Fitzsimmons
2. Date and time of death: March 29, 1995, at approximately 3 a.m.
3. Place of death: Kingston Penitentiary, Kingston, Ontario
4. Cause of death: Asphyxiation by hanging
5. By what means: Suicide

In this instance the jury went on and handed down two recommendations so that the tragedy of Terry's death could be prevented in future. Specifically, those recommendations were as follows:

1. Regular professional assessments of inmates with potential suicide or previous suicide attempts and provide necessary counselling services; and

2. A review board should be formed that would include guards, prison management and inmates to review the procedures around accessing rope and razor blades within the institution including enforcement of the violations.

Dr. Ross McIlquham, the Inquest Coroner, on a separate page of the verdict, outlined the rationale for each of the two recommendations.

The hearing had heard evidence that this was not Terry Fitzsimmons' first attempt at suicide and further that Terry had used razor blades to slash his arms before and used rope commonly available in the prison shop areas to form the noose that led to his death. The coroner explained that inmates are not to have rope or razor blades stashed in their cells, but experience in other cases has shown no serious efforts were made to sanction the collection of such contraband objects.

The list of witnesses granted standing to make representations to the coroner included not only counsel for the Correctional Service of Canada but, most notably in my opinion, Mr. Robert Fitzsimmons, Terry's father.

On reading that Robert Fitzsimmons took the time to attend the inquest and travelled a considerable distance from London to Kingston made me realize that Terry's belief that he had been abandoned by his family was wrong. The family did indeed have unconditional love for their miscreant son. When Robert Fitzsimmons died sometime later, his obituary named his son, Terry as having predeceased the father. This publication was further evidence to me that the family loved and was unashamed of Terry.

The inquest may have been the jury's reasonable conclusions about how a death occurred and their recommendations were put forward in the honest belief they would be considered so that future deaths would be prevented. It was admirable that a family member attended. Terry's father attended despite his son's dreadful acts as proof positive that a parent's love can never be extinguished. However, the inquest proceeded as most do with evidence put forward by the Correctional Service of Canada and the guards' union. These are two groups that could end up being criticized should the shortcomings of either be exposed. No standing was granted to anyone with independent knowledge of corrections and its systems. A jury never heard what solitary confinement could do to a prisoner's mental processes.

The Ultimate Tool of Torture

The jury never heard about solitary confinement. Behind the walls of our prisons—the layers of concrete and steel—lies the ultimate tool of torture: solitary confinement. Without publicity, these units house prisoners in isolated cells for anywhere from days to decades. Supposedly as a means to protect the safety of correctional officers, the situation arguably makes those confined more dangerous. The guards' union does not speak out because that is the way it has always been done. Why risk a reimagined system that does not compromise the mental health of the captive?

The law that sets the standards for Canada's prisons has as a guiding principle that inmates retain the same rights enjoyed by all Canadians save and except for such limitations as are necessary because of the prisoner's incarceration. There were five brutal deaths in the Terry Fitzsimmons story. One wonders if the jury's common-sense recommendations had been in place at the time Terry first went to jail, how many of the five could have been spared. People outside prison walls can be counselled and treated if deemed in danger of self-harm. Was the jury's recommendation so outlandish that they should be ignored? Or were the jury recommendations just shortsighted?

Obviously, deaths from suicide ought to be prevented. Yet was it not just as much a cause of death that Terry's mental makeup had been so altered that suicide became a reasonable method of escape.?

When going before the Parole Board, a key concern is that an offender must show he or she has taken responsibility for the criminal act involved. In Terry's case, he not only took responsibility for his crimes; he administered his own death penalty—twice! Perhaps he understood that he had been so mentally damaged by the system that he could never live a peaceful life in the broader community.

Defending Someone Known to be Guilty

How can a criminal lawyer defend someone known to be guilty? In this case, I suppose my answer is that it is crucial to make known all relevant facts so a court can impose a proper sentence. As with the Fitzsimmons case, there is more relevant information that is necessary to be considered to obtain justice. For those who question my ethics in defending a guilty man, I can honestly say, I did what I believed was right.

So now I turn the question around: I ask society how it can ethically denigrate a human life using concepts like solitary confinement without remorse?

The Office of Canada's Correctional Investigator has looked into prison suicides and found the rates of suicide are six times higher than in general society. Hanging is the most common means of suicide.

The rate of inmate suicides has remained relatively constant since Terry's demise. Terry had gone back inside doing a time that he had no intention of finishing. He took the easy way out—a pine box parole.

PHOTO: KIRSTEN LARA GETCHELL

AFTERWORD
THE TERRY FITZSIMMONS STORY

Keramet Reiter J.D. Ph.D

*P*INE *BOX PAROLE* provides glimpses into a number of often-hidden spaces: client-attorney conversations about crimes and defences, plea negotiations in judicial chambers, and, especially, long-term solitary confinement. The views are far from picturesque, the cringe-worthy moments frequent, and the ethical compass seemingly de-magnetized at points. Nonetheless, the story is one that desperately needs confronting as Canada and the United States (not to mention Denmark and the United Kingdom) grapple with the collateral consequences of overusing solitary confinement at the deepest end of the criminal justice system.

Too often the results are tragic, as they were for Terry Fitzsimmons, the man at the centre of *Pine Box Parole*, and the people he encountered. Like Fitzsimmons, young men in the United States who have spent time in solitary confinement exhibit predictable symptoms of trauma, experience increasing needs to be in total control of the most miniscule details of their surroundings, and ultimately become more comfortable retreating into conditions of solitary confinement. At least some of these young men ultimately commit extreme acts of violence after being released from the extreme conditions of solitary confinement. In 2013, Evan Ebel was released from solitary confinement in Colorado (having spent five years in total isolation). Within days of his release, he killed a pizza deliveryman, and then the Director of the state's Department of Corrections—a vocal critic of solitary confinement, ironically. A few months later, in Nebraska, Nikko Jenkins shot four people in the head in a killing spree immediately following his release from two years in long-term solitary confinement. Fitzsimmons, Ebels, and Jenkins, though, are in the dramatic-but-miniscule minority of the tens of thousands of people who spend time (months and often years) in solitary confinement in the United States, especially. In fact, there are so few of these cases of post-release violence that actually establishing a causal link between the harms of solitary confinement and post-release violence is nearly impossible.

The causal link between solitary confinement and the resulting mental and physical harm to solitarily confined individuals, however, is much stronger. As Hill notes, and Fitzsimmons' story illustrates, suicide rates are higher in prison than in the general population, and higher still in segregation units. For instance, in a study of self-harm in New York City's jail system, scholars found that more than half of all acts of self-harm occurred among people who had spent time in solitary confinement (Kaba et al. 2014). People in solitary confinement are more likely to be seriously mentally ill, and as many as half at any one time exhibit clinically significant symptoms of depression, anxiety, and guilt (Reiter et al. 2020). People in solitary confinement also experience high rates of skin irritation, weight fluctuation, and musculoskeletal pain (Strong et al. 2020); hypertension (likely to lead to long-term cardiovascular burdens) (Williams et al. 2019); and even potential brain shrinkage (Lobel & Akhil 2018; Zigmond & Smeyne 2020; Stahn et al. 2019).

Skeptics, often working within corrections, argue that pars-
ing the effects of incarceration generally from the effects of incarceration's harsher iterations in solitary confinement specifically
is hard, if not impossible (Labrecque et al. 2020). Here again,
Fitzsimmons' story is illustrative. Prison itself certainly created
situations that exacerbated his personal challenges with addiction, mental health, and violence. Imagining that his years in
extreme isolation did anything but further exacerbate this situation defies logic, with or without a well-designed experimental
analysis to prove the exacerbation. Indeed, such well-designed
experimental or quasi-experimental studies evaluating the specific effects of time in solitary confinement are rare for two reasons. First, solitary confinement turns out to be a counterintui-
tively common experience. The extreme practice is supposed to
be reserved for the most challenging prisoners—the ones who
do things like murder fellow prisoners—and is strongly associated with individually and socially harmful outcomes. But, in my
own work in Washington state, I found that 44 percent of people
in prison had spent at least some time in solitary confinement
during their incarceration (Lovell et al. 2020), and national studies in the United States suggest that as many as one in five people
incarcerated in state and federal prisons have spent time in solitary confinement (Beck 2016). The experience is so common that
isolating its impact becomes difficult. Second, even in Canada,
where there are oversight mechanisms like inquests following
deaths-in-custody and judicial commissions of inquiry, like the
one that produced *The Arbour Report* calling out excessive use
of solitary confinement for women, prisons are remarkably resistant to external scrutiny and even more resistant to externally
imposed reform. In the United States, without inquests and commissions of inquiry, the situation is even more opaque.

Much of what we do know about solitary confinement, in fact, comes out of litigation—whether from investigations and defences of individual cases of violence, like Fitzsimmons' (and Ebel's and Jenkins'), or in class action work to improve the conditions of confinement in a given institution or system of institutions, as with the *BC Civil Liberties Association v. Attorney General of Canada* case establishing the unconstitutionality of solitary confinement and the American case of *Ashker v. Brown*, challenging conditions of confinement in California's supermax solitary confinement unit at Pelican Bay State Prison. Terry Fitzsimmons' story, then, contributes to our too-often obscured understanding of the individual, institutional, and societal impacts of overusing solitary confinement. Fitzsimmons' story is also a cautionary tale of both the social risks inherent in failing to mitigate the harms of solitary confinement, and also the daunting challenges in attempting to mitigate those harms.

Keramet Reiter JD PhD is a professor in the Department of Criminology, Law and Society and at the School of Law at the University of California, Irvine. In 2017, she received the American Society of Criminology's Ruth Shonle Cavan Young Scholar Award for outstanding scholarly contributions to the discipline. She is the author of 23/7: Pelican Bay Prison and the Rise of Long-Term Solitary Confinement *(Yale University Press) and* Mass Incarceration *(Oxford University Press).*

Works Cited in the Afterword

Kaba F, Lewis A, Glowa-Kollisch S, Hadler J, Lee D, Alper H, et al. 2014. "Solitary confinement and risk of self-harm among jail inmates." *Am J Public Health,* 104(3):442–7.

Labrecque, R.M., P. Gendreau, R.D. Morgan, M.M. King. 2020. "Revisiting the Walpole Prison Solitary Confinement Study (WPSCS): A Content Analysis of the Studies Citing Grassian (1983)." *Psychology, Public Policy and Law,* doi 10.1037/law0000247.

Lobel J, Akil H. 2018. "Law & neuroscience: The case of solitary confinement." *Daedalus,* 47(4): 61–75.

Lovell, D., R. Tublitz, K. Reiter, K. Chesnut, and N. Pifer. 2020. "Opening the Black Box of Solitary Confinement through Researcher-Practitioner Collaboration: A Longitudinal Analysis of Prisoner and Solitary Populations in Washington State, 2002-17." *Justice Quarterly,* 37(7): 1303-21.

Reiter, K. J. Ventura, D. Lovell, D. Augustine, M. Barragan, T. Blair, K. Chesnut, P. Dashtgard, G. Gonzalez, N. Pifer, and J. Strong. 2020. "Psychological Distress in Solitary Confinement: Symptoms, Severity, and Prevalence, United States, 2017-18." *American Journal of Public Health,* 110: S52-S56.

Stahn, A.C., H.C. Gunga, E. Kohlberg, J. Gallinat, D.F. Dinges, S. Kuhn. 2019. "Brain changes in response to long Antarctic expeditions." *N. Engl. J. Med.,* 381(23):2273–5.

Strong, J., K. Reiter, D. Augustine, M. Barragan, K. Chesnut, P. Dashtgard, G. Gonzalez, N. Pifer, and R. Tublitz, "The Body in Isolation: The Physical Health Impacts of Incarceration in Solitary Confinement," *PLOS ONE,* 15(10): e0238510.

Williams, B.A., A. Li, C. Ahalt, P. Coxson, J.G. Kahn, K. Bibbins-Domingo. 2019. "The cardiovascular health burdens of solitary confinement," *J. Gen. Intern. Med.,* 34(10):1977–80.

Zigmond, M.J. & R.J. Smeyne. 2020. "Use of animals to study the neurobiological effects of isolation." In: Lobel J., and P.S. Smith, eds, *Solitary confinement: Effects, practices, and pathways toward reform.* New York: Oxford University Press: Chapter 13.

PART II

OTHER TRUE CASES

X

CLIFFORD OLSON

SUSAN WOOD

JOSEPH STANLEY FAULDER

ALLAN MacDONALD

DAVID BAGSHAW

INDERJIT SINGH REYAT

INTRODUCTION, PART II

IMPEDIMENTS TO TRUTH-SEEKING

IT IS SAID that all trials are a search for truth. Indeed, the etymology of the word "verdict" is its derivation from the Latin *veredictum* meaning "to say the truth." However, law as it is practiced, places certain impediments to the truth-seeking mechanisms. These breaches can seriously interfere with fair and humane treatment.

There are several impediments in the law that need repair. They include (and this is by no means an exhaustive list):

1. A reluctance to abandon extreme forms of torture such as solitary confinement and the death penalty;
2. An inability to spot and determine how we treat 'natural born killers' who are most likely found to rate high in terms of psychopathy;
3. A failure by not only the courts but society as a whole to understand and accept persons who exhibit body, social, and mental dysphoria;
4. Failure to challenge expert opinion when the basis for belief rests more on academic credentials than scientific expertise;
5. A desire to appease public opinion, especially where the report of a criminal act is horrific;
6. The pressure to shield public institutions from scrutiny when their efforts are below par.

The quest to end solitary confinement has taken years to accomplish. But it is not the only injustice that needed repair. In law school, students read and analyze case law to find the principles of law that can be derived. However, what follows is a series of true cases in which I have to some degree been involved.

The principles of determining truth and imposing fair and humane punishments also require not only looking for legal principles, but also looking at the criminal cases coming before the courts from a social science perspective.

Although my representation of Terry Fitzsimmons had the prime motivation of attacking the concept of solitary confinement, there are other defects in our treatment of prisoners and the application of law that point up the disconnect between how law and punishment is supposed to be applied and the situations in which it is actually practiced.

Solitary confinement was a systemic problem in corrections. The Fitzsimmons story demonstrates the lengthy struggle to find a manner in which the law can be upheld consistent with societal norms of justice. But certainly, there is more to be accomplished.

As stated in the preface to this book, we need to look to psychiatry and social sciences to assist us in dealing with many of the people who now occupy our jail cells. Preferably, adjusting our attitudes towards people suffering from mental illness or simply being regarded as deviant in society would assist greatly.

—*John L. Hill, 2022*

TWENTY ONE

CLIFFORD OLSON
LEGENDARY EVIL

■ ■ ■

KINGSTON PENITENTIARY's closing in 2012 did not end the haunting memories of many of its infamous inhabitants. One of the prisoners associated with the structure is a man who will likely be regarded as one of the evilest men Canada has ever produced. His name? Clifford Robert Olson, the serial killer serving 11 concurrent life sentences for murder.

Clifford Olson asked me to interview him shortly after I took up my duties at Queen's University overseeing a prison legal clinic. I knew he had been convicted of murdering 11 youths, and then sold the information where the bodies could be found to the police so that the families of the deceased could have closure. He claimed he sold the body locations for 10 victims at $10,000 apiece with the last one thrown in as a "freebie."

It was perhaps the first time I entered Kingston Penitentiary. I was dressed in a suit and carried a briefcase. I'm sure I looked to an outside observer like a corporate executive, except that I was on my way to interview perhaps the most hated man in Canada. Correctional staff ushered me into the disciplinary courtroom, a tiny and sparsely furnished space at the entrance to the solitary confinement wing. Once inside, Clifford Olson entered. The guards removed the handcuffs, closed the door, and the sound of the lock turning echoed in my mind.

I had seen newspaper pictures of Olson, but somehow when one hears stories of the perpetrators of heinous crimes there is a tendency to imagine these criminals are much bigger than in real life.

I had two immediate impressions of Olson upon standing beside him and exchanging a few words: he was a tiny man … and he was absolutely charming. Hearing him speak, one would think he had known me for years; there was a friendliness that radiated both through his face and tone of voice that could put one totally at ease.

"I can see that you have a way about you that lets people relax when they are with you," I said. I have no memory of why I said this. It seemed to fit with whatever story he was passing on to me at the time. He nodded appreciatively. "I can see how the young people you raped and killed would be comfortable returning from a bar to your home," I continued.

"I didn't rape any of them," he said in an angry tone. I must have looked somewhat surprised, since I had assumed that his crimes were sexually motivated.

"I waited until their backs were turned and I hit them in the back of the head with a hammer," he said. "They never knew what was coming." Olson's statement was embedded in my brain. I'll never forget it. Nor the fact that he took his action as an act of kindness. It wasn't sex he was after; he just liked killing. Despite Olson's initial display of charm and friendliness at this, our first encounter, his apparent cold-heartedness gave me chills to the bone, and I knew I wanted to leave and be out of there as soon as possible.

The Killing Spree

Clifford Robert Olson was born on New Year's Day, 1940 in Vancouver and raised in nearby Richmond, BC. He was one of four siblings. His dad was a milkman. In grade school he was a bully and a petty thief. He tormented dogs and cats and had few, if any, friends. He dropped out of school after grade 8, living with his parents and playing hockey in the winter. He was arrested and served jail time for a break and enter at age 17. From then on, he continued a life of crime, racking up over 90 convictions and making seven escape attempts from jail. From the age of 17 until the time of his final arrest in 1981, he had spent all but four years in jail.

On May 15, 1981, Olson married Joan Hale. They had a month-old child, Stephen, at the time of the wedding. His bride was unaware he had murdered three children: Christine Weller and Colleen Marian Daignault, both aged 13 from Surrey, BC, and 16-year-old Daryn Todd Johnsrude from Coquitlam. Just days after his wedding, Olson abducted and killed another 16-year-old, Sandra Wolfsteiner of Langley. Then in June, Ada Anita Court, a 13-year-old from Burnaby, became his next victim. A month later, six young people died at Olson's hands: Simon Partington, 9, and Terri Lyn Carson, 15, both from Surrey; Judy Kozma, 14, and Raymond King, 15, of New Westminster; Sigrun Arnd, an 18-year-old German tourist; and a 17-year-old Maple Ridge resident, Marie Louise Chartrand.

The killing spree ended with Olson's arrest on August 12, 1981, as he was in the process of trying to abduct two female hitchhikers near Port Alberni on Vancouver Island.

My memories of my first encounter with Olson are similar to the experience of noted Canadian journalist Peter Worthington who interviewed Olson on several occasions aiming to write a book about the convict.

Did (or could) Olson tell the truth? He assured me that none of his victims was sexually assaulted. Yet he talked openly with Worthington. In those discussions, Olson described how he drugged, raped, and strangled 15-year-old Terri Lynn Carlson and then disposed of her remains in a wooded area along British Columbia's Fraser River.

It was impossible for Olson to give an accurate history of his background or to gain insight into his mental functioning without the aid of professional assistance. Olson did time at a number of prisons: Oakalla in BC, Kingston Penitentiary in Ontario, Prince Albert in Saskatchewan and Ste-Anne-des-Plaines in Quebec. At each of these institutions he was interviewed and tested by a variety of psychologists and psychiatrists. The results were remarkably similar. Olson was considered by the Correctional Service of Canada to be a homicidal psychopath, pedophile, and even necrophiliac, with narcissistic delusions and sexual obsession.

Possibly the best insights were obtained during psychiatric assessments commissioned by Olson's defence counsel, Robert Shantz before Olson went to trial on 11 counts of first-degree murder. Shantz had Olson examined by three renowned psychiatrists: Dr. Tony Marcus, Head of Forensic Psychiatry at the University of British Columbia; Dr. Basil Orchard of the Clarke Institute of Psychiatry in Toronto; and Dr. Julio Ernesto Arboledo-Florez, then Professor of Psychiatry at the University of Calgary and director of forensic services at Calgary General Hospital.

Dr. Arboleda-Florez found Olson to have "an anti-social personality disorder and psychopathic personality." Olson was also, to use the psychiatrist's terms, "a pathological liar" who possessed an "unquenchable thirst for recognition and grandeur," and who preserved his identity through his badness. But he was not psychotic or mentally impaired.

Dr. Orchard found that Olson suffered no anxiety, stress, remorse, or guilt. Rather, he enjoyed recollecting his misdeeds. Orchard described Olson as an individual with a pleasing manner, surprisingly good judgment, an excellent memory, and not delusional. His description included this comment: "A classical picture of a severe psychopath...characterized by his inability to delay any gratification of his desires, his inability to learn from experience or punishment, his inability to have any meaningful relationships, his lack of moral sense, his inability to experience guilt, his inability to perceive others as anything more than objects to manipulate for his own gratification, his chronic conflict with society and the law, his lack of ability to be loyal to any one person, code, or creed, and his total preoccupation with his own desires, to the exclusion of all else."

Dr. Marcus spent the most time with Olson. He found him to be callous and amoral. Marcus' assessment mirrored the others in that he found Olson to be, "a truly amoral individual for whom opportunity, the con, gain, advantage are the only reasons for his operating behaviour…the type of individual who holds allegiance to no one, who would be feared and at the same time despised by both the authority and the underworld."

Showing few neurotic traits. Dr. Marcus saw Olson as "the quintessence of the incorrigible, amoral, anti-social psychopath who does indeed know that he has done wrong and does appreciate the nature and quality of the act, though he cannot respond to these acts with feelings that a normal individual would show." It would be difficult to find a worse case of psychopathy. Olson scored 38 out of 40 on the Hare Psychopathy Checklist.

The Maximum Sentence
Olson was dismissive of these findings. He said of the psychiatrists, "They're all goofs—they're the ones who need treatment, not me. They only know what I tell them." Nonetheless, Shantz had Olson plead guilty to all 11 first-degree murder charges resulting in 11 concurrent life sentences for the deaths of youths aged 9 to 18 years. The life sentences imposed were without eligibility for parole for 25 years. With capital punishment abolished in Canada, it was the maximum sentence.

My meeting in the disciplinary courtroom at Kingston Penitentiary wasn't my last dealing with Olson. I saw him again several years later—this time I was standing outside his cell on a dissociation range. I was not retained by Olson; he just wanted to talk. The bars at the front of the cell were covered with plexiglass so that inmates passing by couldn't reach him as they spat.

This time Olson tried to impress me again by showing me pictures of nude women that he claimed had written to him, supposedly wanting to pay him conjugal visits. He also flashed a letter purportedly written on letterhead of some official in the Government of France, offering Olson asylum should he ever be released from the penitentiary in Canada. I refused to believe any of it and declined his invitation to act as a criminal defence lawyer on his behalf.

American Trial Lawyer Melvin Belli

That last time I had any direct dealings with Olson was when he convinced American trial lawyer Melvin Belli that Olson was actually the Green River Killer. Olson and Belli were photographed together at KP.

Belli was at first reluctant to become involved with Olson. Olson tried to impress Belli with the number of murders he had committed, Belli replied that in the United States numbers carried little weight—that there were now killers who were eating their victims' bodies. It has never been revealed what tactic triggered Belli's agreement to get involved.

It was fitting that Olson wanted Belli as a lawyer and that Belli wanted Olson as a client. If Olson could convince Belli that Olson was the perpetrator of the Green River killings in the United States, Olson's name would be listed along with the celebrity lawyer's other notable clients: Errol Flynn, Mae West, Zsa Zsa Gabor, Chuck Berry, Muhammed Ali, The Rolling Stones, and Sirhan Sirhan, the assassin of Robert Kennedy. Melvin Belli, known as the "King of Torts," had recovered over $600 million in combined settlements. Naming and representing the unsolved Green River murderer of at least 49 teenage girls and women in Washington State would be a momentous triumph for the San Francisco lawyer. For Olson, admitting to the crimes would bring his body count to 60, making him Canada's most prolific serial killer.

Belli sent staff to Canada to interview relevant parties and to confirm Olson's story. Belli instructed Olson that the Belli firm could do what it could to protect his interests in the United States, but that Olson should retain a Canadian lawyer to ensure that he would not suffer any repercussions north of the American border.

I found this out while vacationing in Los Angeles. At about 6 a.m., the phone in a Hollywood and Highland hotel room rang and roused me from my sleep. It was not a collect call.

"Good morning. This is Cliff, Cliff Olson."

"Where are you?" I asked.

"Where I always am. In my cell here in Kingston."

"How are you calling me?"

"I have a cell phone in my cell."

"How did you know where to call?"

"Let's just say I have my ways." Before I could speak further, he gave me a verbal thumbnail sketch of his involvement as the Green River Killer.

"Melvin Belli wants to meet with you," Olson said. "Just drive up to San Francisco and he'll see you tomorrow." The phone went dead.

Not long after that, I also received a call from ABC News in Los Angeles wanting an interview once my meeting with Melvin Belli had wrapped up. They also asked that I say nothing to any other media as "sweeps week" was approaching and the local station wanted the scoop.

Even though I was not retained, my curiosity got the best of me. There was no doubt that if Olson was charged, he could make a strong case to have a Canadian lawyer and it would be almost a certainty he would be eligible to have his Canadian legal fees paid by Legal Aid. I did in fact drive up the Pacific Coast Highway, anticipating being given a briefing on the findings. When I arrived at Belli's temporary law offices (the main location was under repair for earthquake damage), the main investigator told me that Olson had fabricated the whole story.

He obtained what were thought to be little-known details by linking together tidbits of information from several published accounts of the Green River killings.

I thanked the investigator for providing me the results of his search. But I continued to wonder why such a famous lawyer would get involved with somebody who was despised in Canada and totally impecunious. The investigator looked me directly in the eye sensing my naivety. My question was answered in three words: "The movie rights!"

The Faint Hope Clause

In 2001, Gary Leon Ridgway was arrested and named as the Green River Killer. Olson had been stringing me and everyone else along. Nonetheless Olson persisted in the con.

The expected response of a man accused of multiple killings is minimization, that is, either denying responsibility for some or all the killings or admitting to only those for which he was convicted. It astounded me that Olson was proud of his homicides and wanted to increase his notoriety by admitting to many more than he caused.

Olson was a lightning rod for conservative tough-on-crime rhetoric. One Progressive Conservative Member of Parliament, Gordon Edward Taylor (Bow River, Alberta) introduced a Bill in the House of Commons called 'An Act Respecting the Execution of Clifford Robert Olson' on December 12, 1983. The Bill was not allowed with Speaker Gildas Molgat ruling that the proposed legislation was a Bill of Attainder. A Bill of Attainder is inconsistent with Canadian constitutional values since it would be an attempt by the legislative branch of government to intrude on the authority of the judicial branch in determining violations of the law and assessing appropriate punishment. Taylor withdrew his Bill on May 14, 1984.

After serving 15 years in prison Olson opted to make use of a *Criminal Code* section that allowed inmates to bring an application before a jury asking the jury to lessen the 25-year parole ineligibility period to 16 years. The section became popularly known as the 'faint hope clause' since success was difficult. A convicted murderer would have to be able to convince a 12-person jury that parole ineligibility should be reduced by as much as 10 years so that the convict could go before the Parole board seeking some form of release in 15 years rather than the court imposed 25-year ineligibility period.

Amendments had been made to the section of the *Criminal Code* making a plea for reduction of parole ineligibility unavailable to killers with multiple victims. But Olson was convicted before the amendment was in place and he demanded to go before a jury taking advantage of the legal provision that a law cannot apply retroactively.

At his hearing, Olson tried to convince the jury that there was a $1.3 million trust fund in the Melvin Belli firm account that would be divided amongst the families of the victims of his murders. It was a strange move. Why would someone seeking the sympathy from a jury for killing 11 young people now want to impress the jurors that he was so generous to his victims when the Belli firm was establishing his involvement in over 50 other homicides in the United States. The 1996 'faint hope' hearing resulted in no reduction of Olson's parole ineligibility but did serve to garner the hatred of the Canadian public and a desire to see prison reforms put on the back burner. The Harper Conservative government later abolished the provision. As of October 10, 2010, when the provision was abolished, of the 1,508 inmates eligible to make use of the provision, 181 chose to apply: 146 had their ineligibility period reduced and 135 were able to persuade the Parole Board they would be a manageable risk in the community. Olson is the main reason cited why other prisoners sentenced to life imprisonment without parole for 25 years can no longer seek reduction in the time spent in prison by applying for faint hope relief.

My last indirect involvement with Olson was when I was investigating what was described in the press as 'gladiator fights' at the Special Handling Unit (SHU) at Ste-Anne-des-Plaines, Quebec. It was alleged that staff at the ultra-maximum-security institution would release two inmates from segregation and bet on who would defeat the other in hand-to-hand combat. In my Federal Court lawsuit on behalf of inmate Mark Gamble in 1999, it was alleged that the altercations "were nothing more than gladiatorial or human cockfighting events which were staged by the guards to amuse themselves while they watch from behind their protective Plexiglas and steel barriers."

In answer to the Statement of Claim, the Department of Justice stated it had affidavit evidence that Mark Gamble's allegations were simply a pack of lies. The informant was none other than Clifford Olson. I suggested to my colleague at the Department of Justice that he go back and look at the background of his affiant. Once the Olson statement was investigated and it was pointed out who Clifford Olson was, the DOJ promptly withdrew the Olson affidavit.

Savagery

Olson's savagery drew a bitter response from the victims' families and from the public at large. The question remains why this man, given his psychiatric condition, would simply start murdering people at age 40. He had done time before his murder convictions. Why had correctional facilities not identified the monster much earlier and possibly saved numerous lives? I suspect that our court system and correctional facilities are more akin to assembly lines than treatment centres.

I was contacted by the *Toronto Sun*, asking about Olson, a week before he died in the hospital. The reporter asked if I would grieve his eventual passing. I responded that as a human being, "He's deserving of the best medical treatment he can get as long as necessary." But I hastened to add that Olson had done his fellow inmates a disservice by his futile effort to reduce his life-25 sentence by using the faint hope clause that allowed offenders to go before a jury to seek a reduction in the amount of parole ineligibility.

He had also bragged that he was receiving $1,200 a month in old age assistance payments. The Conservative government promptly enacted legislation cancelling these payments. For many elderly inmates about to be released without any prospect of employment, cash savings would give a leg up in re-entering society. As a negative result of Olson's actions, old age assistance payments for elderly inmates were discontinued. My concluding remarks to the *Sun*: "He really did a disservice to his fellow lifers." It had all been just fun for Olson. He never expected to be released. One day, while standing in front of his Kingston Penitentiary cell, Clifford Olson predicted his fate: "I know and you know," he said, "that the only way I'll ever get out of this is in a pine box. A pine box parole."

Olson died inside prison at the Quebec SHU of colon cancer. Olson was born on the first day of January in 1940 and died on the last day of September in 2011. He had spent 50 of his 71 years in prison. I doubt anyone mourned his passing.

Without a doubt, there are 'natural born killers' inside our prisons. They are a threat not only to members of society but also to other inmates. Yet there seems to be a reluctance by correctional authorities and prison rights advocates to see such people as a special breed of criminal. Perhaps instead of constructing supermax facilities, we should heed the diagnosis of psychiatrists and house such people on specially designated prison ranges where they can be held as comfortably as possible for as long as possible.

TWENTY-TWO

SUSAN WOOD AKA ADAM HAZEL

LOVE IS ALL YOU NEED

■ ■ ■

JULY OF 1967 was a joyful time in Canada. Canadians were flocking to Expo 67 in Montreal, in part to celebrate Canada's centennial year. The Beatles released "All You Need is Love"—appropriate for the "Summer of Love."

The summer of 1967 was probably the first childhood memory of 5-year-old Susan Lynn Wood. But her memories of the time were not quite so happy. Born in New Brunswick, Susan was abandoned by her mother at the age of six months. She was taken into care until she was a two-and-a-half-year-old toddler, looked after by paid foster parents. After the money ran out, though, Susan was no longer welcome there, and her great-grandparents offered to take her in.

This was a happy time. Susan developed a strong bond with her great-grandfather until his death from cancer, at which time she moved in with her grandparents and things were never quite the same.

By the time Susan was 12 she already felt that she would rather be a boy. She started mimicking male mannerisms. As her body matured, she would put cardboard under her shirt to suppress evidence of her developing breasts.

Susan left home at age 16 and moved to Toronto, finding a job as a service station attendant and renting an apartment in a converted house. She was able to save enough to buy modest but adequate furnishings. Living alone allowed her to act out her fantasies; she lived and worked during the day as a girl, but in the evenings, she could become Adam Thomas Hazel and enjoy male activities. Today she might identify as being transgender, a term that describes the experience of gender as being not simply male or female. In the 1970s the term was not used or understood. For that same reason, in this story I have chosen to refer to Susan/Adam as 'she/he', (depending on the gender identity at the time) rather than as 'they', which is currently the accepted pronoun for transgender individuals.

Finding a Companion

Susan was short, barely five feet tall, and weighed about 80 pounds. She clipped her hair short so she could dress up as a boy in the evenings. She looked young, and despite that she had no facial hair, she could still pass herself off as a boy using mannerisms honed to perfection.

The acquisition of a female companion rose to the top of Susan's/Adam's list of priorities. And find a date she did! Sandra, the girlfriend, was the same age, and through conversation they found themselves compatible. Best of all, Sandra was willing to see Adam again. Life was good for Susan.

Then disaster struck. Susan was posing as Adam out on a date with Sandra when the two were stopped by police and asked to show identification. The police officers looked at their IDs, looking first at Adam and then at Sandra with a bemused smile. As he handed the documents back, the officer said to Sandra: "You know your boyfriend is not a boy?"

Sandra was shocked. She asked Adam to take her home immediately. When they reached Sandra's house, her father wanted to know why she was so upset. Sandra told him what the police officer had said.

Sandra's father became visibly upset. "Young man," he said in a harsh tone as he glared at Adam, "You are not allowed to see my daughter again unless you can prove you are male."

Adam asked what proof was required.

"Unless you come downstairs into the basement and drop your pants and show me you are male, you cannot see my daughter again," said Sandra's father.

Adam feigned outrage that his masculinity would be challenged and declared outright that he was not willing to have his genitalia inspected.

"Then goodbye," Sandra's father said. "When you're ready to pass the test, you can see Sandra again. If you pass the test." Adam stepped outside, and Sandra's father slammed the door.

Susan was depressed to the point of tears. Would she ever be allowed to see Sandra again? How could she prove to the father that she was a boy? She felt helpless and hopeless as she arrived at her apartment. The thought of never seeing her girlfriend again was agonizing.

As she was lying in bed, a thought crossed Susan's mind: what if she were able to go downstairs and prove she was a boy? She figured all she would need to do was show that Adam had testicles and a penis. Once this was realized, Susan started planning for the great reveal.

The following evening, Susan decided to stalk her prey. She visited a park where she knew there to be reasonable pedestrian traffic after dark. She secreted herself away in some shrubbery.

When a young man passed by, Susan leapt from the bushes and stabbed the young man with a kitchen knife she had brought from home. The man was startled and, not realizing the extent of his injury, ran away. Susan realized her attack had been unsuccessful, and scurried home to avoid any possibility of being seen. The injured man was taken to hospital and diagnosed with a punctured lung—but he lived.

Susan felt no remorse for injuring the passerby. Indeed, it only heightened her resolve to achieve her goal. She formulated a new plan. She had heard when she first moved into her apartment that taxi drivers would sometimes take money to assist in moving heavy furniture. If she could induce a taxi driver to come into her apartment, it would be easier than stalking prey in a public park.

On a Sunday evening, April 9, 1978, Susan summoned a taxi to assist her in moving a portable television within her apartment. The call was answered by 61-year-old Toronto taxi driver Robert Pearson, who was called "Bobby" by his friends Pearson drove cab for Sunnyside Taxi Dispatch. He had driven taxi since 1946 and knew the streets of Toronto well. He knew exactly where to go when asked to show up at a house on Springhurst Avenue, a one-way street running parallel to Lakeshore Boulevard in the King/Dufferin area.

A Simple Task

Pearson wanted to own his own cab. Back in 1957, he posted his name on a list to be considered for a taxi-owner's licence. He and his wife, Irene, realized they could not come up with the money needed if the grant of a taxi-owner licence was approved: $5,000 for the licence, plus another $5,000 to equip the vehicle. Further, Pearson was not in the best of health. He was put off duty in 1977 to recover from a lung operation, and when Pearson's name reached the top of the list to be considered for the ownership licence, he was forced to withdraw his name due to finances and ill-health. Irene Pearson had no marketable job skills. Fifteen years prior, she worked as a cleaning lady, but illness dictated that she could not return to the job.

It was a simple task Pearson was asked to do. He left the cab meter running while he was in Susan Wood's apartment. Susan was always polite and charming with me, so I expect Susan was polite and charming as she gave directions to her hired help. She asked Pearson to pick up the TV and move it to the next room; the television set was not heavy, just awkward to hold.

With the portable TV held against his chest and the bottom of the set held in each hand, Pearson looked straight ahead and waited for directions. Suddenly and without warning, he felt the impact of a baseball bat against his skull. In pain, Pearson dropped the TV and immediately tried to get away. Wood was blocking the exit to the doorway, though, and continued to threaten Pearson with the bat. In that instant, the only plan Pearson could devise was to run to the adjoining bedroom and crawl under the bed. It was the only idea the cabbie could come up with, given the pain and blood dripping from his head.

The bat would be useless now that the cabbie was hiding under the bed. Susan dropped the bat and grabbed the kitchen knife she used in the park the previous day. She swung at Pearson under her bed several times, making contact with each swipe. Eventually, Robert Pearson lay motionless under her bed. Using all her strength, Susan pulled his lifeless body out from its refuge to reap the reward she wanted.

She undid the deceased cabbie's pants and, using the same knife, cut off his genitals. She held the amputated parts under a shower to wash away any blood, laid the parts on a towel, and then removed her own blue jeans and used Krazy Glue to attach the body parts to her lower abdomen. She phoned to let her girlfriend's father know she was on her way to pass the test.

Susan was confident as she approached Sandra's house. Now she could go into the basement and prove she was a man. She rang the doorbell and when Sandra's father answered, Susan advised she was willing to go downstairs in order to reclaim the right to date Sandra once again.

The father allowed her to proceed downstairs, motioning for her to proceed to drop the pants. He looked but had only one comment: "You can buy those anywhere." His prohibition on dating his daughter would stand.

Sandra gave Adam Hazel an affectionate hug as he departed the residence for the last time.

The Meter Still Running

Irene Pearson had become upset that her husband had not returned home in time for supper as he had promised. She placed a call to Toronto Police advising them that her husband was missing. At about the same time, police found an empty taxicab with its meter running, facing the direction of traffic on a one-way street outside an apartment house on Springhurst Avenue. The police asked to enter but received no response. Fearing the worst, police broke through the door and discovered Robert Pearson's mutilated body, concluding immediately that this was the cab driver. Maybe this was a precursor to the death of cab driver Fernand Talbot some years later, by the hands of Terry Fitzsimmons?

It didn't take long to find out that Susan Wood was the responsible tenant, and she was arrested for the murder of Robert Pearson. During police questioning, it was also discovered that Susan had been responsible for the stabbing that resulted in the hospitalization of the young man in the park, and so Susan was also charged with attempted murder. At 16 years of age, she would be the youngest person ever charged with first-degree murder in Toronto.

About a hundred mourners attended Robert Pearson's funeral the following Wednesday, half them taxi drivers. They felt the loss of their friend, but they were also dreadfully aware of the perils of their work. One of the mourners, Glen Ormspry, a longtime friend of Pearson, was interviewed by Dale Brazao, a Staff Writer for the *Toronto Star*, and was quoted as saying "Bobby was a quiet, gentle man who was dedicated to his family. He had a lot of friends, most of whom are here today."

Granted Bail
On April 10, Susan Wood made her first court appearance. She was ordered to remain at the Toronto Metro West Detention Centre until she could undergo a full psychiatric assessment. It came as a surprise to many that Susan was granted bail on July 24 by Mr. Justice Edward Eberle of the Ontario Supreme Court following the conclusion of her assessment. It is unusual for bail to be granted when the charge is first-degree murder. There was no public disclosure as to why bail would be granted, since

allegations made during a bail hearing are usually ordered to be subject to a publication ban pending trial.

Even without knowing why a court had granted release on bail, the taxi drivers in Toronto were outraged. On July 28, they held a peaceful protest outside Queen's Park in Toronto, Ontario's capital building. Attorney-General Roy McMurtry came out onto the lawn to meet with the protesters, telling the cabbies that he had ordered a transcript of the bail hearing to determine if an appeal should be taken to overturn the bail release.

That very day, the Attorney-General ordered the Crown Law Office to appeal the bail decision. Crown lawyers would ask the Chief Justice of Ontario to send the bail decision to the Ontario Court of Appeal. On August 3, Acting Chief Justice Bert MacKinnon granted leave to appeal.

On August 10, 1978, a two-hour bail review took place before a most powerful bench that consisted of Ontario Chief Justice William Howland, Justices Charles Dubin and Arthur Martin. Crown Counsel Doug Hunt argued for revocation of bail, and defence counsel Hugh Silverman asked that bail be kept in place.

The Court made an immediate decision, holding that Susan Wood would have bail revoked and await her trial in a provincial remand centre. Susan had been at liberty for two and a half weeks before the bail revocation took place. She sat quietly in the courtroom, wearing a jean suit and jogging shoes as the decision was read. She stood and brushed her shoulder-length brown hair from her face as she was taken into custody.

In Ontario at the time, there was usually a preliminary hearing in provincial court to determine if there was sufficient evidence to proceed to trial. Even though the facts of the case were well known, defence counsel ordinarily calls no witnesses, preferring to use the preliminary hearing as an opportunity to get further disclosure of facts to be used by the prosecution— and to test the Crown witnesses and pin them down on the testimony expected at trial. In Susan Wood's case, a preliminary hearing date was set for August 25 and it was over on the day it started. The 16-year-old was ordered to stand trial for the slaying of Robert Pearson and the attempted murder of the young man in the park.

Lists of Experts

Hugh Silverman was a respected Toronto criminal lawyer who would later go on to become a provincial court judge. (He is perhaps best remembered for striking down a provincial law that made it illegal for retail stores from operating on Boxing Day and eight other statutory holidays). It was speculated that Hugh Silverman would use the insanity defence.

Bringing an insanity defence, (now known as NCR, not criminally responsible) to a jury is problematic. Section 16 of *The Criminal Code of Canada* specifies that a person is not guilty by reason of insanity if the accused person suffers from a mental disorder that renders that person incapable of appreciating the nature and quality of an act or omission or knowing that it was wrong. In 'lawyer speak', such a determination is relatively easy. For psychiatrists, however, the distinction is much more nuanced. Therefore, before going to trial it is important that the lawyers know with some certainty what the psychiatrist will say and how the expert testimony can be presented to a jury in order to achieve a verdict of "not guilty by reason of insanity."

Most defence counsel maintain a list of experts who can be counted on to deliver opinion evidence in a manner compatible with the defence cause. When it came to psychiatric/psychological expertise, there was no better team than the "dynamic duo" of Dr. Allan Long (who had a Ph.D. in Psychology) and Dr. Jerry Cooper (who was a medical doctor and psychiatrist). Both had extensive courtroom experience and could provide expert opinion that a lay juror could readily grasp.

Crown attorneys were also familiar with these two, whom

were sometimes mocked as being "hired guns" for the defence. Dr. Cooper has been quoted in a *Globe and Mail* article as saying, "When I look at a case, I always ask the lawyer what he wants. When a lawyer is happy and his client is happy, then I'm happy. The thing is, I don't need it. Who can buy me? I won't go by a script. I don't mind a guy rehearsing me, but no one tells me what I am going to say. When people tell me I'm a hired gun, I laugh."

The fact remains that a defence lawyer can use reports that coincide with the defence theory of the case, and when the opinion runs counter to that theory, the opinion can be ignored, and the author never called to the stand.

Five Psychiatrists

Susan Wood's trial began on December 14, 1978. Now 17 years old, Susan stood in the prisoner box dressed in blue jeans, a plaid shirt and heavy construction boots. She seemed to project an aura that she was rough, tough, and masculine. Yet, she was emotional, frequently wiping tears from her eyes with a wad of tissue. Tears ran down her cheeks as defence counsel entered a plea on her behalf: "Not guilty by reason of insanity."

The facts of the case were read into the record by Toronto Police Sergeant Julian Fantino. (Fantino would later go on to become Chief of Police in London, Ontario, York Region and eventually the Police Chief in Toronto. From there he became Commissioner of the Ontario Provincial Police, and eventually turning to politics to become Member of Parliament for the Toronto riding of Vaughan. He would also be appointed to several positions in the Stephen Harper Conservative government.) The 36-year-old police officer delivered his statement factually and without commentary, lacking any sense of emotion for the victim or the accused.

Defence counsel Silverman agreed that the facts of the case were substantially accurate. Then the tough work began. A jury, having heard the grisly account of Robert Pearson's killing and mutilation, would have to find Susan insane at the time of the murder.

Five psychiatrists were called to give expert opinion evidence. One after another they were grilled on the stand, as to the type of expertise counsel was asking the court to accept. Each gave a full and complete description of the university degrees held, their work experience, and publications. Each in turn was accepted by the court to testify as to their opinion of Susan's insanity.

Four of the five psychiatrists were of the opinion that on April 9, 1977, Susan was incapable of appreciating the nature and quality of her act. Psychiatrist Dr. Peter Rowsell testified that Susan was mentally tormented and sexually confused. Opining that on April 9, Susan likely knew what she was doing and even understood that her actions were wrong. But she was so divorced from reality, she likely believed that the cabbie was "more a thing than a person."

Of course, the defence called Drs. Long and Cooper.

Dr. Long seemed sympathetic in his psychological analysis of the accused woman. He swore that Susan was of the right age for treatment. She was young and "plastic", she had the ability to relate, she could be a "nice little girl," she was a person living in two worlds, male in one world and female in the other. Having a year-long relationship with Sandra had kept her motivated to continue this double life. Her real world was that of Adam Hazel, and it was in that world she felt love and connection to society. Her troubled childhood as a girl was not one that she would willingly revert to.

In what appeared as a contrasting viewpoint, Dr. Jerry Cooper said there was a very poor prognosis for recovery. It would take many, many years before any substantial recovery could take place and Susan could be able to function on her own in society without the risk of harm. Cooper did not see Susan as a "nice little girl." Instead, he found that in talking to her, "one got the feeling you were dealing with someone from another planet."

"People like her deteriorate." Cooper swore. "The treatment is always very difficult. You can't cure the illness, but after many, many years of treatment you can hope that the individual will be able to function." Dr. Cooper laid blame for Susan's unusual behaviour, claiming it originated from the abandonment and rejection she felt as a child, saying that it was "likely that anyone with this background would suffer mentally."

The combination in outlooks in the Cooper and Long testimony was a godsend to defence counsel Silverman. For jurors who could find sympathy for Susan Wood, the Long testimony held out hope for recovery. Jurors who saw Susan as an evil menace to society, could be assured that she would be locked away in a psychiatric hospital for a very long time.

With trial evidence concluded, the prosecution and defence delivered closing arguments. The trial judge, High Court Chief Justice Gregory Evans, delivered his charge to the jury, laying out the various options: they could find her guilty of first-degree murder, which requires planning and intent; they could find her guilty of second-degree murder, which is more impulsive; or they could find manslaughter, where no intent is required. The last option would be to find Susan not guilty by reason of insanity. Then he commented: "In light of the evidence, I would think you would have considerable difficulty in concluding that she was not insane."

The jury readily agreed. In accordance with the jury's finding, Chief Justice Evans ordered that Susan be taken to the St. Thomas Psychiatric Hospital in St. Thomas, Ontario to be kept and treated until she had recovered. The warrant to hold her would be in place until the provincial cabinet authorized the Lieutenant-Governor of Ontario to grant her release.

The Chief Justice thanked the jury for its participation in the legal proceedings and discharged them, but it was not over. Immediately after the jurors left, Susan Wood was again standing before the Chief Justice to answer to the charge of attempted murder. This, of course, was in relation to the stabbing of the young man who suffered the collapsed lung. This time, Hugh Silverman opted to have the charge dealt with by judge alone, without a jury, and once again entered a plea of not guilty by reason of insanity.

Chief Justice Evans heard the factual summary of events giving rise to the charge, and, on consent of counsel for both sides, agreed that the evidence heard at the murder trial be used in the newest proceeding. Evans took less than half an hour to make a second finding of not guilty by reason of insanity.

Both Crown counsel and defence expected it would be many years, if ever, before Susan Wood would be able to walk freely in society once again.

Requesting a Licence

Robert Pearson's widow was having a tough time financially. In 1979, she was 57 and lived in a top-floor apartment in a house owned by her brother-in-law. She could not work but was in receipt of Mother's Allowance since she was caring for her 15-year-old grandson, Robbie who she had raised from childhood. Within a year the boy would be 16 and would have his support, a monthly family benefit of $297, cut off. Robert Pearson had no life insurance at the time of his death.

Mrs. Pearson came up with a plan. She would petition the Metro Toronto Licencing Commission to consider giving her a taxi owner's licence as a tribute to her deceased husband. If Mrs. Pearson could obtain a licence, she could rent it to a driver and live modestly on the income.

She received support for this project from Ward 7 Alderman for the York Borough, John Nunziata. (Nunziata would later enter federal politics and become a Liberal Member of Parliament in 1984, the year the Liberal Party was almost wiped out by the Brian Mulroney Progressive Conservative landslide.) Nunziata was a student lawyer at the Parkdale Community Legal Services. The Parkdale clinic was the first community-based legal clinic in Ontario and allowed law students at Osgoode Hall Law School to get hands-on experience with clients who could not afford private counsel. Nunziata took the bold step of asking Toronto cabbies to support the cause by signing a petition, even though some would surely see Mrs. Pearson's attempt to secure a licence as "butting in line," when many had waited years to have the opportunity.

Nunziata appeared with Irene Pearson before the Licencing Commission in February 1979, stressing that life had been hell for Pearson's widow. Nunziata argued that she had limited income from welfare, suffered from insomnia and high blood pressure, and had a moral right to have the benefit of a licence, since the tragedy of her husband's murder was a direct result of trying to do the job he did.

The three-person Commission panel disagreed. Although Commission Chair Peter Clark expressed regret and confirmed the negative decision was most difficult, it would violate the existing licencing by-law to allow Mrs. Pearson to jump queue and receive preferential treatment. To make an exception would require council to change the by-law, a recommendation the Commission was unable to make. The object was to ensure that one licence would be granted for every 850 residents in the coverage area.

Nunziata dismissed the decision as a "slap in the face" to a victim of crime. But Nunziata had not emptied his legal toolbox, and assisted Irene Pearson in making application to the Criminal Injuries Compensation Board.

In May 1979, Irene Pearson learned that her application for compensation for the death of her husband had been approved. The award was not major, but certainly an improvement from the welfare she was forced to give up. Irene Pearson would be compensated $1,000 to partially reimburse her for the $1,500 cost of the funeral, $5,000 for loss of her husband's income, and (as of May 1), $500 per month for the rest of her life.

Face-To-Face With Susan

While all this was going on, Susan Wood was kept in a locked ward of the St. Thomas Psychiatric Hospital. She had been in what could be considered "maximum security" for about a year when she made contact with my office.

I drove to the hospital from my office in London, Ontario. The hospital, constructed in 1937 on land that had been six area farms, was a light-coloured two-storey brick complex with what I recall were the longest halls of any building I had ever visited. The grounds were vast and open, giving the over-all impression of a safe and comfortable place to live, that is until one was admitted to the locked ward. There was bustling activity and encounters with heavily medicated patients.

It was there that I had my first face-to-face meeting with Susan Wood. Susan was bright, talkative and cheerful, much different from the person I expected to see. She was not on any discernible medication.

"I hope you didn't have trouble getting in," Susan said while greeting me. "One of the patients got agitated about half an hour ago. He hit one of the staff workers and had to be medicated."

"Are you okay?" I asked.

"Oh, I'm fine. I never have any trouble. I'm on good terms with everybody in the ward. I like them and they like me."

As our discussion continued, it became obvious that Susan was becoming tired of the conflict between staff and some of the more psychotic patients. She wanted out of the ward but could not move without the approval of what was then known as the Lieutenant Governor's Board of Review. She had asked for a hearing and wanted me to assist.

She proceeded to give me a summary of her case with which I was able to do some research and devise a timetable that I brought to Susan at our second meeting.

"We will be able to get you off the ward if we can convince the Board that you are a manageable risk to be housed in the hospital off the locked ward." I told her that we do that by asking that the warrant that confines you to hospital be loosened and proposed what I called a three-year plan. I advised that at our first hearing, the Board would ask whether she'd recovered. Most people going before the Board and wanting out will jump at the question and say they have recovered from their insanity.

"I don't want you to do this," I cautioned. "When the question is asked, I want you to answer 'Partially.' That will give me the opportunity to pitch for the loosening of the warrant to have you moved to an open ward. The following year, if you continue your good behaviour, they will ask you the same question. Again, I want you to answer 'Partially'. I would then propose that you be allowed access to the hospital grounds and escorted trips into the city of St. Thomas. On the third year, when asked about your recovery, you will finally be able to agree that you have recovered."

Susan was amazed that she could potentially be free in three years.

"But it's all up to you," I warned. "Each year, you must get a glowing report from hospital staff. You seem to like staff now, and they like you. The records I have read are fine, so we're good to go for year one. But the next two years are totally up to you. Be pleasant, and do as staff want, and we'll press ahead."

As expected, the first appearance before the Board was easy. It was no trouble to persuade the Board that Susan could be managed in the general population of the psychiatric hospital.

Susan continued her treatment and remained polite and cooperative with staff. On the second year's Board, she was able to say that she had partially recovered. The Board allowed her access to hospital grounds and supervised visits into the city.

I read the paperwork as I prepared for the third hearing. Again, Susan had impressed the staff. She and I decided we would take the leap and claim full recovery.

Hearings before the Board are usually informal. The hospital had coffee and cookies on a table to munch on as we awaited the start of the hearing. We took our seats across a table from the three-person Board, which consisted of a psychiatrist, a lay person, and the Chair, a Supreme Court judge. All three smiled politely as we assembled.

Questioning Susan, and the positive review of a hospital staff member, went as expected. I could sense a favourable decision. But there was one final question put to Susan by the judge. I cast my eyes downward, not expecting it.

"When two women have sex," the judge asked, "who does what to whom? "

Susan and I had never talked about it, and I worried that Susan could give an answer that could upset the hospitable tone that had been prevalent throughout the hearing.

Susan answered immediately.

"Having sex with another woman should be no different than sex between a man and a woman," she said. "If the two parties have respect for one another, the object is for each person to give and get pleasure from the other." She left it at that. The judge gave a nod that he was satisfied with the answer.

The decision on year three was that the warrant would be cancelled. Susan would be free to restart her life wherever she chose to reside.

Susan looked at me and smiled. As we stood up at the conclusion of the hearing, Susan hugged me and buried her head in my chest. "Thank you," she said as she released her arms. She gave me another warm smile, and I left the hearing room.

I never saw or heard from Susan Lynn Wood from that day forward. To my knowledge, she has never come into conflict with the law.

I like to think she is living happily and hopefully with a partner who can give her love. After all, that's all she really needed.

I now realize that this was a case where a crime could have been prevented. The horrific slaying of an innocent cabbie need not have occurred if our attitudes in society were more accepting of a person's desire to be seen in the context with which the person is most comfortable. It is an example of failure by not only the courts but society as a whole to understand and accept persons who exhibit body, social, and mental dysphoria. We may claim that attitudes are shifting but there is still a call to maintain 'conversion therapy' clinics as though LGBTQ+ issues are still socially intolerable.

TWENTY-THREE

JOSEPH STANLEY FAULDER

A TALE OF TWO FAMILIES

■ ■ ■

My dreams and fond schemes of wine, women and such
Have been with me since I was a child.
These fantasies nursed, have made me accursed.
And were the source of my running so wild.
—Joseph Stanley Faulder

WHENEVER A CRIME IS COMMITTED, there is a ripple effect. A victim is not only the person on whom the crime is perpetrated, the family of the injured person can also suffer. The same goes for the perpetrator of crime. That person's family can also endure the agony of the crime from the time of arrest onward. In some cases, the whole community can experience the pain.

So it was with two families living a continent apart, one in the United States and one in Canada. Both families endured the pain of loss, but the incident had implications that disturbed international relations.

The Phillips

One of those families was the Phillips family of Gladewater Texas. The Phillips were a prominent family in a small eastern city 90 miles east of Dallas. Loyce Phillips was born October 14, 1898 and died February 5, 1975, at age 76 of heart disease and diabetes. He married Inez Scarborough, one year his junior, and together they had one son, Jack Loyce Phillips, born in 1925.

Loyce was very civic minded, serving a term as Mayor, as did his son Jack who also served as Mayor of Gladewater. Jack served in the United States Army Air Force during World War II. He attained the rank of Second Lieutenant, piloting B-17 aircraft. Following the war, he attended the University of Texas at Austin. He married Barbara Wampler in 1946 and when Jack graduated with a Bachelor of Science degree in geology, the married couple returned to Gladewater.

The Phillips father and son partnered in the oil and gas business. Loyce brought in his first well in the 1930s. Jack made the business an enormous success. He found 14 oil and gas fields in Texas, Louisiana, New Mexico, and Mississippi. With a daughter, Nancy, he recruited two grandchildren into the family business, Jack L. Phillips Co. He also contributed to his community, spending 22 years as President of the Gladewater Round-up Association, and served as a director on four bank boards. The family became extremely wealthy.

The massive Phillips wealth allowed Jack to pursue his travel to exotic locales in Africa. He loved venturing to Africa and taking his family on safaris. His south-Texas ranch held over 15 species of exotic game. Jack also was set up to breed native whitetail deer and quarter horses.

Jack was extremely devoted to his mother, Inez. Inez and her husband Loyce lived in a sprawling white brick bungalow in Gladewater. The house was surrounded by pecan trees. Loyce and Inez were very happy in their home. Despite being elderly, they were in the process of adding an addition at the time Loyce passed away.

The Faulders

The other family was the Faulders. Joe and Eleanor Faulder lived in Alberta, Canada. Joe was a rail mechanic for the Canadian National Railway. Joe and Eleanor had three children, a son named Barry born in 1929, a daughter named Patricia born in 1932, and another son named Stan born in 1937.

Like Jack Loyce Phillips, he had his father's given name but like the Phillips clan, Stan never used the father's first name. He was named Joseph Stanley Faulder, but everybody referred to him as Stan.

When Stan was 3 years old, he went for a car ride on a country rode near the family home in McLennan, Alberta, about 400 km. north of Edmonton in Peace Country. His mother was driving. Stan started fiddling with the door handle while sitting alone in the back seat of the family Hudson as it rounded a corner. In those days, kids were not nestled into car seats nor did they wear seat belts. The car door swung open, and Stan tumbled out of the moving vehicle. Some say his head struck the car door as he fell. No one knows for sure, but Stan suffered a serious head injury. It was touch and go whether he would live or die for a few weeks. Stan eventually recovered or "sort of" recovered.

After the accident, Stan suffered petit mal seizures. He endured bouts of depression abnormal for kids his age. Sometimes he would have blackouts which his family called "Stan's spells." At age 7, he was caught stealing. He stole a couple of cap guns from Woolworths on a dare. He could offer no explanation for his misdeed. Police sent him home after an intense lecture. He would not admit he was dozing; he never admitted suffering mental blackouts.

Stan's spells continued as he grew older. When he started high school, the family moved to Jasper, Alberta. His grades at school fell. By age 14 he started drinking. Perhaps it was his father's influence — his dad was an alcoholic. At 15, he was arrested for stealing a wristwatch. For that he spent six months at a boys' home. Two years later at age 17, he was arrested for theft once again. This resulted in six months in jail.

Even though he was getting into trouble, Stan was well-liked. In summer months, students would arrive in town

seeking employment at Jasper Park Lodge. Stan would immediately befriend the newcomers and help them manoeuvre the
trails and climb the mountains and then party with the younger
crowd, singing, dancing, and playing his guitar. One associate
described Stan as the person everybody wanted to party with.

Others commented what a kind-hearted young man he
was. A woman caught in a blinding snowstorm credits Stan's
caring attitude for saving her life in rescuing her during a
blizzard.

At age 27, Stan received a penitentiary sentence of two
years. He was caught in a stolen vehicle and rather than turn
in the person who committed the theft, Stan took the rap. He
asked for psychological/psychiatric help while doing time at
Stony Mountain Prison. The help he was given involved enroll-
ing him in an experimental programme where he was administered LSD.

Stan got out of prison in 1962 seemingly totally rehabilitated.
He immediately found work in Jasper driving heavy machinery. The following year he married Lorraine and together they
had two daughters. Stan adored his children. Both Stan and
Lorraine drank, sometimes to excess. Stan drifted from job to
job. Alcohol and finances placed a heavy toll on the relationship and by 1971 the marriage was doomed. Stan and Lorraine
divorced in 1973. The court ordered that Stan would be entitled to two visitations a year with his daughters. This intensi-
fied his drinking while he sank into deep depression.

Stan headed to Vancouver for employment, but his working life was sporadic. He eventually drifted south, across the
border, into the United States. He worked for a while as a
kitchen assistant in a Reno, Nevada casino, but that job too
was short-lived.

Stan's family tried to track him down. They tracked down
and contacted a friend in Vancouver shortly after Stan had left.
The contact had no forwarding address. The family decided it
was best to wait it out and allow Stan to contact them if he was

of a mind to do so. It would be 20 years before they heard about Stan again. With the lapse of time, the thought was that perhaps he had died. Lorraine, Stan's ex-wife and his daughters, Krista and Camille coped as a family unit while Stan was drifting throughout the United States. It proved to be a tough go for Lorraine. She worked hard but a good chunk of her salary had to be spent on babysitting. Camille was 7 when Stan left and, in the years ahead, she was charged with the responsibility of looking after Krista while mom was away at work.

Hustling at Juke Joints

Stan's departure was particularly tough on Camille. All that was left for her to remember him by were a few snapshots. She could not understand why Stan had left. Camille has been quoted as saying, "My father and I were very close, and I can remember fighting with my mother until I was 16 when she could finally explain things to me and make me understand about marriages and how things break down and what happened. I fought with her for those nine or ten years and blamed her, initially as a small child, for sending my father away."

By 1975, Stan had made his way to Texas. When he met people in Longview, an oil town in the northeast part of the State, he introduced himself as Stan Cotter. There were a variety of establishments featuring music, dancing, gambling, and drinking known as juke joints to serve the workers from the oil fields. Stan Cotter found he could raise cash hustling pool at one of these venues on a strip known as the Whiskey River Bend. It was at one of the juke joints called the Hurricane Club, that Stan met up with Stormy.

Stormy Summers was the alias used by Lynda McCann. Stormy, a sometimes sex worker, could not be missed in the bar. She weighed 240 pounds and had swastikas tattooed on each hand. Her boyfriend or husband was Ernie McCann, a member of a local outlaw biker group called Destiny's Legion. Ernie was not present when Stan ran into Stormy. That night she was with another man named James Moulton. The three sat down at a table and ordered drinks. In the course of conversation, it was revealed that Moulton had been laying tile for an old lady who lived alone in Gladewater. Her husband had passed away a few months previously and she was ripe for the picking. What's more, she had installed a floor safe brimming with cash and jewelry.

As the conversation went on, the three became obsessed with how easy it would be to break in and steal the valuables. The lady was rich, elderly, and except for her, no one else was at home to put up a fight. The three got in a car, drove to Gladewater and cased the property.

A few evenings later, on July 8, 1975, Stan and Stormy made a return trip to Gladewater. This time the intention was to rob the old lady. Stormy went by herself to the back door. She knocked and when Inez Phillips opened the door, Stormy apologized but explained her car had broken down and asked if she could use the telephone to get help. Inez readily agreed and allowed Stormy to enter the house.

Once inside, Stormy pulled a gun on Inez Phillips and allowed Stan to gain entry. Stan was to search the property and find the floor safe. He began his search.

Then there was the sound of gun fire. A bullet was fired but it hit no one. The 75-year-old widowed homeowner had decided to put up a fight and needed to be restrained.

What happened next was open to question. Nonetheless, a woman who was hired as a caretaker found the body of Inez Phillips with a large gash on the back of her head, her hands bound with tape and a kitchen knife protruding from her chest.

The floor safe was untouched. It contained only costume jewelry of minimal value and no cash. There were no fingerprints left behind. This was not a case where forensic evidence could help find the culprit.

Jack Phillips was devastated. He had lost his father only months before, and now his dear mother was gone as well.

Police had no leads. He did the only thing he could think of doing. He posted a $50,000 reward for information leading to the arrest and conviction of the person or persons responsible for this tragedy. James Moulton came forward and named Stormy Summers and Stan Cotter.

Stormy was picked up. She minimized her involvement in the robbery and placed most of the blame on Stan. She was charged and convicted of conspiracy to commit burglary and given a ten-year non-custodial sentence.

Stan was arrested and charged with murder after getting into some trouble and being arrested by Highway Patrol in Colorado in 1977. He was extradited to Texas and once back in Longview in Texas Ranger custody, subjected to four days of gruelling interrogation. In the end, he signed a statement that read: "I went back to check on Mrs. Phillips. She was moaning and groaning and kicking. I felt the back of her head and the skull felt crushed. I went to the kitchen and got a knife. I went back to the bedroom and stabbed Mrs. Phillips. I stabbed her in the center of the chest." By signing the statement, four days of interrogation came to an end.

With a confession in hand, the prosecutor, Otis Hill, felt it was an open and shut case. Stan Faulder, whose identity and Canadian citizenship was now confirmed, would be represented at his murder trial by Vernard Solomon.

Right to Remain Silent

If this were not a true story, the full blame for a conviction could be placed on the shoulders of Vernard Solomon for giving ineffective counsel. In fact, Vernard Solomon was a "Super Lawyer," a designation of his peers bestowed three times in *Texas Monthly Magazine*. In January 1975, he was certified as a Specialist in Criminal Law and maintained that rating until his death on September 15, 2018 from complications suffered after a truck accident 10 days previously.

Faulder suspected his family in Alberta or wherever they

may be now would be further upset to learn he was in custody facing a murder charge. So, he just did not bother to give any of the information to Vernard. He also did not tell his lawyer that he took responsibility for an auto theft, even though he was not the thief, and spent time in prison in Canada as a result. (Texas police had obtained Stan's criminal record from the RCMP, but no thought was given to notifying the Canadian consulate that one of its citizens was in custody charged with murder.) Nor did Stan mention the traumatic brain injury he suffered as a child. Vernard Solomon had a client so depressed he was not willing to give the lawyer useful information to mount a successful defence.

What confronted Solomon was a confession as the only real piece of evidence that could be used to convict his client. Solomon knew that Otis Hill would be exploiting that statement to maximum effect to convince a jury beyond a reasonable doubt that Faulder was a killer.

The defence lawyer learned that during the police interrogation, Faulder had asked for "a couple of days" to think through his story. The wily defence counsel said this statement should be interpreted as Faulder asking for the right to remain silent. Solomon argued that the constitutional right to remain silent had been breached. Solomon had to attack the confession. And that the confession, the only piece of evidence linking Faulder and Inez Phillips' death should be ruled inadmissible.

The trial judge rejected the argument and the jury convicted Faulder. A death sentence was imposed. However, Solomon appealed the ruling. An appellate court agreed in a judgment handed down in 1979 that continued questioning was a violation of Faulder's rights and the confession could not be used against him.

That ruling did not sit well with the Phillips family. With the verdict overturned, Jack Phillips was extremely disappointed as was his family. Phillips sought legal advice and found there was a little-used provision in Texas criminal law that would permit private prosecution. Jack did not want to see his mother's killer accept a plea bargain that public prosecution would likely offer. Jack had money and he would use it to his advantage. He hired Otis Hill, now in private practice because of his knowledge of the case and Phil Burleson, also a former prosecutor. These men were excellent advocates and could be counted on to get the job done. A fee, reported to be as much as $155,000, was no problem for the Phillips family.

Money to Testify

Because they were excellent advocates, they soon realized this prosecution would be much more difficult than the first trial. This time there was no confession to put before the jury. To be successful, they needed eyewitness testimony. That meant Stormy Summers would have to be called to recount events. To facilitate the process, Jack offered Stormy $15,000 "relocation expenses" and immunity from prosecution for murder. With the promise of cash, Stormy was certainly willing to repeat the description of events set out in the confession document that had been ruled inadmissible and could not be entered into evidence.

Jack Phillips denies money was ever paid to the witness. He claimed she simply wanted to testify but was afraid to do so. In the event Faulder was acquitted, he might want retribution. Once convicted, money to find her a new place to live became unnecessary. No one has been able to trace if Phillips paid money as the result of his offer to Stormy.

Yet there was another problem. Stormy was a participant in the robbery and for her testimony to be admissible, there needed to be corroboration. No problem. Stormy's husband Ernie was willing to say he overheard the conversation at the Hurricane Club. Of course, Ernie McCann needed $2,000 to compensate for lost wages while he might have to be in court. At the conclusion of the trial, even without the confession, on the testimony of a swastika-tattooed sex worker and her outlaw biker husband, Joseph Stanley Faulder was convicted of murder.

Now Jack Phillips could spend his money for the real prize. Once a conviction is entered, the sentencing phase can begin. Texas has the death penalty but in order for it to be imposed, a jury must first conclude that there is no possibility of rehabilitation. That would require the expert opinion of a psychologist who could predict future behaviour. Fortunately, for the Phillips family, such an expert was available.

The expert was a psychiatrist named Dr. James Grigson. He was more often called Dr. Death. During his lifetime (1937 – 2004), Grigson testified for the prosecution in 167 capital trials, most of them resulting in the imposition of the death penalty. His testimony was almost identical every time he was called upon in such cases. He would spend 90 minutes interviewing the convicted person and then enter the witness stand and swear under oath that the person he just interviewed was a "severe sociopath who will continue with his previous behaviour and will commit other similar criminal acts if given the opportunity to do so."

Jurors believe they are hearing considered and expert evidence. Lawyers and judges know that often experts' conclusions are in line with the desires of the party that hired them. A former Assistant Texas Attorney General in a *Washington Post* article explained it this way: "Expert witnesses are bought and sold.…The prosecution buys them, and the defence buys them. It is up to the jury to decide which is believable."

The jury, with this evidence, believed that Joseph Stanley Faulder was a severe sociopath and not only killed Inez Phillips but would likely, given the opportunity, kill again. Faulder was sentenced to death. He was then and for all foreseeable time to come living out his days alone in a cell measuring 1.5 x 2.7 metres as inmate No. 580. The 1981 murder conviction and a death sentence were the grand prize for the Phillips family. For Jack Phillips it was the return on investment he most relished.

All would no doubt have been forgotten except for the intervention of lawyer Sandra Babcock. Fresh out of Harvard Law School in 1991, the cause of death row inmate Stan Faulder became one of her first files. It had been passed on to the clinic where Babcock was employed by Vernard Solomon. Babcock dug in deep and with fresh eyes set out to find things that may have been missed or learn things Solomon had not been told while he was in charge of the case. One of her first moves was to seek out the Faulder family and to advise the Canadian consulate that one of its citizens has been on death row for 10 years.

Emotional Turmoil

Sandra Babcock was working with the Houston-based Texas Resource Centre that took on the Faulder case as it did with other capital cases. On November 1, 1991, the Centre was able to reach Stan's sister, Pat, now Patricia Nicholl, aged 60 when she received the call. "It was a terrible jolt," she told the *Calgary Herald*. The family presumed Stan was dead since it had been so long with no contact.

The rest of the Faulder family also was jolted to have news that Stan was alive and was awaiting execution. But the news evoked different emotions.

Camille was the eldest daughter when Stan left her mother. "To hear that he was suddenly alive and, in this situation, it's a really hard feeling to describe," Camille told the *Edmonton Journal*. "It was very emotional...an emotional turmoil. It was scary. It was like a shock. You don't know what you feel. Because after 20 years we really don't know this person anymore. He was our biological father, and he was with us for a period of time, but 20 years after the fact, we've all grown up and started our own lives. I knew that we felt badly for him."

The younger daughter, Krista and the girls' mother felt differently. They gave up on Stan and believed at the time they received the news that he should die. Krista and her mother found it difficult to excuse the sense of abandonment after Stan left in 1973.

Both Camille and Krista grew into responsible adults holding down good jobs. Camille worked as a schoolteacher and Krista was a financial clerk with Canadian Forces at the time they were informed about Stan. Krista was only four when Stan departed. As an adult, Krista believed in capital punishment, even for a man she cannot remember and was unwilling to change her viewpoint just because of the biological connection.

"I've had a few phone calls from people that are just, you know, they're just completely horrified that I feel the way that I do because he's my father. But they don't understand the whole story and I don't think my opinion should change just because he's my father. You have to understand," Krista continued, "that this man abandoned us. He abandoned myself and my sister. I understand he has been in prison for fifteen years, but there was a period of about six years when he had every opportunity in the world to contact us and chose not to. I'm not going to lie to him. I'm going to tell him exactly what I think and with that type of crime, I was very horrified."

Camille and Krista's mother, who remarried, moved to British Columbia. The mother no longer used the Faulder surname. Krista was upset for her mother, whom she described as "terrified" that Stan had re-emerged to disrupt the lives of the family members. Krista claimed, "It's a real fear for her physical well-being. She lived with him for seven years and she saw it. I can't say anything about that, because I don't remember. But from that seven years, she was just hoping and praying he would never show up. Now that he has, of course, well, she's scared. She doesn't even want anyone to know who she is."

Camille was a fervent opponent of capital punishment. Yet she was determined not to let the rift in the family interfere. She explained, "We've dealt with it really as much as we can and we've agreed to disagree and just carry on with our lives as best we can until something happens, until the judges in Texas make a decision."

Camille attended the Huntsville penitentiary with her aunt, Pat, in July 1992. "It (talking with Stan) was like talking with an old friend," the daughter commented.

Ideologies

Even though Stan Faulder's family was notified in November, 1991 of his plight, the first press mention of a Canadian on Texas' death row was in the April 28, 1992 edition of the *Calgary Herald*. The newspaper account mentioned that Faulder admitted hitting Inez Phillips with a "small club" and stabbing her with a kitchen knife while she was "bound and gagged." The paper never mentioned that the admission had been ruled inadmissible by a Texas appellate court and the description of the incident that resulted in his conviction and sentence was from the questionable duo of Stormy Summers corroborated by her husband upon receiving money for their testimony. It did note the matter was under appeal by Sandra Babcock.

Legal nuances were irrelevant when it came to ideology. With the last execution in Canada taking place in 1962 and a 1975 vote abolishing capital punishment in Canada, the Faulder case provided the soap box necessary to argue the merits of the death penalty. Proponents for the restoration of capital punishment included right-wing journalists and politicians including David Frum and Art Hanger.

David Frum, a thoughtful conservative commentator and journalist, expressed the sentiments of many conservative thinkers when he wrote: "My own view is that only a society with a shocking contempt for the value of human life would refuse to execute a man who could beat and then cold-bloodedly drive a knife through the body of a defenceless elderly woman."

Art Hanger sat as a Member of Canada's Parliament from 1993 to 2008 representing the Northeast Constituency in

Calgary, Alberta. He was a leading spokesman for ultra-conservative law and order positions. As a Justice critic for the Reform Party (a precursor to Canada's present Conservative party), Hanger was opposed to any government involvement to save the life of a Canadian on death row. When Canada decided to intervene, Hanger asked, "Why is our government continuing to interfere with the truth in another country?" For Hanger, such intervention stood in the way of the orderly Texas corrections' administration of justice.

Sandra Babcock continued the fight to save the life of Stan Faulder. By raising the complaint that the Texas government was in breach of the Vienna Convention on Consular Relations which specified that foreign nationals should have access to emissaries of their home country, she allowed for Canadian government intervention. David Frum denied any damage was done when Texas assumed Faulder was an American because he held a Texas driver's licence. The Canadian consulate could have ensured Faulder had good legal representation, but Frum argued he did have exceptional legal representation from one of the best advocates in the State. To Frum, failure to notify Canada was a "harmless error."

But was it? Once notified, the Canadian government was able to intervene. Once Canada became involved, Secretary of State for Foreign Affairs Barbara McDougal, a Minister in Brian Mulroney's Progressive Conservative government, took immediate action and wrote to the Texas governor, Ann Richards, requesting that the punishment be commuted to life imprisonment. The Canadian Embassy in Washington filed a formal letter of complaint with the US State Department that Texas had "knowingly" omitted Faulder's name from a list of Canadian citizens held in custody that the Consulate General receives annually. Richards later denied the request because Faulder, through Babcock, had not exhausted all avenues of appeal.

George W. Bush and PM Jean Chrétien

By 1995, Texas had a new Governor, George W. Bush and Canada had a new Prime Minister, Liberal Jean Chrétien. Chrétien's Foreign Affairs Minister Lloyd Axworthy had the Canadian government intervene in the legal proceedings brought by Babcock.

Indeed, Governor Bush was receiving correspondence from around the world, although most of it came from Canada. The Texas State archives records 3,521 letters to Governor Bush about Stan Faulder. At Minister Lloyd Axworthy's behest, US Secretary of State Madeline Albright wrote to Governor Bush asking for clemency. Other notables such as Archbishop Desmond Tutu and Amnesty International are included in the list of correspondents. Although mostly pleading for Faulder's commutation of sentence, there are letters for the opposite including letters from Art Hanger and Jack Phillips.

It is not surprising that Stan Faulder's fate was a matter of public concern. It is also not surprising that opposition Members of Parliament would rise in the Canadian House of Commons to put on record their opposition to the demand for clemency that External Affairs Minister Lloyd Axworthy had proposed. However, there is a cardinal rule that in dealing with foreign jurisdictions, Canada speaks with one voice. It may not be technically treasonous but it is surely shameful if an elected Member of Parliament ignores this convention to undermine the stance of the Canadian government.

Yet my research has uncovered a letter written by Art Hanger on House of Commons stationery where he expressly undermines the policy of the Canadian government. That letter, dated November 27, 1998, reads as follows:

> Dear Governor Bush:
>   Congratulations on your overwhelming victory in these past mid-term elections! A well-deserved Republican triumph.

I have been following the case of Mr. Stanley Faulder a native of Alberta who is convicted of murder in the State of Texas. His execution date scheduled for December 10,1998. The Canadian government has appealed to you to show clemency for Mr. Faulder, arguing that he was never informed of his rights to see a Canadian consul. Mr. Faulder was tried and convicted of murder.

The Canadian government wants to see Mr. Faulder's sentence commuted to time served and brought back to Canada. If returned to Canadian authorities, Mr. Faulder would most likely be released without serving further time. They will also argue that he has already served 21 years in prison.

I believe it important to voice a different point of view than that expressed by the Canadian Foreign Affairs Minister. As an opposition Member of Parliament, I cannot accept the reasoning that Mr. Faulder should be spared the death penalty because he is a Canadian.

He was tried twice and found guilty. He was refused clemency for good reason because there was no just cause to grant clemency and the US Supreme Court refused to hear the case.

It is unfortunate that a Canadian entered your jurisdiction to commit such a heinous crime and I feel deeply for the family and community upon which this terrible act has impacted on them. I believe, as do others in our Parliament and our society, that Texas justice should prevail and that the death penalty for a convicted first-degree murderer would be deemed an appropriate punishment.

It would be of great advantage to discuss this matter further with you. In appreciation and observance of your Thanksgiving holiday, I will be pleased to contact you once again early next week.

Yours sincerely.
Art Hanger,
MP Defence Critic Opposition Party Calgary Northeast

Art Hanger was not the only opposition member to make such contact. Jay Hill, another Reform Party MP also sent an email to the Governor that reads as follows:

> Dear Governor Bush,
>
> I am writing to inform the Governor that the Canadian Members of Parliament who have been traveling to Austin seeking a stay of execution for Stanley Faulder do not represent the wishes of all Canadians.
>
> I, along with my colleagues in the Reform PArty [sic] of Canada (The Official Opposition) have been calling for a national binding referendum to reinstate capital punishment in Canada.
>
> The following is a statement I made in the House of Commons on May 26th, 199[sic] and the corresponding press release which was circulated nationally.
>
> Canadians have no business telling the State of Texas how to govern your land!
>
> Sincerely,
> Jay Hill, MP
> Prince George-Peace River, BC

The views of Art Hanger are consistent with his reactionary stances to crime and punishment. In March 1996 he announced that he supported a return to corporal punishment and even booked a trip to Singapore to investigate the efficacy of caning as a deterrent to crime. Public outcry caused him to cancel the trip.

It was Jack L. Phillips that sent the most disturbing letter to the Governor. It spoke directly to the pain the Phillips family was enduring. He speaks personally and emotionally to the Governor and predicates his views with his Republican connections and Christian values. The letter dated December 1, 1998 deserves to be reproduced in full:

Dear Governor Bush:

I wrote you last on April 22, 1997 when Mr. Faulder was then scheduled for execution Please know that I would not impose on your time again unless the matter was of extreme importance. Because of the seriousness of the matter described below, I take the liberty of writing you again to make you aware of the following information and to urgently seek your help.

By way of introduction, we have met on three occasions. The first was at the Houston airport shortly after the great political announcement concerning your father, our President, was made. We had a brief and enjoyable visit. The second was in the Tyler office of our mutual friend, Leonard Davis, with a small group when you were first considering running for Governor. I am so glad that you later made a positive decision because you have truly been an outstanding good Governor of this great State. The third was in Austin at your Birthday Party on July 17, 1998.

Now to the point:

On July 9, 1975, Joseph Stanley Faulder brutally tortured and murdered Inez Phillips, my 75- year-old widowed mother. He entered her Gladewater home at gunpoint after church while she was canning fruit in her kitchen. In the process of robbing her and burglarizing her home, he tied her up and bound her with tape. He bludgeoned her with a homemade blackjack fracturing her skull in several places.

After two hours of torturing my mother, he got a 12-inch butcher knife from the kitchen and went to her bedroom where she was taped and bound on the bed and stabbed her in the chest with such force and determination that the knife penetrated through her heart and through her whole body with the point of the knife coming out her back. This is the way her maid found her the next morning.

That was 22 years ago. Before my dad's death, I promised him I would take care of my mom. My mother was a beautiful Christian lady in every sense of the word, just as your lovely mother is. She dedicated her life to helping others. The District Attorney related that it was the most brutal, senseless murder he had ever heard about. For 22 years, I have not had a good night's sleep, as I live with the feeling that somehow I could have done more to protect my mother. Two separate juries have sentenced Mr. Faulder to death, he has been to the Texas Court of Criminal Appeals twice, he has been to the Fifth Circuit Court, he has been to the Supreme Court, and all courts and juries have upheld the death sentence.

The Prime Minister of Foreign Affairs [sic] of Canada, Mr. Lloyd Axworthy, a staunch opponent of the death penalty, met with Secretary of State Madeleine Albright yesterday and requested that she write you a letter and request clemency for Faulder. To my amazement Madeleine Albright did write you and the Board of Pardons & Parole asking for a thirty (30) day reprieve of his death sentence so that you could consider the clemency petition. A member of the Canadian Parliament, a Mr. Art Hanger just called me and is faxing a letter that he has written to you requesting that you not give Mr. Faulder clemency. Mr. Hanger also states that about three-fourths of the people in Canada are for the death penalty. If you were to commute Mr. Faulder's sentence to life, you would be opening the doors and he would walk out a free man, as he has already served a fifteen-year life sentence based on the time he was convicted.

When Mr. Faulder was first apprehended he was carrying a Texas drivers license showing a Longview, Texas address. Of course, he was assumed to be a US Citizen living in Texas. It was some time later before it was found that he was truly a Canadian Citizen disguised as a Texan. It was found that he had a long criminal record in Canada and he personally requested that the law officers not notify his country or his family of his incarceration for murder. They now claim he should be set free because his government was not notified. The courts have already ruled that the Vienna Convention is not an issue for reversal.

Mr. Faulder's defense had their own psychiatrist analyze him and evidently it was so bad that they refused to put the psychiatrist on the stand. The state had him analyzed by two psychiatrists and each stated that he was a psychopathic killer and would surely kill again. If you were to free Mr. Faulder I feel that I would be receiving the death sentence and surely I would be his next victim.

I enclose an article from the Tyler Morning Telegraph dated November 27, 1998 wherein they quote the Toronto paper "I don't say that I shouldn't be here. I say that the death row should not exist. Period." Joseph Stanley Faulder. It is quite obvious that this man has been proven guilty, he now even relates this in a newspaper and thinks it is all right for him to kill in Texas but that he should not be killed. If the above were true it would appear that a Canadian citizen would have more rights than a Texas citizen.

Governor Bush, I urgently and respectfully implore you to please not let the letter from Madeleine Albright, at the request of the Canadian government, interfere with the carrying out of justice and punishment for this most brutal murder. Canada and Madeleine Albright should not control justice in Texas. The wheels of justice have ground very slowly these past twenty-two (22) years. Two long and laborious trials and two different juries from different Texas counties have heard the evidence and rendered a proper sentence. The Supreme Court and Appellate Courts have also ruled in this case. Please, don't put my life in jeopardy and cause me to fail my mother a second time.

I know you are a just man and I believe that I know your decision and that this letter is really not needed,

I feel however, that I must make all possible effort for justice. If necessary, many of your friends and I would be happy to come to Austin and meet with you on this matter.

Thank you for your favorable consideration of my plea and request.

Sincerely yours,
Jack L. Phillips

Keeping Stan Alive

Sandra Babcock continued her quest to keep Stan Faulder alive. A ruling that an execution date would be postponed was not treated as a victory. Babcock was a seasoned soldier and a court-ordered delay meant that there was another battle yet to be fought.

Sandra Babcock had done excellent work by convincing one court after another of the need to delay the execution date. December 10, 1998 appeared to be Stan's ninth and final appointment with the executioner. Stan was comfortable knowing his death was fast-approaching. His religious convictions gave him strength. "We don't have a vengeful God," he believed. "There is a time for judgment, and its not here on Earth. If I don't make the grade there, that's something I'll have to deal with then."

A week before the scheduled date, Stan's sister, Pat Nicholl left Jasper, Alberta to see her brother in Huntsville, Texas. The siblings stared at each other through a thick glass panel and spoke of Stan's family, his daughters and the grandchildren he never met. Faulder took the meeting with stoicism. "We've said our goodbyes for the time being," Stan said. "We're set on both sides. I'm okay with that. I prefer it that way. Goodbyes are very hard, you know, under these circumstances."

An execution date of December 8, 1998 was at hand. Yet again, Babcock pulled a rabbit from her hat. The December date was cancelled. A new date in 1999 would have to be established. Fifteen minutes before the time for his execution, the Supreme Court of the United States ordered a stay. A prison spokesperson told a CBC news crew on scene to cover the execution that Faulder's comment was, "Far out! That suits me." It was left to Sandra Babcock to convey Faulder's message to his supporters. She told CBC reporter Anna Maria Tremonti that Stan offered his thanks to the Canadian people for their letters. Babcock then expressed her own reaction: "I have mixed feelings. I'm really, really happy. But about a half an hour ago I had to go and say good-bye to my client for the last time. He believed he was going to die. I think that's cruel and unusual punishment."

George W. Bush was exploring the possibilities of running for the US presidency and was spending time on the road promoting "compassionate conservatism." Interventions from people of influence such as Albright were seen as unnecessary bumps in the road to the White House. When asked about the request for a thirty-day reprieve that Albright had submitted, Bush dodged the issue. He responded, "I can understand her concerns and desires. The good news is, in our state people get treated fairly. People just can't come in our state and cold-blooded murder somebody. That's unacceptable behaviour, regardless of their nationality." Bush was quick to add that until the State board of Pardons and Paroles makes its decision, any action by him would be premature.

Ordained as a Minister

These delays allowed onlookers to get a better impression of who Joseph Stanley Faulder really was. According to Dr. Grigson, Faulder was a severe sociopath who would definitely kill again. If anyone wants to kill, prisons are the place to do it. Violence is a continuing threat in penitentiaries. But Stan Faulder kept to himself and eventually studied and in 1982 became an ordained minister. He would also write poetry and craft boxes and toys from matchsticks to sell to guards and other inmates so he could purchase canteen supplies.

People who did time with Faulder heaped compliments on the man. Danny Dean Thomas spent a year in a cell beside Faulder. They would talk to each other by holding shaving mirrors outside the bars. Hours passed as the two men conversed in this manner.

"He's a real decent guy," Thomas stated. After a year as neighbours, Thomas opted to work in a prison factory that made uniforms for the guards. He became thus entitled to a larger cell and additional privileges. Thomas understood Faulder's refusal to do the same: "He doesn't want to work for the state that's trying to kill him."

Danny Dean Thomas was found dead in his cell on August 31, 2009, the day before his 54th birthday. One account described his death as caused by boredom in the long wait on death row to meet the executioner. He was 26 when convicted and sentenced to death for murder.

Another death row neighbour was John Skelton. The two lived side-by-side for five years, 1985–1990, and they knew each other well. He described Faulder as "a real mild person, pleasant to talk to."

"He's never argumentative. You just can't feature him being involved in anything like that," Skelton said. "But I'm sure he didn't do the actual killing anyway." It was through their getting to know one another that Skelton sensed that Faulder's "confession" was really contrived to spare Lynda McCann (or Stormy Summers as she was known).

Skelton was released from prison when he was finally acquitted on appeal for murdering his business partner. But Skelton didn't give up on Faulder. He wanted to know the truth and now that he was a free man, he decided to track down McCann. "I think he's innocent of the charge. He was fond of that woman. She is the one I am sure killed Phillips. We talked about it. I went down to Louisiana and tried to locate that old gal and never did find her."

Skelton tried to convince Faulder to write to his family. Faulder always refused. Stan told him that he "didn't want his family to know where he was. He didn't want to hurt them any more than he already had."

All the while, Sandra Babcock pushed on bringing motions in court at all levels looking to get a judgment if not to free Faulder but at least delay the death penalty from being carried out for as long as possible. The Canadian government, to the dismay of critics such as Art Hanger, joined in by filing interventions in support of Babcock's cause. Babcock left her job with the Texas Resource Centre in 1995 and moved to Minnesota where she started a five-year stint as a public defender. She continued to represent Faulder on a pro bono basis. Her dedication can be understood in a response she made when asked why she became and continues to be such an avid opponent of the death penalty. She traced her motivation to an attendance as a second-year law student to a conference for students interested in doing public-interest work. "I heard a talk by Bryan Stevenson," she answered, "who works at the Equal Justice initiative in Alabama. When he was giving his talk, one of his clients had just been executed. In the midst of his speech to a room full of students who were complete strangers, he started to cry because he had lost his client. I was blown away by his commitment to the issues and by his involvement, both at an intellectual level and at a personal level. And I said to myself that I wanted to work with people like him."

Today Sandra Babcock is a Clinical Professor at Cornell Law School and remains highly admired by her colleagues in the legal profession.

Defence of the Wrongly Convicted

In late 1998, a conference on the death penalty was held in Chicago. In attendance was a representative of a Toronto group, the Association in Defence of the Wrongly Convicted

(AIDWYC, now known as Innocence Canada). AIDWYC had been formed to challenge wrongful convictions by a group of volunteer criminal and prison law lawyers and academics determined to see justice properly administered. The honorary head of the Association was Rubin 'Hurricane' Carter, a man who was a former middleweight boxer who had spent twenty years in prison before being exonerated.

I was appointed to the Board of AIDWYC while living in Toronto and in the spring after the Chicago conference I was asked to come by Rubin's home for coffee. I recall approaching Rubin's residence not far from the Dupont subway station. The steps leading up to Rubin's house were boxes of spring flowers ready for planting. Carter was dressed in jeans and a work shirt enjoying pleasant weather and gardening. I sensed the matter he wanted to discuss bore some urgency that would necessarily delay his garden work.

Once inside the house, Carter briefed me on the Faulder case and the role AIDWYC was prepared to play. My task was to accompany two internationally respected psychiatrists on a junket to Austin, Texas to meet with the head of Texas Board of Pardons and Parole and with Governor George W. Bush. Another delegation arranged by AIDWYC had been tasked with dealing with impressing the Board and the Governor of the general merits of commuting the death sentence to life imprisonment. Ordinarily, AIDWYC adopts cases where there is demonstrable factual innocence. This time, however, we were not to suggest that Faulder was innocent, merely that he was brain-damaged and if the Governor would grant a 30-day reprieve, a new MRI scan would be taken, and psychiatrists could state definitively that Faulder was ineligible for execution under Texas law.

On arrival at Austin, Texas, psychiatrists Stephen Hucker, Julio Arboleda-Florez as well as the head of the Texas Society of Psychiatric Physicians accompanied me as we entered the capitol building. In the days before September 11, there was no apparent security. We were directed to the stairs immediately on our left to access the Governor's office. Upon arriving at the reception desk, we were each asked to sign in. As I did so, I noted the name of a Reform Party Canadian Member of Parliament had undertaken the same trip a week earlier. I had no doubt Texas officials had been given the reasons why Faulder should die.

In Texas, the entire 18-member Board of Parole must agree unanimously to recommend a pardon before the Governor can act. Indeed, the Governor is limited to deferring execution only 30 days if new material is sufficient to cause a reconsideration by the Board.

The meeting was amiable with the psychiatrists putting forward a compelling case that Faulder suffered from and continued to suffer the ill-effects of brain injury. Persons who had brain damage similar to that suffered by Faulder could act impulsively and irrationally especially under stress. The injury could affect a person's ability to form the wrongful mental intent (lawyers call this the *mens rea*), that is a necessary element of a crime. It became apparent to those of us watching the proceedings, however, that the argument was having little effect. The meeting ended. I was interviewed by a television camera crew hired by a Canadian station. It was also obvious that the Texas reporter was disinterested in the topic. She had seen it all before.

A new date of June 17, 1999 was set after a flurry of new court applications had been considered.

Once again, Faulder was given the opportunity to have a last meal consisting of items that were kept in the prison's food supplies but nothing extraordinary would be prepared.

Four members of the Phillips family arrived at the Huntsville penitentiary. They were escorted into a closed room with a large window that allowed spectators to view the lethal injections being administered. Jack Phillips stood closest to the window. Faulder had made his goodbyes to his family the previous weekend. He didn't want his family to see him die.

Prison officials had advised the press of the ritual that is involved. The prisoner is given a first injection that puts him to sleep. A second injection causes the diaphragm and lungs to seize and stop. A third injection of potassium chloride stops the heart and death is instantaneous.

No one witnessing the procedure has spoken out about how the audience reacted while the injections were given. We know only that Faulder closed his eyes, coughed twice, let out a deep gasp and ceased to move.

Personal Questions

Just hours before the lethal substances were pumped into Stan's veins, Lorne Honickman, a Toronto lawyer and journalist asked me to be a guest on his supper-time phone in show on CITY TV in Toronto. The Faulder case was discussed, and the lines were opened for me to speak to members of the viewing audience. One man whose voice, I thought, sounded youthful was outraged that Canadians would be involved in moves to prevent the State of Texas from exacting its penalty. He asked, "How would you feel if a member of your family was murdered?"

I expected we would be talking legal theory. The question was personal and caught me off guard, so I responded in a very personal manner. "I have a cousin whose 8-year-old little girl was abducted, raped and murdered, and stuffed in a dumpster in the Town of Mount Forest several years ago. The murder was vicious and grotesque, but I'll tell you that if I had any reason to believe that the man who was convicted of the crime was convicted or sentenced unlawfully, I would be first in line to fight for his rights." The unexpected answer silenced the caller, but I sensed he was testing my emotional involvement in the case. I did not learn until the next day that the execution had been carried out. I met Toronto criminal lawyer Marlys Edwardh at the entrance to the Courthouse in Toronto. She expressed her condolences. I was somewhat embarrassed that I suddenly was feeling grief on Stan Faulder's passing. After all, lawyers are supposed to maintain boundaries and not get caught up in the emotions of a case.

Then it came to me that the caller to the TV show the previous evening was right. This is about families and family connections. The Phillips family and their supporters were grieving the loss of a mother. The Faulder family and their supporters were shaken by his loss. Where the two groups differ was that the Phillips allies were supporting the taking of Faulder's life as a means to obtain closure. The Faulder family understood there is no such thing as closure. Neither side comes out a winner. Believing that closure will mend the suffering of crime victims is denying the concept that two wrongs don't make a right.

The execution of Stanley Faulder was a direct result of a jury's acceptance of the evidence of Dr. Grigson where his expert opinion rested on personal ideology but was untested because the court accepted academic credentials rather than scientific expertise. The concept of 'an eye for an eye' rests on desire to appease public opinion especially where the report of a criminal act is horrific. Canada has ended the brutality of capital punishment but the public's desire for retribution for heinous conduct persists.

Whenever a crime is committed there is a ripple effect. People in society may be horrified that a crime has torn the fabric of the country's social network. Politicians may get involved to promote a particular agenda. Everyone is touched by it; but most of all, it is the families that suffer most.

TWENTY-FOUR

ALLAN MACDONALD

TRAPPED

■■■

A STORY ATTRIBUTED TO INDIGENOUS FOLKLORE asks what would happen if a bear met a wolf in the woods. The fable suggests that the wolf could be easily taken down by the brute strength of the bear in this one-on-one struggle. But suppose the bear confronted a pack of wolves. The bear, the story suggests would be at a severe disadvantage.

The bear and the wolf encounter is an allegory for the conflict between Allan MacDonald and Thomas Coffin after a tragic conflict that took place at the Commodore Bar in the municipality of Penetanguishene, Ontario on May 31, 1997.

Background
Allan MacDonald (the bear) was a 49-year-old former North York, Ontario firefighter who had moved to Penetanguishene and became Chair of the local Police Services Board. The town was attempting to cancel its local police service and opting to contract with Ontario Provincial Police for municipal police protection. During the negotiations, the local police were represented by Constable Thomas Coffin (the wolf). Negotiations were tough, long, and protracted. Each side dug in its heels to secure their respective positions.

About a month following the labour negotiations and after the OPP had been granted the policing contract, Coffin and

MacDonald met again. This time it was police officer Coffin confronting impaired driver MacDonald. A criminal charge for drunk driving was laid and a conviction was ultimately secured. As a result of the conviction, MacDonald was forced to surrender his driver's licence.

The charge impacted not only MacDonald's position as Chair of the Police Services Board but also threatened his firefighter job and perhaps a generous pension MacDonald hoped to receive. The fact that it was Coffin who laid the charge grated on MacDonald's mind to the point of obsession. The conflict between MacDonald and Coffin became personal.

On the evening of May 31, 1997, MacDonald learned that Thomas Coffin was at the Commodore Hotel having a few drinks with his companion, Constable Steve Roden. MacDonald, armed with a gun entered the hotel bar, placed the barrel of his gun at the back of Coffin's head and pulled the trigger. The 31-year-old father of three died instantly. MacDonald was pursued out the door by Constable Roden and a bar patron. As they approached MacDonald, MacDonald took aim but the gun jammed. MacDonald was overtaken, arrested, and immediately charged with the murder of Thomas Coffin as well as the attempted murder of Steve Roden.

The bear had taken down a lone wolf but now it was time for the pack to assemble. Even though the bear's leg was figuratively in the trap, there was no giving up. MacDonald refused to confess to the killing even though it had been witnessed by several people present at the bar. MacDonald's only concession was allowing his hands to be swabbed for gunpowder residue.

The Trial
The fist-degree murder trial was scheduled to be held in Barrie, Ontario before Justice Peter Howden. MacDonald had retained the services of criminal trial lawyer Dan Brodsky. Brodsky had the reputation of being extremely talented in criminal defence work and was seen as a major obstacle if the Crown prosecutor

were to get a conviction. The prosecution saw the need to take extraordinary measures.

Crown prosecutor Lorne McConnery hoped a confession would seal MacDonald's fate. McConnery therefore hired psychiatrist Dr. Angus McDonald to interview the accused being held in custody awaiting trial. McConnery failed to seek a court-ordered psychiatric assessment. He simply sent Dr. McDonald in cold to obtain whatever admissions he could.

The psychiatric report disclosed the first meeting between the psychiatrist and the accused. Allan MacDonald asked Dr. Angus McDonald for help.

"Indeed, almost the first thing he [MacDonald] told me was to ask me if I had any desire to help him," the psychiatrist wrote. He then stated, "I indicated that I did, but was uncertain as to whether or not I could be helpful under the circumstances and asked what help he might require. He responded rather intently. 'Kill me…kill me now.'"

Of course, defence counsel Brodsky objected to allowing the psychiatrist's evidence to go before a jury. Justice Howden agreed. The judge found it appalling that a Crown prosecutor would employ such tactics and commented that it was a repetition of a scheme found loathsome by another court in the past.

The judge held that MacDonald was particularly vulnerable when visited by the psychiatrist. "Of course," Justice Howden ruled, "his only choice at that point was continuation of a conversation with an intelligent person from a caring profession, albeit identified as being from the authorities, or returning to his cell and perhaps losing a much-desired opportunity…to be transferred from the jail to the mental health centre."

Not only had the prosecution's tactic of inducing an incriminating statement from a vulnerable accused failed, it also caused Dr. McDonald to face criticism from his profession.

Daniel Brodsky won the pretrial battle of excluding Dr. McDonald's evidence but he still had to go to war with a determined prosecution team wanting to avenge the death of

Thomas Coffin by restricting the liberty of Allan MacDonald for the longest period possible.

Brodsky realized that with so many witnesses to the shooting, it would be impossible to deny that MacDonald had been the assassin. If the intention to kill Coffin was planned and deliberate, a conviction for first-degree murder would be inevitable. The ability of the Crown prosecutor being able to prove beyond a reasonable doubt that MacDonald's actions were premeditated was open to question. If the jury could find reasonable doubt, a conviction for second-degree murder was possible. It might even be possible that a jury could conclude that MacDonald suffered so much mental anguish that the judge should leave it open for the jury to consider manslaughter that can, but need not, involve a life sentence.

Options to Consider

The difference between first-degree murder and second-degree murder is the sentence that is mandatory in each case. A conviction for murder carries with it a life sentence. The difference is the date on which the prisoner can be eligible for parole. First-degree murder has a mandatory sentence of life imprisonment without eligibility for parole for 25 years. If Brodsky could convince the jury there was no planning and deliberation and have them agree to second-degree murder, the sentence would still be life imprisonment but parole eligibility could vary between 10 and 25 years. In the event of a manslaughter finding, MacDonald could expect a prison term of a fixed number of years.

During the six-month trial, Brodsky called evidence to show that his client suffered from depression, loneliness, and alcoholism. The shooting happened spontaneously without planning as MacDonald's mental state was so troubled that the lethal confrontation between MacDonald and Coffin was inevitable. Brodsky argued that MacDonald's mental condition fell short of the legal definition that would support a not guilty by reason of insanity defence but certainly was ample to support a second-degree conviction.

Crown attorney Michael Minns painted a picture of a cold-blooded execution by a predator seeking revenge for an earlier impaired driving charge. He was able to call upon witnesses who told of MacDonald's dislike for Coffin.

A jury of nine men and three women was called upon to decide the facts. It was a trial where the photographic evidence of the scene was graphic and the narration of witnesses using terms describing Thomas Coffin as bleeding "like a firehose" aroused mental images far more graphic than camera images. A jury could not help but notice the despair and tears of Coffin's wife and children as witness after witness testified. MacDonald's sister Pat was the accused man's sole supporter in the court-room gallery.

After six hours of deliberation, the jury returned a verdict of guilty of murder in the first-degree. Justice Peter Howden imposed the mandatory sentence.

As MacDonald was taken from the prisoner's box to the cells of the Barrie courthouse, Brodsky faced media questioning outside the courtroom. He expressed his disappointment:

"My client is upset not because he was found guilty of an offense, but that he was found guilty of an offense that did not recognize the extent of his psychiatric state. His wish in this case was to be convicted of that which he believed he was guilty of, which is manslaughter. He always expected to be punished."

After waiting in local custody throughout the appeal period, the caged bear was off to federal penitentiary. First stop was the Millhaven Assessment Unit where it was decided that placement at Fenbrook Institution, about 100 kms. from his former home at Penetanguishene would give him best access to his family and a support network. Fenbrook Warden Mike Provan sensed public pressure should the move take place. When Fenbrook would not accommodate him, he was placed at Joyceville Institution northeast of Kingston, Ontario.

Imprisonment

A cop-killer in prison can expect no sympathy from custodial staff. MacDonald's case had been widely publicized. One way to make life difficult for a prison inmate is for a correctional officer to lay an institutional charge. Such charges are not for violating the *Criminal Code*. They are for an alleged breach of prison rules as laid out in the *Corrections and Conditional Release Act*. One such rule is that an inmate must not be disrespectful or abusive to a staff member in a manner that could undermine the staff member's authority.

Sometime in 2004, Allan MacDonald was on his way to cell count. It was alleged by a correctional officer that MacDonald laughed on his way. It was not stated if the correctional officer meant that MacDonald had laughed at her or whether MacDonald had been reacting to something he found humorous. In any event, the guard commenced internal disciplinary proceedings stating that MacDonald's act of laughing "undermined this writer's authority."

The institutional charge was classified as 'minor' and was adjudicated by a Correctional Supervisor. Had the charge been classified as 'serious', it would have had to be tried before an outside authority (often a lawyer under contract) called an 'Independent Chairperson' at a proceeding taking on all the trappings of a criminal court.

In the case of MacDonald, the inmate Offence Report and Notification of Charge went before a Joyceville Correctional Supervisor who on the basis of the written complaint and without hearing evidence entered a conviction and imposed a penalty of a warning or reprimand.

For MacDonald, a conviction, even though the penalty did not involve a fine, loss of privileges or time in segregation, was no laughing matter. Even minor charges are recorded on an inmate's file and can pose a stumbling block should the inmate be considered for a transfer to lesser security or when the inmate gets an opportunity to apply for parole.

A Challenge to the Disciplinary Charge

Allan MacDonald asked for my advice on how he could challenge this conviction. Unfortunately, I could not suggest anything that could be done immediately. Any challenge to the conviction would have to be processed through the internal grievance system. It was understood that before judicial review could be sought, MacDonald would have to be denied relief by grieving the fact of his conviction first at the institutional level, then to the regional level and finally to the national level and be denied a remedy at each stage. The process is time consuming and at every level it is correctional authorities that must rule upon the propriety of the actions of one of their own.

MacDonald grieved to the higher level after being denied relief and eventually all three levels of the grievance procedure system had been exhausted. We were then allowed to apply to the Federal Court to have the conviction of the disciplinary offence reviewed. It was argued that MacDonald had not been given the opportunity to defend himself and that it was not up to him to ensure that the officer who laid the charge was present at the hearing and be subject to cross-examination.

On July 31, 2007, the judgment of the Federal Court was handed down. The judge held that, "in the circumstances of this case, there was no onus on the Applicant to list the Charging Officer [as a witness]."

The application for judicial review was allowed. But the judge went further. She not only quashed the conviction, but ordered that the matter not be retried using correct principles and also ordered that all records pertaining to the conviction be removed from the prison files. Further it was ordered that Canada pay $2,500 for MacDonald's costs.

Who's laughing now? It is one thing for the Correctional Service of Canada's personnel to be found wanting but the financial sting of having to pay for the error was a swipe of the bear paw that cut deeply.

Fighting the System

MacDonald remained at Joyceville from January 2001 to January 2005. A reduction in his security level allowed MacDonald to once again be considered for transfer to Fenbrook Institution. Relatives and friends would be much likelier to drive 100 km. from Penetanguishene to Gravenhurst where Fenbrook is located that make the 400-km. trek to Joyceville.

The transfer to Fenbrook did not go well. The Fenbrook Institution Warden had taken calls from the widow of the slain officer and from the Canadian Police Association that opposed MacDonald's being at Fenbrook. The warden also knew that when MacDonald was originally 'pen placed', the inmate held the designation as a High Profile Offender because of media and community interest in his case. It is much more convenient for penal institutions to be ignored by the surrounding community than to attract attention.

The Correctional Service of Canada decided it would be much less controversial to bend to public pressure and return MacDonald to Joyceville by way of an involuntary transfer—a transfer to which the inmate does not agree.

On January 12, 2006, Allan MacDonald was served a Notice of Involuntary Transfer. There had been no change in MacDonald's correctional plan and he met the criteria for placement at Fenbrook. At the root of the decision was an attempt to bend to the views of the Canadian Police Association hoping to make MacDonald's stay in prison as uncomfortable as possible. The wolves were now assembled in a pack.

Yet almost six months after the earlier Federal Court judgment that struck the disciplinary offence, on January 7, 2008 the Federal Court once again ruled in MacDonald's favour. Justice Orville Frenette concluded that the Correctional Service of Canada "has not demonstrated any basis from which the Warden could have drawn the conclusion that Mr. MacDonald should have been transferred. The sole factor to which he refers in the Notice of Involuntary Transfer does not have any support in law or policy." He ordered the involuntary transfer to Joyceville Institution annulled. The court also awarded MacDonald $4,000 in costs.

This judgment outraged MacDonald's opponents. If the figurative pack of wolves was made up of victims and police, the pack now expanded to include a much more vicious addition —public outrage.

The tool used to create public unrest was the populist media. The incentive to kindle the fires of outrage was the cost awards the court had ordered paid from the public purse.

Press Reaction

A March 16, 2008 headline in the *Toronto Sun* read as follows: "Cop-killer Allan MacDonald's efforts to line up a cushier life in prison grate tens of thousands of people the wrong way." The news article suggests it was the newspaper's involvement that caused Fenbrook to deny MacDonald a place to serve time after spending only a few months at Millhaven Institution's maximum-security assessment unit before he sought transfer to medium-security Fenbrook. The perception that medium-security Fenbrook was 'cushier' than Joyceville was based on Fenbrook's location in the Muskoka area, often referred to as Ontario's cottage country (although inmates do not get to enjoy the amenities). The article fails to advise readers that at the time, Joyceville was also a medium-security institution, one with a prison farm that allowed suitable prisoners to work outdoors tending crops and farm animals. The article cites the opposition by the 31,000 members of the Police Association of Ontario and the people who had signed the Association's on-line petition.

The newspaper never suggested to its readers that the Correctional Service acted against the law and was called out by the courts for not upholding the rule of law as required of all government actors. Further no mention was made that whenever a suit is launched in court, an order of payment of costs is made against the unsuccessful party. Rather, the impression left to enrage readers was that institutions were being forced to be 'soft on crime' and to squander tax money by paying out enormous sums to the most undeserving. Demands for changes to the law flowed into Ottawa.

The Aftermath

Once a person is sentenced to imprisonment, a correctional plan is devised. The object of such an exercise is to determine what factors led the person to offend in the first place. It may be psychiatric problems, lack of education, poor job skills—you name it—in order to treat someone, the underlying problem must be understood.

Once the criminogenic needs are analyzed, a prisoner can be sent to an institution most adept at dealing with the deficiency. Various institutions offer various programs. Except in minimum-security prisons, there are walls or fences to separate the offender from the rest of society.

We tend to believe that protest can resolve legal issues. However legitimate it may seem to believe that a personal stance should guide government action, in the end, unless there is compliance with the law and acceptance of court orders, protest devolves into vigilante behaviour. That is anathema to the rule of law.

Yet the demand of the howling wolves was far too great for government to ignore. To prove that it was willing to get tough on crime, the Harper Conservative government changed the rules to make it mandatory that anyone convicted of murder should spend a minimum of two years in maximum security. There is no rationale that keeping a person locked away in a maximum-security institution will enhance public safety or indeed address any of the criminogenic deficiencies that caused the individual to break the law. But it keeps the wolves from howling.

TWENTY-FIVE

DAVID BAGSHAW

KIDS WHO KILL KIDS

■■■

WHEN PARENTS ARE FORCED to bury their own child, it seems to go against the very order of the natural world. While a child's death is sometimes inevitable such as in cases of fatal illness, tragic accidents, or natural disasters, there is perhaps a greater degree of heartache when the loss was preventable. Consider the heartache that a parent must endure when a mother or father hears that the reason for a child's death is premeditated murder.

Stefanie Rengel was a talented 14-year-old enjoying the winter holiday break from Rosedale High School of the Arts. She enjoyed spending time with her family, who lived together in a two-storey house in Parkview Hills (a quiet neighbourhood in the Toronto's East York district). At home was Stefanie's stepfather James Hung, her mother Patricia Hung, and Stefanie's three brothers, Ian (age 12), Eric (age 4) and Patrick (age 2).

Stefanie's mom, Patricia had split from her first husband and began dating James Hung in the year 2000. Patricia and James were both law enforcement officers with the Toronto Police Service. The whole family had adapted well together despite the marital breakup.

The only big drama in Stefanie's life concerned her breakup with boyfriend Steve Lopez, whom she had dated casually and only briefly. Before Steve, there was David Bagshaw, whom she had also dated only briefly.

By all accounts, Stefanie was a happy teen. She sometimes dyed her hair unusual colours and wore eye-catching clothes. She was very talented. During the 2007 Christmas vacation, the family had rented a karaoke machine that allowed Stefanie to belt out Avril Lavigne's "Slipped Away" with much gusto.

The whole family stayed up late on New Year's Eve, every family member wearing a smile as the clock ticked closer to 2008. The future seemed bright for Stefanie and her brothers.

Stefanie Rengel's Last Words

According to published reports, things were normal at home. New Year's Day started out like any other day. It was cold and snowy in Parkview Hills, but that did not prevent Stefanie from spending the afternoon at a friend's house and returning home for dinner. "A few Doritos won't wreck my appetite," she thought while brother Ian gobbled down a grilled cheese sandwich. Then her cell phone rang.

Stefanie wondered who would be so inconsiderate to call at a traditional mealtime, but no name came up on her phone. She immediately deduced that it must be her ex-boyfriend, Steve.

"Is that you?" she demanded. The voice on the other end of the phone was upset. "Meet me," the male caller pleaded and then repeated, "Meet me." Stefanie ended the call and put on her boots. "I'll be right back," she said to her brother as she dashed through the door without a coat. She wore a black sweater that her mother had gifted her for Christmas.

Suddenly a male figure emerged from the bushes that grew on a street median. Stefanie looked up as the man raced towards her, too alarmed to notice that he was carrying an eight-inch kitchen knife.

Stefanie suffered a total of six stab wounds. One stab punctured her left breast, carried through the chest cavity, and hit the inside of her back. Other slashes perforated her right lung and sliced her liver. A blow to her stomach caused its contents to drain into her peritoneal cavity. Stefanie collapsed on the snow.

A few minutes later, a 34-year-old accountant named Gavin Shoebottom drove by to find Stefanie lying in agony on the side of the road. He was aghast at the severity of the wounds. "Hold your stomach," he yelled, racing back to his car to get a blanket and call 911. The 911 operator advised Shoebottom to put pressure on the wounds and assured him that an ambulance was on its way.

"It hurts," Stefanie whispered, thankful for the assistance she was receiving.

"Who did this to you?" Shoebottom asked.

Stefanie found it difficult to speak. Her organs were shutting down. "Bags...went that way," were her words as she pointed up the street, indicating the direction in which her attacker had fled.

"Come on, sweetie, you're okay." Shoebottom told her, wondering to himself how much longer it would be before the ambulance arrived. Paramedics finally arrived, loading Stefanie into an ambulance and rushing her to the Toronto East General Hospital. There, she was pronounced dead. News reports would label her "Toronto's first homicide of 2008."

Melissa Todorivic

Melissa Todorovic was in many ways the antithesis of Stefanie Rengal. Both lived in Toronto's east end and were about the same age, but Melissa was full of self-doubt about her looks and body image and doubted that she could ever find love. Where Stefanie could be counted on to have a houseful of friends on occasion, Melissa found it difficult to form friendships. Melissa was smart but worked hard to maintain her reputation as a straight-A student. She hated the fact that she wore glasses and braces and went through bouts of bulimia after becoming convinced that she was too fat. She was not content with her curly hair either and would spend lots of time with a straightening iron trying to enhance her appearance. Most of all, she needed a boyfriend to validate herself.

Melissa had had boyfriends in the past, but the breakups came hard. She once cut herself after losing a boyfriend. One previous relationship referred to her as a 'Klingon'—not the *Star Trek* alien, but the type of person who would always try to 'cling on' to a relationship. She would monitor boyfriends' e-mails and threaten them with physical harm should they make a break with her.

David Bagshaw

David Bagshaw had no idea of the person he was involving himself with when he began dating Melissa. He appreciated her in part because she was smart. David was not much of a scholar, himself being diagnosed with ADHD and pre-scribed Ritalin since the age of three to calm his behavior. In school, he often acted out and was frequently reprimanded for aggressive behaviour. He was often absent and was pun-ished for swearing and fighting with other students when he did attend. From time to time he would even strike Melissa, who resented that David was sometimes unfaithful with her.

Most of all, David appreciated Melissa for the sex, which was consensual between them. When David was dating Stefanie Rengel, there was an absence of sexual intimacy. Indeed, what ended the relationship was an email David sent Stefanie requesting oral sex. Stefanie's mother main-tained tight control over Stefanie's internet contacts and ordered Stephanie to say goodbye to David once and for all after seeing the offensive message.

David's home life had also been problematic. His par-ents, Ronald and Cindy Bagshaw, were separated. When David was 14, he struck his mother, who reported the inci-dent to police. While the charges were dropped, David agreed to enroll in an anger management class. Living part time with either parent was not going so smoothly for David during this time, and at age 15 he lived in a group home for three months.

Ronald Bagshaw was not fond of Melissa; he found her suspiciously controlling. She was barred from visiting David at the father's house, but Melissa was so possessive of her new boyfriend that she installed spyware on his computer to track his communications.

Then there were the rumours. Bagshaw had made an off-hand comment on one occasion that he thought his former girlfriend, Stefanie, was pretty. Melissa became obsessive about Stefanie as a result, scouring Facebook to scrutinize pictures of her imagined rival. The subsequent hearsay didn't help either. Melissa's cousin repeated that Stefanie had reportedly said that David Bagshaw was 'bad news', and that he had supposedly been flirting with other girls behind Melissa's back.

Even Melissa's parents urged her to break off her association with David. Instead of dumping David, Melissa stepped up her motivation to hold onto the relationship. "Who's going to look at somebody with braces and glasses when there are so many pretty girls in high school?" Melissa asked her mother.

Competition Ramps Up

Melissa started to consider that perhaps the best way of competing with Stefanie would be to eliminate the competition. The idea was put into writing as early as May 22, 2007 when Melissa accused David of trying to rekindle his relationship with Stefanie. During an online chat session, Melissa became enraged that David was cheating on her.

"I'm going to fucking stab her if I want to," Melissa texted to David. "Then I'll just kill her."

The next day, David jokingly offered to provide Melissa with a knife. Melissa responded that she already had one. ("I even brought it to school today LOL" was Melissa's exact response.) Melissa's jealousy was so deep that she began to fantasize maybe her brother could rape Stefanie, or perhaps David and Melissa could abduct her imaginary rival to a place where Melissa could torment her before killing her.

Talk of what Melissa believed would be Stefanie's just desserts occupied more and more time as David and Melissa conversed. Melissa even related to David a dream in which she "took a knife and cut off Stefanie's boobs" before slitting lengthwise through her torso and throwing her mutilated body from a balcony.

In the fall of 2007, Stefanie started grade 9 at Rosedale Heights School of the Arts on Toronto's Bloor Street East. She liked the new school, quickly making many new friends and forgetting about David completely.

Melissa wanted Stefanie dead, but figured that David could atone for his errant behaviour by doing the deed himself—with Melissa directing, of course.

A First Threat

On the evening of October 20, 2007, David Bagshaw walked to Stefanie Rengel's home and phoned her from the driveway. He asked Stefanie to come out to speak with him, a request Stefanie accommodated and exited the house. He let his cell phone drop to the ground.

Her mood was as chilly as the night air. She demanded to know what David wanted, but David could not take the actions Melissa had directed.

"Melissa wants me to stab you," David confessed. "When she calls, tell her I tried so that she'll stop pestering me to kill you." David left.

Stefanie was angry and indignant. She picked up David's cell phone, went back in the house, and described the incident to her mother, Patricia.

Patricia phoned Melissa to try to resolve the situation. She tried to reassure Melissa that Stefanie was not attempting to mock her and that the comment about David having a roving eye was intended to protect Melissa from any potential heartache.

Melissa did not accept the apology, and in fact became so hostile and indignant with Patricia that Patricia threatened to get a restraining order. Ultimately chalking the whole event as teenage melodrama, Patricia did not involve the police.

Melissa and David continued to message one another.

"What about Stef?" David asked.

"Bang, bang," Melissa replied.

"I need a bang first," David texted, hoping to lighten the mood. "I wanna bang you."

"I want her dead, David LOL. We've been through this. Even if it takes you a week."

By December, the talk centred on getting a gun. Melissa demanded that David take whatever steps needed to be taken to find a revolver.

"I need a mask and gloves," David protested, fearing that Stefanie's parents would recognize him.

"Cut fucking leotards," Melissa replied dismissively, unimpressed by David's tepid objection.

It was only when Melissa threatened to curtail all sexual activity with David that he agreed to try again.

New Years Eve

It was supposed to happen New Years Eve. Stefanie was inside the house partying with her family and taking turns singing karaoke, while David lurked in the backyard. He was spotted by a neighbour and suspected of being a prowler, but no report was made. Melissa was kept in the loop; David and Melissa called or texted 65 times during the evening, with Stefanie never leaving the house. David gave up and went home.

Melissa was outraged by David's lack of success. She refused to pick up his calls or respond to his texts.

David continued his texting: "where are u," "ur cheating", and "why won't you answer me." By 3 p.m., Melissa felt she was once again in control. She called David and the two spoke for a quarter of an hour. She reminded David that unless he developed more of a backbone than she had seen until now, she would "go on top" with another guy.

The blackmail worked. By 5:51 pm, David called Melissa to tell her that he was on his way to Stefanie's house with a knife. The two kept in telephone contact while David secreted himself away in bushes close to Stefanie's house. At 6:08 pm, David made the fateful call to Stefanie. Stefanie walked outside.

"I see her," David said to Melissa before ending the call.

Melissa called Stefanie's number fifteen minutes later and was satisfied that the call went to voicemail. She assumed the murder had been completed.

David buried the knife and his bloodstained coat under the snow in a nearby friend's yard. He then verified the kill to Melissa.

"I love u hunny," Melissa texted. "I can't wait to see you." Melissa suggested that David take a taxi to her house to collect his reward. Once there, Melissa demanded that David act out the slaying. Then they had sex.

Not Much of a Whodunnit

Word got out that Stefanie had been slain. A friend of Melissa's texted her that Stefanie was gone and asked Melissa if she was concerned that police would regard her as a suspect. "Who knows I wanted her dead?" Melissa replied. "Cuz I only told u and David so unless u told someone, only u should. But I never did anything and neither did David. We fucked tonight. LOL."

It didn't turn out to be much of a whodunnit. By 7:15 pm., Det. Sgt. Steve Ryan of Toronto Metro Police was interviewing Stefanie's parents and brothers along with several of David's friends. The bizarre relationship between David and Melissa took shape, and a search warrant was granted that authorized the seizure and examination of computers belonging to Stefanie, David, and Melissa for forensic investigation.

Melissa, accompanied by her mother, was brought in for questioning at 54 Division. Melissa remained calm and collected despite the nature of the interview. She declined the right to speak to a lawyer. It was late in the interview when Melissa casually admitted that she had asked David to kill Stefanie. At that point the interview ceased.

Melissa and her mother were present as her rights were read to her and she was charged with first-degree murder. When she was re-interviewed the following day, she admitted that killing Stefanie was more her idea than David's. The only time tears came to her eyes was when she admitted that she had told David that she wanted Stefanie dead and that she might break up with him if he didn't kill her.

Melissa maintained her composure throughout a three-week trial. Her lawyer was noted criminal trial lawyer Marshall Sack, an experienced sole practitioner often involved in high-profile murder trials. His silver hair, brushed back into a ponytail, contrasted with his black barrister robes. The Rengel murder case would be listed as one of his major cases when he died in 2011.

The defence theory that Sack put forward was that Melissa had no real intention of killing Stefanie. Indeed, she was not present at the murder scene. The theory, however, was shaken by the introduction of over 30,000 pages of instant messaging transcripts and her admissions upon arrest. Nonetheless, it took twenty hours of deliberation over three days for the jury to return a guilty verdict.

At her sentencing hearing, Dr. Phil Klassen, a forensic psychiatrist and deputy clinical director at the Centre for Addiction and Mental Health, testified that his examination of Melissa indicated symptoms of borderline personality disorder. To make things abundantly clear to the jury, Dr. Klassen suggested that her mental state was much like the Glenn Close character in the movie *Fatal Attraction*.

Before sentencing, Melissa read a prepared statement without making eye contact with Stefanie's family. "Every day I wish that I could go back in time and change everything I said, and have Stefanie be alive with her family again…I want you to know I take full responsibility for my part."

Puppet and Puppet Master

The Crown attorney moved to have Melissa sentenced as an adult rather than as a youth. Despite being only 15 years old when the crime was committed, she was declared to be a continuing threat to society without much-needed psychiatric intervention and lifelong monitoring.

The prosecution wanted Melissa sentenced as an adult. The Crown's move was of great significance. If sentenced as a youth, the maximum sentence would be six years, with four of those years being served in the community and no supervision at the expiry of the sentence. Best of all, no criminal record. The Crown's application was successful. Justice Ian Nordheimer found that Melissa didn't acknowledge an "unequivocal acceptance of responsibility for the crucial role she played in the death of Stefanie Rengel." The sentence imposed was life in prison with no chance of parole for seven years. She would be under state supervision for the rest of her natural life, even if released, she could be returned to prison for violations of the conditions of her parole.

"The puppet master is not less blameworthy than the puppet," Justice Nordheimer stated. "Indeed, I would suggest that the master is more culpable since he or she puts the wheels in motion and stands back under a façade of dissociation while the scheme that they have created unfold."

Those words must have cheered Heather McArthur, who represented David Bagshaw. McArthur was a brilliant Toronto lawyer who was later appointed as an Ontario Superior Court Judge. The Crown also applied to sentence Bagshaw as an adult; he was four days shy of his eighteenth birthday when the stabbing occurred. As the 'puppet.' to use Nordheimer's terminology, it would be expected that Melissa would be found more blameworthy, thus giving David a lesser sentence. Further, David pleaded guilty to the crime, which often serves as a mitigating factor in sentencing.

Such was not the case. Although Justice Nordheimer accepted David's remorse and expression of empathy, the Judge concluded that even though David was the "more reluctant of the two partners in this evil endeavour," he could have, and should have, ended his relationship with Melissa and alerted authorities of the planned killing. Two psychiatrists attended at the sentencing hearing, neither of them concluding that David would not reoffend. On September 28, 2009, David was sentenced to life in prison with no parole eligibility for 10 years.

David Bagshaw was taken from the courtroom and subsequently held at the maximum-security Sprucedale Youth Centre, located in Simcoe (about 90 minutes west of Toronto). Sprucedale is the highest level of closed detention for youth in Ontario, and houses some of the most violent youthful offenders in Ontario. The facility is clean and well-run and differs from a standard maximum-security penitentiary in that it offers programs and opportunities. For some who see punishment as the main goal, this attempt to provide rehabilitation seems abhorrent. There is an indoor pool, a gym, weight room, shared kitchens, and video games. The young offenders are allowed late nights on weekends and are permitted to order fast-food deliveries from KFC and McDonald's.

Apart from regular social activities, the young men held at Sprucedale receive schooling and programming designed to rehabilitate their errant ways. David was doing particularly well at Sprucedale.

Then he turned 21. On his birthday, January 5, 2011, he was forced to vacate Sprucedale, as he was no longer eligible to be held and treated in a provincial facility. Next stop: Millhaven maximum-security institution near Kingston, Ontario. Millhaven houses some of Canada's most notorious criminals, including its J Unit that confines the worst of the worst. The

Millhaven Assessment Unit was being used as a centre where the inmate would be interviewed to make a final decision on the degree of supervision and treatment requirements necessary. Inmates would then be sent to a prison that matched the security level and treatment opportunities available.

The Stephen Harper Conservative government, holding firm on its 'tough on crime' stance, altered the Commissioner's Directive (the rules by which Canada's prisons are run) to include a provision that required all persons convicted of murder to spend their first two years in maximum-security.

Request for an Override

David Bagshaw contacted my office before leaving for Millhaven. He was fearful of what awaited him there and seemed extremely anxious that he would be placed at Millhaven fulltime. Upon receiving the call, I looked up the *Commissioner's Directive* (CD) setting out the two-year maximum-security rule and found that the same CD provided that in certain cases —in the discretion of the Assistant Commissioner responsible for correctional operations and programs—an override could be granted.

On December 10, 2010, I wrote to the Assistant Commissioner, Chris Price asking that he grant an override and allow Bagshaw to be considered for placement in an institution other than Millhaven. The core of my argument was that two years in maximum was unnecessary, since Bagshaw had already spent almost three years in maximum-security Sprucedale. Further, it would not be in the interests of public safety to nullify the gains he had made in his rehabilitation while at Sprucedale. I included a comment in my letter that Bagshaw "remains immature emotionally despite his chronological age. Placement at a maximum-security institution would be disruptive of the gains he has made at Sprucedale."

The Assistant Commissioner responded by letter dated January 5, 2011, advising that he would leave any decision concerning an override with the Millhaven Assessment Unit. He advised that my letter would be forwarded to the Millhaven Assessment Unit for consideration in the penitentiary placement process.

An intake officer at Millhaven is required to complete a Custody Rating Scale. The CRS, as it is known, awards points for numerous risk factors. The problem, however, is that the points system makes it impossible for a person who has committed murder to obtain a score any lower than that which would specify maximum security.

It seemed to me that by looking solely to the CRS for penitentiary placement, the power that authorized the Assistant Commissioner to allow an override was meaningless.

Placement was made at Millhaven on January 20, 2011. I wrote a second letter to the Assistant Commissioner on January 25, repeating my concerns that Bagshaw was emotionally immature and could be susceptible to bullying by more hardened inmates, thus putting his health and safety at risk. No response was received from the Correctional Service. On February 8, 2011, I again wrote to the Assistant Commissioner, this time requesting reasons for the Assistant Commissioner's refusal to use the override. These are decisions that, if wrongly made, that can be challenged in Federal Court. The letter obviously put the administration on notice that there was the possibility of judicial review in the Federal Court.

On February 10, 2011, I received a fax from Senior Deputy Commissioner Marc-Arthur Hyppolite that deferred all authority for decision-making to the Warden. It read as though it was a template answer to queries on pen placement.

> In keeping with Commissioner's Directive (CD) 705-7–
> Security Classification and Penitentiary Placement, the
> decision-making authority for offender security classifi-
> cation and placement remains with the Warden. As such,
> I am forwarding copies of your correspondence and my

replies to the appropriate Warden for consideration in further decision-making. I would in addition, point out that the institution is to provide the offender with the reasons for the proposed placement in writing two days prior to the final decision; then, the offender has an opportunity to provide a rebuttal which is to be considered by the decision-maker. As well, if an offender disagrees with the final decision, he or she can appeal the decision using the grievance process.

With no decision taken by the designated Assistant Commissioner on the override provision, a decision was taken not only to place Bagshaw in maximum-security Millhaven Institution but, worse yet, to hold him in the notorious 'J Unit', where he would be at the mercy of hardcore criminals.

In filing a notice of Judicial Review in the Federal Court I felt certain that I had at least two substantial grounds on which to attack the process that was used: first I could argue the fairness and reasonableness of the decision, and then I could challenge the process used being a violation of the doctrine of *delegatus non potest delegare,* the Latin term meaning that when the law states a particular individual is to make a decision, that individual cannot delegate the decision-making authority to another.

Sometimes legal arguments get overtaken by facts. As I feared, Bagshaw was bullied by inmates in J Unit, even though he had the build of an NFL linebacker. On March 20, 2011, a group of J Unit inmates decided to attack one of their numbers, 34-year-old Steven McDonald. Bagshaw had no idea what the confrontation was about but was bullied into participation. As guards approached to quell the disturbance, a homemade knife (or "shiv" as it is called inside) was shoved into Bagshaw's hands so that he would be forced into taking the rap for the outburst.

However, the guards took the confrontation to be more serious than it was. Armed with AR-15 rifles, the guards let loose with two shots. One bullet struck 29-year-old Jordan Trudeau in the chest, killing him. The second shot hit and wounded Bagshaw, causing non-life-threatening injuries. Bagshaw was transported to hospital, treated, and returned to Millhaven.

A press release issued by the Joint Forces Penitentiary Squad detailed that an altercation had taken place but that the prison guards had not done anything wrong and did not use excessive force in quelling the outburst.

CBC reported on April 7, 2011 that Bagshaw was charged with attempted murder of an inmate at Millhaven Institution. The Regulations to the Corrections and Conditional Release Act provide that 'outstanding charges' can also be considered in assessing an inmate's security level. It thus came as no surprise that Mr. Justice Near of the Federal Court dismissed my Judicial Review application. However, he was highly critical of the Correctional Service in determining when the override provision could be used.

Once the Court's decision came down, there were two repercussions: Firstly, the case drew national attention for challenging the Harper tough on crime policy, and secondly, it reactivated interest in the Rengel killing.

Reawakening the Stefanie Rengel Murder

The reawakening of the Stefanie Rengel killing drew international attention. I received a call from a production company advising that NBC was preparing a documentary on four different cases on "kids who kill." My cooperation was requested in on-camera interview for use in the show.

I attended Millhaven to be sure that David would consent to my talking about his case on American television. He said he had no problems with my speaking about any aspects of his crime. Indeed, he filled me in on several details of which I was unaware when I had taken on his case.

I travelled to Los Angeles and underwent a lengthy interview in a high-rise studio on Wilshire Boulevard. I could tell by the questions asked that the documentary would concentrate on the gorier aspects of the slaying rather than on the psychological motivations of the perpetrators.

The *Toronto Star* also found out about the decision of an American network to dredge up details of the killing of the cop's daughter. Understandably, Stefanie's family were opposed to re-opening the emotional wounds they had suffered. The newspaper was taking the position that the NBC report would be exploitive and sensational. It came as no surprise when I learned that NBC had relented and decided to drop the Bagshaw/Todorovic segment of their production.

Manipulation and Unwillingness to Abide by Rules

As of 2022, David Bagshaw remains in prison. Melissa Todorovic was released on day parole, which is granted by the Parole Board when it believes an offender is unlikely to reoffend and can rejoin the community. She lived for some time at a halfway house under the supervision of a community parole officer. Grants of day parole come with conditions, the foremost being to keep the peace and to be of good behaviour. This condition includes being open and transparent with one's parole officer. Other usual conditions include not associating with persons an offender knows (or ought to know) has a criminal record. For people like Melissa, it is not unusual to find a condition that she not involve herself romantically with anyone not approved by her parole officer.

Nothing seemed out of place when Melissa left her halfway house. She never mentioned to her parole officer that she was meeting with a guy named Kirk. It only came to light when Kirk mentioned to his probation officer—yes, Kirk has a criminal record—that he was dating Melissa Todorovic. The name rang a bell with the probation officer, who recalled that Melissa had served time for the Rengel killing. Melissa's parole officer was notified, and a search of her room at the halfway house uncovered a Valentine's Day card that Kirk had given her. A note inside the card contained Kirk's apology for not satisfying Melissa and not treating her well.

Melissa claimed she was dissatisfied with Kirk's sexual prowess, setting her sights on Kirk's best friend, Dennis. Once her dishonesty and lack of transparency were found out, the day parole was suspended in March 2019 and Melissa, now 26 years old, was returned to the Grand Valley Institution for Women in Kitchener to await a decision of the Parole Board of Canada on whether to cancel the suspension and re-release her to a halfway house, or to revoke her parole and return her to prison.

Melissa hoped for the former. Having lost the support of the halfway house where she was staying, Melissa proposed that she be reinstated in her day parole and required to stay in a halfway house in Kingston.

A post-suspension hearing was held in the board room at Grand Valley Institution in August 2019. The presenting parole officer commented to the Board that Melissa secretly involved herself with not one, but two men and was "manipulating them against one another." This was said to represent Melissa's unwillingness to abide by rules, and a strong hint that she could return to her criminal ways.

Melissa was teary-eyed throughout the hearing. She admitted to dating two people without the knowledge or approval of her parole supervisor. "I knew it was wrong," she admitted. "I didn't have people to talk to. I liked people complimenting me and giving me attention and I didn't want that to end."

Melissa was asked to leave the room while the Board came to a decision. When called back into the hearing, she sat without emotion as the Board delivered its decision to revoke parole.

Two teens who plotted and killed another teen will likely remain imprisoned well into their adulthood.

The murder of Stephany Rengel was horrific and needless. There was and should be sympathy for the family of the victim.

All too often, however, we confuse our emotion to render a sympathetic response with the emotion of inflicting vengeance on the perpetrator of the violence. This is where our correctional system breaks down. Once a person is arrested and convicted of a crime, however monstrous, that person should be treated in accordance with law. But those laws should not be vengeful.

We have seen in the Allan MacDonald case that forced maximum security for at least two years after a murder conviction was brought about by a desire for public vengeance. It is often said that "hard cases make bad law." The Bagshaw case is a case in point. He was rightly convicted of his crime but the gains made in his years in a youth facility were washed away in the mandatory two years at a maximum-security penitentiary. He could have benefitted by continued rehabilitative programming that he received when first incarcerated. Melissa Todorivic did not seem to benefit from her stay in prison and was properly returned. Not everyone can be rehabilitated but, at least for public safety, our institutions should not impede the process.

TWENTY-SIX

INDERJIT SINGH REYAT

AIR INDIA: TERRORIST OR VICTIM?

■ ■ ■

H E SPENT HIS FIRST 30 YEARS building a lifestyle that most Canadians would consider successful. Born in India, Inderjit Singh Reyat emigrated first to the United Kingdom and then to Canada, training and eventually finding work as an electrician in British Columbia. He bought a home for his wife and family. He then spent the next 30 years mostly in prison, trying to hold on to what he had achieved.

No one could guess that the mild-mannered, gentleman wearing a turban could be considered violent. Reyat was polite and charming as I recall from our first meeting before I assisted him at a parole hearing in 2005.

The Explosions
The morning in the seaside village of Ahakista, County Cork, Ireland started peacefully on June 23, 1985. At exactly 8:12 a loud noise broke the morning's tranquility. Air India Flight 182, a Boeing 747 that had taken off from Toronto flying to London en route to Delhi was blown from the sky. All 329 passengers and crew were killed. Only 131 bodies were recovered from the ocean. Most of the dead were Canadians, many from Toronto.

At about the same time, an explosion at Tokyo's Narita Airport killed two baggage handlers who were unloading cargo from another Air India passenger jet, bound for Bangkok.

Terrorism was not on most people's minds before September 11, 2001. The disasters over Ireland and in Japan were separate and took place long before the notion of terrorism became ingrained as a fact of life in North American minds. Yet, it is a little-known fact that Canada's security agencies, the Royal Canadian Mounted Police (RCMP), Canada's national police force and the Canadian Security Intelligence Service (CSIS), the country's national security system, had foreknowledge of the tragedy.

Sikh extremism had its roots in India and was largely unknown in North America in the latter part of the 20th century. Sikh immigrants to Canada began arriving in the early 1900s, and were welcomed as law abiding.

However, in India, the British Raj was dispersed from India in 1947, and the independent state of Pakistan was formed as a result. Sikh leaders were pressing for similar treatment and wanted to form a separate Sikh state (to be called Khalistan). Several Sikh radicals continued the movement and collected weapons, establishing a base in the Golden Temple—often referred to as the 'Sikh Vatican', in Amritsar, Punjab, 28 km. from the Indian border with Pakistan.

By June 1984, Prime Minister Indira Gandhi decided it was time to subdue the discontent. She launched Operation Blue Star and attacked the Sikh separatists. About one thousand Sikhs were killed and portions of the Temple were destroyed.

The militant Sikhs sought revenge. In October of that year, Indira Gandhi was assassinated by her Sikh bodyguards, which touched off widespread rioting in which more than two thousand people were killed.

Canada's Sikh Community

There was also discontent within Canada's Sikh community. As it would later be shown, the national security provided by the Royal Canadian Mounted Police and the newly formed

Canadian Security Intelligence Service (CSIS) were not working in sync.

Canadian security forces focused on Talwinder Singh Parmar. Parmar resided in his British Columbia mansion, passing himself off as a humble sawmill worker and a persecuted "simple Sikh preacher," as he described himself. Parmar was suspected of commanding a small army of assassins holed up in a heavily fortified four-storey bunker inside the Golden Temple Complex in Amritsar, Punjab, India.

There was a history of violence against fellow Sikhs who would not do the bidding of Parmar. Sukhdev Singh admitted to carrying out more than forty killings on Parmar's direct orders. The dead included insufficiently observant Sikhs, poets, Hindu-Sikh peace activists, left-wing intellectuals and innocent Hindu shopkeepers.

Even after the Air India bombing, the extremist reign of terror continued. A reporter, Tara Singh Hayer, was shot and crippled in Surrey, BC. In 1998, he was assassinated. Hayer had agreed to be a Crown witness and testify against others involved in the Air India bombing. To date, no one has been arrested for his killing. The determination of the extremists and the intemperance of their methods is more reminiscent of traditional organized crime groups than religious activists.

Reaching Out to Reyat

It was against this backdrop that Parmar reached out to Inderjit Singh Reyat. Reyat was a devout Sikh, born in India in 1952, who came to Canada in 1974 after living and working in England for six years and obtaining British citizenship. Reyat had immigrated to Canada from England along with his wife and four children. He was a trained electrician and worked for Auto Marine Electric Ltd., a company on Vancouver Island. When not at work, Reyat was the clerk of works at the Sikh temple in Duncan, British Columbia. He was devoutly religious, and no doubt perplexed by the attack on Sikhs in his native India. Most of all, he was devoted to his wife and kids.

In 1985, Reyat met with Parmar. Reyat was honest in his admission of faith to the Sikh religion, and was disappointed with how his fellow Sikhs were being treated in India. Parmar became satisfied that Reyat was sufficiently observant and made an unusual request of Reyat. Parmar wanted Reyat to obtain dynamite and an ignition device. Reyat knew instantly that the need for such material was to construct an explosive device—and he knew that he could not say no to Parmar. Reyat knew instinctively that showing ambivalence or empathy for anyone Parmar despised would incur Parmar's wrath. It wasn't just his own life at stake, but much more pressing for Reyat was that a refusal could jeopardize his wife and family's safety. Nonetheless, Reyat realized the damage that could come from such an explosion. He took it upon himself to ask Parmar if his intention was to cause death to any person. Parmar simply laughed off the suggestion, assuring Reyat that the intention was simply to create an act of civil disobedience that could magnify the Sikh separatist cause in India by "destroying something big" like a bridge or a rail line. Reyat's skill as an electrician was surely the reason he was being enlisted.

Reyat had qualms about what he was being asked to do. Going to police about the meeting was unthinkable. No explicit threats were made but—as with organized crime—much is left unsaid. He would comply with the request.

Reyat went to businessman Ken Slade, owner of Drillwell Enterprises, with some trepidation. As an employee of Auto Marine Electric, Reyat saw Slade about three times a week to do work on Drillwell's fleet. Slade had sympathy for minority groups. Slade and Reyat bonded as friends.

I believe that Reyat resented that he had to use this connection to meet Parmar's expectations. Yet, although my client never told me this, Reyat appreciated that a failure to comply might mean his own death, or harm to his wife and children. Distasteful as it was to betray his friend Slade, it had to be done.

After being assured that Reyat knew how to use dynamite, Slade gave Reyat a few sticks. Trading dynamite with local loggers was not uncommon for Slade, but Reyat's request seemed unusual. However, the bond that developed between the two men satisfied Slade that Reyat's intentions were honourable.

CSIS wanted to follow Parmar. A counter-terrorist investigator, Ray Kobzey, later told a public inquiry that investigators on the ground had a difficult time convincing their superiors that tailing Parmar would be fruitful. Kobzey testified that there was fierce competition for scarce resources. Those in authority believed agents should be deployed to seek out spies from the Soviet Union and Eastern European countries rather than wasting time on Parmar—despite the fact that internal documents labelled Parmar as "the most radical and potentially the most dangerous Sikh in the country."

Funding was granted for a single day of surveillance. Police watched as Reyat, Parmar, and another man, later identified during a Hamilton, Ontario prosecution as Surjit Singh walked into a wooded area on Vancouver Island on June 4, 1985. Police heard a loud noise that they suspected to have been the discharge of a gun. With this evidence obtained, the surveillance was continued until July 21, 1985, two days before the Air India bombing. Russian espionage was still deemed more critical at that point.

Murky Evidence

Here the evidence gets murky. At the time, police were adamant that no follow-up was taken, as they confused the sound of an explosion for that of a gunshot. But later, two RCMP officers told a British court that they heard a bang similar to the sound of the detonation of a blasting cap. They testified to examining the area and finding a stick of dynamite suspended less than a metre above the ground, plus two aluminum blasting cap shunts. It took three years for this information to finally become public.

The Air India and Narita Airport explosions happened on July 23, 1985. It was only then that police and CSIS linked the observation in the wooded area with the deadly attack on innocent civilians.

On November 6, 1985, 35-year-old Reyat was charged along with 41-year-old Parmar. Reyat was accused of an array of weapons and explosive charges as was Parmar. Both were granted bail. Reyat was later found guilty and a $2,000 fine was imposed. The judge did not find any connection between Reyat and the aircraft explosions.

With the legal hurdle out of the way, Inderjit Singh Reyat and his family returned to Coventry, England where he quickly found employment with his old employer. Talwinder Singh Parmar was discharged when the prosecutors admitted there was insufficient evidence to bring him to trial.

The Main Driving Forces
Although Parmar was discharged from his Vancouver Island weapons charges, he continued to experience legal difficulties and was arrested along with six other Sikhs on June 14, 1986 in Hamilton, Ontario, charged with conspiracy to commit terrorism in India.

Despite the fact that Parmar was an unemployed lathe operator, it was suggested that as head of the Babbar Khalsa (Lions of the True Faith) group, he was indeed the ring master in a savage terrorist organization.

Only later did Canadians learn that in the days leading up to the Air India disaster, police and CSIS had identified Parmar's main associates as the driving forces behind the bombing: Ajaib Singh Bagri and Ripudamen Singh Malik.

Police took particular interest in Ripudamen Singh Malik, believed to be the financier of the militant separatists. The problem surfaced that none of the investigative agencies were working together. CSIS believed the duty of an investigative agency was the collection of intelligence and not the collection of evidence, which they deemed was a police responsibility— or at least, that was the excuse offered when it was discovered that several wire-tapped conversations had been erased even after the bombing occurred. Nothing remained of extensive written summaries of the nature and content of the calls.

It was later discovered that someone had been deeply troubled with the potential use of explosives in Air India flights. A phone call warning of the bombings was received by Canada's Department of External Affairs. James Bartleman, then in charge of the intelligence and analysis branch of the department (later to become Lieutenant-Governor of the Province of Ontario), recounted how he had read an intelligence briefing days before the bombing.

"I saw in [a package of intelligence briefings] a document that indicated Air India was being targeted that weekend— specifically the weekend of the 22-23," Bartleman said. He was shocked by the reaction of a senior RCMP officer when Bartleman showed the officer the document.

"He flushed and told me that of course he'd seen it, and that he didn't need me to tell him how to do his job."

It was never discovered who was so worried as to come forward with the tip.

The accusations against Parmar were never proven, and in the end Parmar returned to India, where many believed the real justice was done. Parmar was arrested by Indian police, whose record says that he died in custody. Yet the assumption is that he was brutally tortured to reveal who was involved in the Air India disaster. He refused to give up names until the pain became too agonizing shortly before he died, and he gave up the name of the man at the bottom of the totem pole— Inderjit Singh Reyat, the man who knew the least about the disaster.

Families and Friends of the Victims

In Canada, the families and friends of the victims of the Air India bombing were outraged that there seemed little by way of police action to bring the perpetrators to justice. Once Parmar pointed the finger at Reyat, the Canadian government was under the gun to take action.

The Government of Canada advised British officials of the desire to extradite Reyat from the UK to face two charges of manslaughter and five counts of possessing explosives in connection with the Narita explosion. On February 5, 1988, as he was driving to work at the Jaguar plant, Reyat was arrested by Scotland Yard to face an extradition request from Canada.

Reyat's team in England was able to stall extradition for almost a year. In the interim, families and friends of the Air India bombing were both furious and frustrated. They demanded action. Reyat's defence team took every legal step imaginable to prevent Reyat's return to Canada, including an appeal to the House of Lords (the UK's highest court). But in a terse one-line endorsement in November 1989, the House of Lords dismissed the Reyat appeal without reasons and granted extradition to have Reyat tried in Canada on charges resulting from the Narita Airport bombing. Once extradition was granted, the Canadian public demanded action.

Reyat's flight from London touched down at Vancouver International Airport on December 13, 1988. Tight security surrounded Reyat as he was whisked away for a brief appearance in British Columbia Supreme Court and the start of a marathon trial in Vancouver.

The 62-day trial with more than ninety witnesses and four hundred exhibits was largely circumstantial. Forensic scientists and police testified that Reyat had purchased or had access to items similar to nine bomb components. It was later found that police buried evidence from defence counsel that Reyat was not the purchaser of the Sanyo tuner.

The verdict delivered on May 9, 1991 was that Reyat was

guilty on all counts. With no more evidence than had been before another court where Reyat had been convicted and fined, a 10-year sentence was imposed

A 10-year sentence was seen by the public as lenient, given the massive loss of life. The public backlash forced the sentencing judge to caution that the term of imprisonment imposed was solely for the Narita bombing, and not tied to any other bombing incident. The judge also noted that Reyat had spent 40 months in pre-trial detention. If a two-for-one consideration was taken for time spent in pretrial custody, doubling the 40 months as 'good time' reduction would be the equivalent of handing down a 16-year sentence

Keeping Reyat locked up did nothing to temper the public distaste of how Canada's investigative and law enforcement agencies had let the public down. A CBC *Fifth Estate* documentary that aired on February 1, 1994 only exacerbated the outrage.

American Intervention

The Fifth Estate investigative report revealed that the American CIA and FBI had covered up what they knew about Canada's Sikh terrorists, who were operating with the help of Pakistani authorities. The United States did not want to jeopardize their use of Pakistan as a base to provide money, weapons, and training to Afghan rebels (then in conflict with Soviet troops). Public disclosure that Pakistan was supportive of Sikh terrorists could have led Congress to deprive money being sent to Pakistan to aid in the Afghanistan war.

American information identified Manjit Singh, known also as Lal Singh, as being the passenger who checked baggage under the name 'M. Singh' onto the London-bound Air India flight, and who checked a bag labelled 'L. Singh' that was headed for Japan.

Other Sikhs bought weapons with the help of a Pakistani secret service agency and were trained in the United States.

Fred Camper told *The Fifth Estate* that he trained mercenaries in the US and that Lal Singh was one of the individuals he trained.

Former CIA Director Robert Gates did not accept *The Fifth Estate* report. He denied that the United States was involved in any coverup and said that the CIA knew nothing of Pakistani involvement with the Sikhs until long after the Air India explosions.

Throughout Reyat's 10-year imprisonment, police continued their attempts to get Reyat to divulge information. Reyat told the *Globe and Mail* in a 1996 interview that a member of the RCMP Air India task force offered to drive Reyat from the medium-security BC Matsqui Institution to a minimum-security prison "in a limousine" if he would divulge the name of the man who accompanied Parmar and Reyat into the woods where the explosion was tested. Reyat further understood that he would be offered immunity from prosecution on the Air India plane bombing if he cooperated. Doug Henderson, RCMP staff sergeant in charge of the Vancouver-based Air India task force, denied that police offered immunity, although he admitted that immunity was discussed in the request for information.

Henderson would later testify that he believed Reyat was "a pawn manipulated by others" and that he had conveyed to Reyat his honest belief that Reyat had been used.

Parole was denied when Reyat became eligible after serving two-thirds of his 10-year sentence, with the Board turning him down on grounds that he had not taken responsibility for his actions. Following that, Reyat never re-applied for parole and rightly believed he would serve every day of his 10-year sentence.

As Reyat's manslaughter sentence was due to expire, it was decided to charge Reyat as well as Ripudaman Singh Malik and Ajaib Singh Bagri with the aircraft disaster that killed more than three hundred people. But one hurdle stood in the way—Malik from Vancouver and Bagri from Kamloops were charged with murder on October 27, 2000. Reyat was in England and was not charged but was named as an unindicted co-conspirator.

Canada had received permission from England to try Reyat on the Narita airport bombing but had not included the airplane bombing in its extradition request. Once again, England had to be convinced that there was a triable case to permit the Canadian courts to proceed. It took until June 2001 before the warrant permitting Canada to proceed with murder charges against Reyat was signed. Once he had completed his 10-year prison sentence, Reyat found himself facing a possible life sentence for murder of the crew and passengers aboard Air India Flight 182. The trial promised to be the longest and most expensive in Canadian history.

The Motive of the Crown

It was an open secret that the real motive of the Crown to hold Reyat past his warrant expiry date on the manslaughter convictions was to pressure him to turn against Malik and Bagri and give evidence that would see the millionaire and his associate convicted. The Crown prosecutors went so far as to offer Reyat immunity if he were to testify against Malik and Bagri—a so-called 'talk-and-walk deal.'

Reyat turned down the immunity offer, figuring that he would rather plead to some lesser charge than be labelled as a rat by his peers. It came as no surprise that the pressure to make a deal was put into high gear. Reyat could avoid a life sentence; he wouldn't be stuck with inordinate legal expenses, and he could count on police support for future parole if he would plead to manslaughter.

The deal made sense to Reyat, but he adamantly refused to testify against his co-accused. He stuck by his guns: that he had never known Parmar's intention, and that he did not participate in the bomb making.

The compromise reached between the prosecutor and

Reyat's own conscience was that Reyat would plead guilty to manslaughter and be called as a witness at the Malik and Bagri trial, where he would answer questions truthfully.

In February 2003, Crown counsel and Reyat's defence counsel hammered out what would be an agreed statement of facts to support a guilty plea to the lesser charge that included the offence of manslaughter. The Agreed Statement explicitly noted that Reyat had no intention of harming the Air India victims.

After a delay of 18 years, prosecutors finally had a conviction for the Air India bombing. Reyat was sentenced to five years for manslaughter.

Reyat's transfer to penitentiary was somewhat delayed because he was subpoenaed to testify against Bagri and Malik in their murder trial. Once called, Reyat said no more than he had admitted to from the time of his first arrest.

Reyat was to be the essential witness needed for a successful prosecution of the co-accused. The trial of Bagri and Malik commenced before a BC Supreme Court judge on April 28, 2003, and concluding December 3, 2004.

Longest Trial in Canadian History

On March 16, 2005, Justice Ian Bruce Josephson acquitted Malik and Bagri in what had been one of the longest trials in Canadian history—and a $57 million expense to the taxpayers. The acquittal was good news for the two accused men, but the judgment proved to be a disaster for Reyat. In handing down his decision, Josephson commented that he found Reyat, the chief witness for the prosecution, to be an "unmitigated liar." The judge found Reyat's evidence to be "patently and pathetically fabricated in an attempt to minimize his involvement...while refusing to reveal relevant information he clearly possesses." Although the judge had every right to comment, he was never taken to task that three prior prosecutions had upheld Reyat in his statement that he did not know anything of the plot beyond what he had stated earlier in the Agreed Statement of Facts. When he failed to provide the evidence necessary to establish the Crown's case, the two co-accused walked. With Bagri and Malik free to carry on, Reyat would thenceforth be known as "the only man convicted in the Air India bombing."

Reyat was not granted parole during the five-year sentence. After serving two-thirds of the sentence, he would be considered for statutory release to serve the remainder of his sentence in the community under the supervision of a parole officer.

However, Canada's *Corrections and Conditional Release Act* provides that even though an offender would ordinarily be entitled to be released, the Parole Board can review a case and detain an inmate past the statutory release date if, in Reyat's case, "the commission of the offence caused the death of or serious harm to another person and there are reasonable grounds to believe that the offender is likely to commit an offence causing death or serious harm to another person before the expiration of the offender's sentence according to law...."

It was when a referral was made to the Parole Board of Canada that I was retained by Reyat to assist him at his detention hearing. Having participated in many detention hearings in the past, I realized that a persuasive risk assessment was needed to show that Reyat would be a manageable risk in the community.

To this end, I contacted Dr. Karen De Freitas, a well-respected psychiatrist in Ontario who could be called upon to provide an honest, in-depth answer regarding the degree of risk posed by Reyat. Dr. De Freitas interviewed Reyat for two hours at Kingston's Collins Bay Institution, as well as reviewing Reyat's institutional case file, in January 2006. On February 3, she delivered her seven-page report.

The bottom line in her report was that if Reyat were to be released in June on his statutory release date, he "will not likely cause death or serious harm to others."

That report conflicted with the Correctional Service

of Canada's Assessment for Decision, which stated that Reyat "remains a serious risk" if he gets statutory release next June, and that he should be held in jail until February 2008 (when his full sentence for manslaughter is complete).

The *De Freitas Report* reasoned and gave insight into Reyat's thought processes. "He is aware that he contributed to the tragic loss of life and he regrets this," De Freitas noted. "He is also aware of the suffering that his family has endured because of his actions. He believes that his father committed suicide in part because he was not available to help him because of his incarceration. He is aware of the shame he has brought his wife and children."

De Freitas noted that Reyat was a model prisoner throughout his time in penitentiary, working as a baker in the prison's kitchen and holding religious services with another Sikh prisoner. The report noted that Reyat held no commitment to the Sikh separatist movement and that he had lost touch with current events in the region.

De Freitas went on to say that Reyat seemed genuine in his distancing himself from Sikh politics, commenting that, "While it is difficult for me to assess the truth of this claim, it is certainly plausible that his own very serious legal problems have taken precedence in his mind."

A Charge of Perjury

Reyat maintained his story that he had no inkling that Parmar intended to use the dynamite and timing device in a manner that would cause loss of life. To Reyat, Parmar "seemed respectable." Reyat again told the psychiatrist that he prays every day for the Air India and Narita bombing victims—but does not feel that he was the one who killed them. None of this was new. It was the exact same position presented to other courts and accepted by all except Justice Josephson.

Even though the RCMP agreed to provide a letter to the Parole Board as part of the guilty plea negotiations leading to the Air India manslaughter conviction, my review of the file showed that the RCMP had reneged on that promise. It was only with some extreme prodding that the RCMP agreed to release the letter stating it had no objections to Reyat's release.

The failure to provide a support letter was the least of Reyat's problems with the RCMP. The force has a policy that until a charge is laid, it will neither confirm nor deny that a charge will be laid. It therefore came as a shock that the RCMP let it be known to three media sources that a charge of perjury would be laid while Reyat was about to go before the Parole Board. Neither Reyat nor I had been notified about the pending charge until news broke of the RCMP intention. A conviction for perjury could lead to a sentence of up to 14 years. Worse, knowledge by the Parole Board that a release would be futile would substantially diminish chances of success at the upcoming gating hearing.

I wrote to RCMP Commissioner Giuliano Zacardelli, complaining of the leak that I felt sullied the reputation of the RCMP. Zacardelli never replied.

Reyat decided to go ahead with the hearing despite the apparent obstacles. The Board and the Institution were notified that the hearing would proceed. The Government of Canada chartered a jet so that families of the victims could attend the hearing. The Board was inundated by media requests to sit in on the proceedings, and a special room on an upper floor of Collins Bay Institution was outfitted with chairs to accommodate a large crowd. Three other rooms were set aside for security reasons and visitors to the institution were kept clear of any encounters with Reyat.

It was a most unusual hearing. Members of the media were scrambling to get any updates they could, and the previous evening I had met up with CBC reporter Terry Milewski for an interview at his request. He had set his hotel room up as a makeshift studio complete with lighting, a cameraman, and a sound man. All that was lacking was hair and makeup.

Upon arrival at Collins Bay Institution the next day, I met with Reyat in an anteroom prior to the hearing. He was remarkably calm. He understood the questioning would be tough, but he said he was there to tell the truth and was prepared for any outcome.

Behind us in the hearing sat about 120 observers. While it is not unusual for one to three observers to be present, having an entire audience felt somewhat unnerving.

Once the institutional parole officer read the CSC position and answered a few questions from the Board, it was time for the main event: the questioning of Inderjit Singh Reyat. Michael Crowley, the lead Board member, started off a hearing that would eventually last some six hours—almost triple that of an average hearing.

I became concerned during Reyat's questioning that some of his answers were skewed from his previous testimony. Was this because of nervousness and the unusual forum in which he found himself? Would anyone notice? His position about Parmar and the provision of material remained more or less the same, but the Board was adept at spotting inconsistencies. Reyat became emotional during the hearing. At one point he broke down in tears, which required a brief interruption of proceedings. Upon resumption, Reyat explained his emotional upset, saying that he had become emotional because "of the people who died," and continued by saying, "My thinking was different; I was young. My thinking has greatly changed."

The Board then heard three representatives of the victims. Their statements were heart wrenching.

When it came time to make submissions, I focused my attention on the crystal ball the legislation forced the Parole Board to peer into—Would Reyat cause death or serious harm to another before the end of his sentence? I also realized that the Board had been put in an impossible position. If it went by the letter of the law, it would be like a slap in the face to the victims represented in the hearing room, who simply had enough of government ineptitude and delay.

Reyat was escorted to a holding cell to await the Board decision. I walked out of the room with Terry Milewski. All the way to the door I was able to gauge from Milewski's reaction that the hostility toward Reyat was overwhelming. The unspoken sense I got was that the victims—and the Canadian public—needed their pound of flesh, and that Milewski thought Reyat was a liar for his inability to give straight answers to events that should be indelible on his mind. I was apprehensive that this would be critical for the Board's decision.

When we returned to the hearing room, Michael Crowley came right to the point in summarizing the Board's decision.

"Mr. Reyat," Crowley began, "the Board has deliberated, and we have decided to detain you until your warrant expiry date. We found you today to be evasive and contradictory in your answers...and you have minimized your role in our view for this horrific crime."

An appeal to the Parole Board's Appeal Division merely rubber-stamped the decision of the panel that ordered Reyat's detention. A further appeal to the Federal Court was made arguing that the Board must find a "pattern of persistent, violent behaviour" had been established. I urged the Federal Court to find that no such pattern existed, and the Board decision should be overturned. Madam Justice Snider deftly handled this objection by noting there had been two bombings and even though Reyat was not involved in either, the two bombings constituted a 'pattern' sufficient to comply with the legislation. The judicial review in the Federal Court was dismissed on May 29, 2007.

Shortly after his March 3, 2006 detention hearing, Reyat was transferred to British Columbia to face perjury charges. Reyat completed his prison sentence in British Columbia in 2008 and was transferred to a provincial jail while awaiting trial on the perjury charges.

In September 2008, Reyat received some good news: the BC Court of Appeal overturned the decision to refuse bail and ordered his release from custody. Further, there would be no appeal of that decision.

Reyat was convicted in the fall of 2010 on the perjury counts. On January 7, 2011, he was sentenced to 9 years—reduced to 7 years, 7 months with credit for time spent in custody on the charges. Nonetheless, it was the longest sentence ever imposed by Canada for perjury. Appeals to the British Columbia Court of Appeal and ultimately to the Supreme Court of Canada were dismissed.

The Reyat matter came before the Parole Board of Canada shortly before Reyat was scheduled for release. His case was reviewed by a single member of the Board in what is referred to as a 'paper decision', that is, a Board member makes a decision solely on the paperwork generated by the Correctional Service to determine what conditions, if any, should attach to the offender's release.

This time, only a single member of the Board conducted the review. A decision was signed on January 14, 2016 to impose a residency condition on Reyat. Instead of being released to the community, there were a number of listed requirements including not to reside at his home but rather to live at a Community Residential Facility (CRF) until the end of his sentence or unless sooner released by decision of the Board.

In coming to the decision, the Board member noted that the CSC documentation indicated that Reyat's association with a terrorist organization was identified as "inactive while incarcerated although not disaffiliated and [Reyat's] affiliation has not been terminated."

Even while granting Reyat release, the decision still diverted the blame for the Air India explosions to the only individual the government had been able to convict. Yet it seems that he was being punished not so much for the explosions but for withholding information. Clearly, that is not how the criminal justice system operates. Everyone has the right to be presumed innocent until found otherwise by a court of competent juris- diction. It is up to the prosecutor to investigate and bring forth sufficient evidence that a person is indeed guilty. It is a perver- sion of justice to imprison an individual for not providing the evidence that the state is required to muster.

The Major Report

While Reyat sat being considered the villain in the Air India disaster, a Commission headed by retired Canadian Supreme Court Justice John C. Major pointed out who should take the lion's share of the blame. The report was highly critical of the RCMP and CSIS, who had been too busy with fighting to maintain their turf than to keep Canadians safe.

It also noted shocking breaches of security at Canada's air- ports, including a breakdown of the X-ray machine at Toronto and a failure to inspect a bag when a beeper went off (signaling potential explosives). After the bombing, a 1986 CSIS security report indicated that 10 of 159 people scanned as employees of a cleaning company at the Vancouver airport had connec- tion to the international Sikh Youth Federation and the Babbar Khalsa organization—both groups linked to Sikh terrorism. CSIS admitted that the lapse in security screening "could prove embarrassing and fatal" should any of the cleaners become involved.

The security situation at Toronto's Pearson airport was similarly lax. The *Major Report* accepted the testimony of Brian R. Simpson, then a summer student about to enter law school, that despite the fact that Burns Security was supposed to maintain access to planes, Simpson had no trouble entering the Air India jet, checking out washrooms and even sitting in the pilot's seat. He confirmed with me that the code used to unlock secure doors was easily broken.

The Major Report found that although CSIS had wire- taps listening to conspirators plotting an atrocity to coincide with the anniversary of the 1984 slaughter of Sikh militants at Amritsar's Golden Temple by the Indian army, no one understood a word of the Punjabi farming dialect and that it took up to six weeks to get a translation.

It was common knowledge in the expatriate community that some violence was to occur, and that people were warned not to fly Air India around the Golden Temple massacre dates. Indeed, it was reported that CSIS was warned of the impending bomb threat but took no action to pass along the information. Evidence was given to Justice John Major that testy relations between the RCMP and CSIS was not solely the fault of CSIS. One RCMP officer was ordered not to turn over information to CSIS, on grounds that, "We do the work and they get the credit."

Despite Major's highly critical report, there has never been acknowledgement that anyone in the RCMP or CSIS received a demotion or pay cut. Indeed, one CSIS operative who did not pass along the bomb threat later became Lieutenant-Governor of Ontario.

Investigative Incompetence

There is no doubt that the Air India bombings were horrific and cannot be condoned by any right-thinking individual. However, using public outrage as a cover for what has been found to be investigative incompetence is scandalous. Reyat pleaded guilty and was fined for delivery of the dynamite. All other sentences and his 30-year ordeal in prison should be seen as a drift away in Canada from the Rule of Law. In effect, Reyat suffered punishment because of his action in delivering dynamite without it having been found beyond a reasonable doubt that he intended the deaths that would ensue.

Inderjit Singh Reyat is now safely at home with his wife and family. He suffered almost 30 years in prison having to worry about his family's safety from attack—either by vicious Sikh separatists who might want revenge, or from members of the Canadian public who hold him responsible for the deaths of over three hundred citizens. He was punished with a fine for his cooperation in providing explosives. It is doubtful that he realized he would become the fall guy for Indian terrorists and Canadian security agencies, each with different motives but working towards the same end—finding a scapegoat. He was caught in the middle.

In Conflict with the Criminal Law

When I commenced my university studies, I had no intention of becoming a lawyer. I can truthfully say that I came into the profession with no intention of changing the world or how it operated. But over the years of devoting my career to representing people in conflict with the criminal law, I found that one need not condone wrongdoing to appreciate that as human beings we all deserve to be treated justly and humanely.

I also learned that our whole system of justice is centred on truth-telling. At the start of Part II, I tried to identify where impediments to truth upend the notion of justice to which we all should be committed. These impediments include a desire to appease public opinion especially where a criminal act is horrific and there is pressure to shield public institutions from scrutinywhen their efforts fall below par.

I am told that a good story teller never preaches. I am hopeful that in recounting my experiences with Terry Fitzsimmons and the individuals named in Part II, that the reader might come to share my concern for fostering a change in attitudes towards prisoners and eventually change laws when it comes to correctional systems. It will be a big fight to do so, but, as Claire Culhane often said, "It's the best fight in town."

ACKNOWLEDGEMENTS

The writer gratefully acknowledges the assistance provided by Nathan Wisnicki who edited previous drafts of the manuscripts and offered helpful suggestions. I also want to extend my thanks to Raphael Rowe for agreeing to the inclusion of his Foreword and to Professor Keramet Reiter who contributed the Afterword. They serve as inspirations in the fight for justice. Certainly, I am thankful for the trust and assistance of Dr. Lorene Shyba of Durvile Publications Ltd. In Calgary, Alberta. Her kind words and insights sustained me on the road from keyboard to printed page.

I am also appreciative of the contributions and critiques offered by Jo-Anne Johnson and Marilyn Pagnuelo who also reviewed the material.

Dr. Stuart Grassian reviewed and revised that portion of the text dealing with his interview in Boston. For this, I am most appreciative.

Most of all, my thanks go to my wife, Roxann Hill, who offered many helpful suggestions, poured over the manuscript, and brought to my attention any overuse of legalese, ensuring that the story could be read by non-lawyers as well as those in the profession.

I am tremendously appreciative of my former clients who shared with me their own personal stories of how the judicial and correctional processes impacted them. This has allowed me to obtain insights into the criminal and correctional systems that one can never study in textbooks and case law. I am especially appreciative to the late Terry Fitzsimmons for urging me to make his story public.

Sitting at a computer for hours on end can make one lose all concept of time. I am therefore very thankful to my English Cocker Spaniel, Hedy, who frequently slept in an armchair beside my desk and every so often would make sure I knew when it was time to take a break and go for a walk outside.

The Durvile True Cases Series

1. Tough Crimes: True Cases by
Top Canadian Criminal Lawyers
Edited by C.D. Evans and Lorene Shyba

2. Shrunk, Crime and Disorders of the Mind:
True Cases by Forensic Psychiatrists and Psychologists
Edited by Dr. Lorene Shyba and Dr. J. Thomas Dalby

3. More Tough Crimes: True Cases by
Canadian Lawyers and Judges
Edited by William Trudell and Lorene Shyba

4. Women in Criminal Justice: True Cases By and About
Canadian Women and the Law
Edited by William Trudell and Lorene Shyba

5. Florence Kinrade: Lizzie Borden of the North
Written by Frank Jones

6. Ross Mackay, The Saga of a Brilliant Criminal Lawyer:
And His Big Losses and
Bigger Wins in Court and in Life
Written by Jack Batten

7. Go Ahead and Shoot Me!
And Other True Cases About Ordinary Criminals
Written by Doug Heckbert

8. After the Force: True Cases and Investigations by
Law Enforcement Officers
Edited by Det. Debbie J. Doyle (ret.)

9. Pine Box Parole: Terry Fitzsimmons and the
Quest to End Solitary Confinement & Other True Cases
Written by John L. Hill

ABOUT THE AUTHOR

John L. Hill is a triple graduate of Queen's University in Kingston, Ontario, Canada and also holds an Honours B.A. and M.A. in political science and a J.D. from the School of Law. He earned an LL.M. in Constitutional Law from Osgoode Hall Law School in Toronto. He has lectured internationally on prison law topics at conferences of the International Association of Psychiatry and the Law. Now retired from practice, Hill writes op-ed columns for *The Lawyer's Daily* on prison law topics.